SURVIVAL

A Guide To Staying Afloat In The Deep Waters Of Life

By

Victoria Alai

SURVIVAL 101: A GUIDE TO STAYING AFLOAT IN THE DEEP WATERS OF LIFE
by Victoria Alai

First Edition

Published by EveryoneCounts.World
Sunnyvale, California

www.EveryoneCounts.World

Cover design by Alex McDonell, awm-art.com

Photography: Laura Jaye, laurajayephotography.com

Editors: Suzanne Reamy, Laura Jaye, Jodi Burke, Safa Alai

Illustrations: Victoria Alai, Alex McDowell, Elizabeth Eckes

Author services by Pedernales Publishing, LLC.
www.pedernalespublishing.com

Library of Congress Control Number: 2021906469

ISBN: 978-1-7369708-2-9 Paperback edition
978-1-7369708-1-2 Hardcover edition
978-1-7369708-0-5 Digital edition
978-1-7369708-3-6 Audiobook edition

Printed in the United States of America

10 9 8 7 6 5 4 3 2 1

IGWT-HJF

xx-v13

Dedication

To You

Wishing you health, happiness, prosperity, love, sanity, peace, and abundance today and always.

You are not alone!

Table of Contents

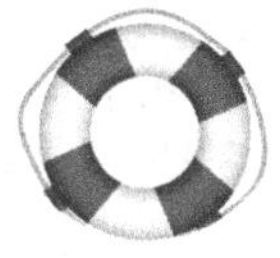

Foreword

We often hear people joke when we deliver our first child, "They don't give us a book on how to parent." Well, folks, I'm here to tell you that we now have a book on how to "re-parent" ourselves and thrive in this thing called life. Welcome to *Survival 101*—your guide to living and experiencing a happy, joyous, and prosperous life!

When Victoria and I first met, we were both at a crossroads in our lives, looking for a path that would lead us towards a happier and freer way of living. Little did I know that when I met Victoria thirty-plus years ago that we would end up walking this absolutely amazing "upward path" together and grow on our journey of healing and "thriving."

As she will share with you throughout this book, the twists and turns her life has taken echo my journey, a journey that Victoria witnessed and supported. My path took me overseas to work with developmentally disabled individuals at the community mental health center in Jakarta, Indonesia, to Ulaanbaatar Mongolia to work on international adoption, then back to South Dakota to work in child and family services and mental health and addiction recovery.

All the while, Victoria was by my side, walking through many of the practices you will read about in this book as we grew and shared what we were learning and experiencing along the way. I was brought to tears of joy many times while reading this book, having walked this walk with Victoria, knowing her journey and her desire to humbly share her upward path, with the deepest desire to help as many people as possible find a happy, joyous and free life.

Seeing this book come to fruition fills my heart with joy. Victoria is an amazing mentor, teacher, channel of universal life force energy, supporter, and guide. I am truly honored to have the opportunity to write this forward, and even more so to be blessed in sharing this life and friendship with Victoria. In the pages that follow, you will find that Victoria has a keen understanding of all the various aspects of living a peace-filled prosperous life. This book is written by someone who has walked the path and utilized all the tools in this book firsthand to support her current flourishing way of living. She discusses our needs simply and tangibly, starting from "visible needs," as she labels them, such as basic needs for food, housing, and income to "invisible needs" for emotional, mental, and spiritual support. She reminds us, time and time again, that she is there to support us on our journey from surviving to thriving and having an amazing life.

Victoria has pulled together ideas from multiple practices. By combining essential aspects of a wide range of simple techniques for living and healing, she has promoted novel ideas such as the "Dream Team," otherwise known as your support network, "visible and invisible" needs which must be met for a thriving life, and steps for a personal "Upward Path." She lays out step-by-step instructions on how to move into a prosperous, thriving way of living, including all aspects of functional adult life. And while doing so, she takes us along her journey in a way that makes us want to keep reading, follow the path, and thrive.

For those of you exploring the early pages of this book, this path holds great promise for your physical, mental, and emotional freedom. This book invites us on a journey of internal exploration to look at new ways of thinking and acting in life. Thankfully, whether comfortable or not, we are all on this journey together, and Victoria has found a way to make it into our hearts and homes in a way like nothing else out there. May you enjoy and learn as much from Victoria as I have.

–Jodi Burke, Licensed Clinical Social Worker and
Licensed Addiction Counselor

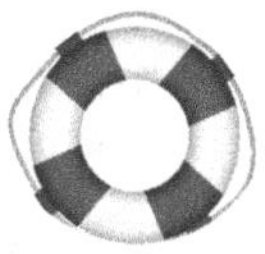

Introduction

If you are reading this book, then you may be in a pinch.

Are you experiencing stress and challenges or hoping to alleviate some kind of pain? Are you reading this book for yourself or to find help for a friend or a loved one? Do you feel like you are drowning inside even though you "appear" to have everything together on the outside?

Whether you are struggling to keep a roof over your head and food on your table or you are in a major life transition and feeling lost, this book is meant to be a guidebook for any situation you find yourself in. *Survival 101* can help you stay afloat and navigate the shallow as well as the deep waters of life.

This book is about survival. It's not about surviving on an island with a group of strangers with whom you must compete for dominance or negotiate alliances, even though some of us may feel like we are living this scenario in real life. It's deeper than that. It's about the conscious and unconscious needs that drive our thoughts and actions and how we strive to get those needs met, gracefully or not. But it's also about hope. Because no matter what your circumstances are or where you come from, I believe you can successfully meet your needs.

My primary motivation in writing this book is to share my experiences—some extremely painful and some joyous—so that you might pick up ideas, tips, and beliefs to help you reach a happy, abundant, and free place in your life faster than I did. Who knows, maybe some of the ideas in this book will help you start a new career or a business that employs other people. Or you may discover deep underlying needs that are not being met in your relationships and find yourself completely transforming in that important area of life.

In this guidebook, I share the principles, tools, and steps with you that have helped me personally survive and walk a path to thriving. I also share life resources I have found to support others and perspectives from inspiring people who have influenced my own journey. Throughout the book, we will primarily look at ways to fill both visible survival, like food and water, and invisible needs, such as validation and love. We are also going to explore how these visible and invisible needs are interconnected.

As you are reading through *Survival 101*, you might notice a tonal difference between each of the four sections. This book offers a mixture of practical, mental and emotional strategies; Part I and Part III lean towards a psychological and emotional point of view, whereas Part II is a practical survival mindset that reads more like a how-to field guide. The final section, Part IV, is a workbook you can dive into and come out with a solid plan. While I believe starting from the beginning of the book will give you the highest return, you might benefit from jumping ahead to specific sections that offer you immediate support and then come back to where you left off.

In my experience, the mindset required to "survive" or meet physical needs is very different from the contemplative mindset needed to meet emotional needs. I have adapted each section of the book to best serve the need in question. It's one thing to survive physically and another to survive mentally, but when you combine a solid approach for both physical and mental survival, you wind up with options you might never have dreamt of before—ones which yield lasting and abundant results in your life.

Everyone's Survival Experience Varies

Although I consider myself an ordinary person, I feel I have gained deep insight on multiple levels as I learned to survive and thrive. I have been addicted to self-help for decades as I explored how to heal from pain and trauma. I credit the painful events and relationships of my life with providing the fuel I needed to survive and ultimately thrive. So, in this book, I am striving to be part of the solution together with you.

You might already be thriving in many ways and find yourself with only one or two areas of life that need "tweaking." If you are cruising along in that boat, wonderful! That's inspiring! Maybe reading this book will give you a few extra tools to use in your personal life or ideas on how you can support others who may be struggling.

I find myself today living abundantly in all areas of my life today, with rarely an issue that pulls me into survival mode. However, I continue the habit of learning as much as I can on how to become even more happy, joyous, free, prosperous, and abundant. One of my friends once told me:

> "If you think things are good now, just wait. This is the tip of the iceberg of how good things can be if you just keep your personal growth work going."

She was right! I am currently doing everything I can to be present and aware, for myself and those around me. Today, my visible and invisible needs are filled ninety-five percent of the time. When the circumstances call for it or something bothers me, I continue to dig deeper to discover what misunderstandings I'm operating out of or how I can unhook from other people's behavior and beliefs.

Note: My circumstances can and have flipped overnight in some cases.

By following basic survival principles, I know that I can survive in any economy or change in industry. Even if my ego takes a hit while I adapt, I can be healthy and happy. I believe there are principles that anyone can adopt to move even closer to a happy and thriving life: acceptance and generosity.

The Key to Getting Started is Accepting Life as it is Today

I find I have to start with wherever I am right now to survive and become open to thriving. The clarity of seeing and accepting my present circumstances, including the people in my life or the job I have today, and then working with what I've got, has been the key to unlocking survival, stabilizing my life, and ultimately thriving. So, I do the best I can with where I am today.

Giving Back to Others is Key

I want to share how I reached an abundant life with you and your friends because it helps me continue to be thankful and learn, especially from you. It's not "if" but "when" you survive and thrive that matters. When you reach your thriving place—as NO DOUBT you will— consider immediately finding someone else who can adopt what you have learned to better their life.

I have found that sharing what I have learned can help other people, especially if I share information when asked. I have drawn on countless others who shared their wisdom freely before me. Now I get to experience sheer joy when I see the spark light in others' lives like I'm sure it will in yours! No matter what I share, being willing to be open with what I know helps me solidify the lessons I've learned. Beyond helping me retain the knowledge I share, nine times out of ten, I learn something from the other person about myself, my life, or the world.

I find there is a paradox in giving of myself:

The more I am willing to share what I've learned and experienced in my life, the more abundance, peace, and happiness I enjoy.

I invite you to join me on this journey, to get clarity, to heal and gain trust that you already hold everything you need inside of you to live a happy, prosperous, abundant, loving life no matter your current circumstances.

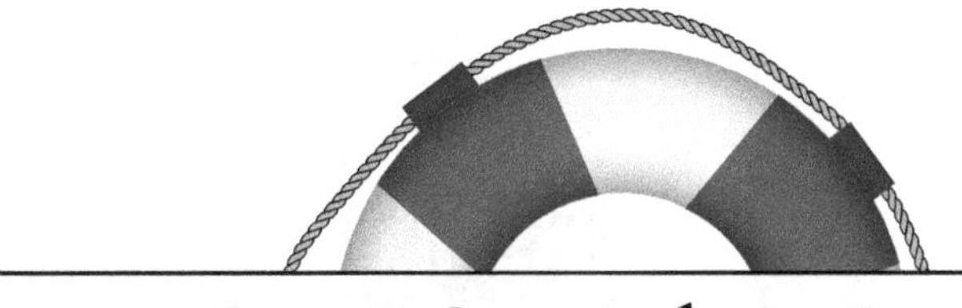

Part I: Survival 101 Basics

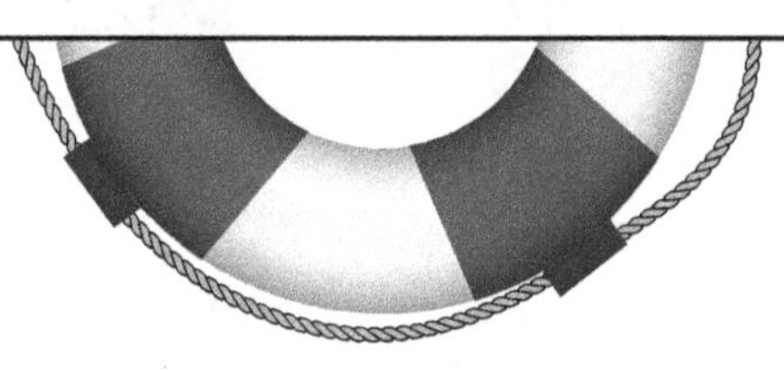

Chapter 1: What is Survival?

Let's reflect for a moment on what "survival" means. The concept of surviving, in theory, seems straightforward. It goes like this. We start by being born, we arrive in the world, and all our basic physical, emotional, and security needs are taken care of by people who, ideally, we can trust. These caregivers have our best interests in mind. Over time, we learn to take over the responsibility for our physical, emotional, mental, and spiritual needs. In our late teens and early twenties, we get an education and move into an abundant and prosperous life through meaningful work. We then create a home, get married or enter into a long-term relationship, and, perhaps, start a family of our own.

We plan, implement those plans, then pause, review, pivot, plan, and implement again throughout our lives. We repeat this cycle over and over until we retire. Hopefully, after retirement, we pass away from natural causes surrounded by loving family and friends leaving behind a thriving legacy. This path sounds logical and straightforward in theory, but how many of us take such a straight path to create a thriving, abundant, and prosperous life?

In reality, most of us seem to end up on crooked paths that lead to unique outcomes. In many homes, some start their lives with one or more parents absent or struggling to support a child. This struggling parent may actually harm the child's development, and so a survival mindset may kick in early for many children.

What is Surviving?

Survival, to me, is a reduced state of life that focuses on the mere act of staying alive and getting basic needs met. I feel like I am "surviving" when I find myself in a scarcity mindset where resources are few and there is not enough to go around. I believe I can barely keep my head above water when I am in such a frame-of-mind. It feels like whichever direction I turn, I'm faced with a new and urgent life or death decision, even if, technically, I'm not in a life-or-death situation.

Survival for me is driven by fear, where all I can do is focus on getting my basic needs met

Realizing and accepting I am in survival mode, is the spark that leads me to change my life. I change by observing my circumstances, making the clearest decisions I can, and taking action to follow through on my decisions. Once I have taken action, I step back to see how that action worked. Each action I take towards survival helps me stabilize my life overall, and each part of my life that stabilizes reduces my anxiety and fear, giving me more hope for an even fuller life. When enough of my visible and invisible survival needs are met, I look up one day and realize I'm not just surviving but thriving.

What is Thriving?

I know I am thriving when I find myself living in a reality where most of the time, I experience peace, sanity, happiness, equality, unconditional love, respect, unity, prosperity, abundance, freedom, purpose, gratitude, safety, and service. In my thriving world, relationships reflect patience, tolerance, kindness, and acceptance. **Knowing, accepting, and trusting that I am and always have been perfectly okay, is the foundation of my thriving life.** I believe what my good friend Dr. Sue Nesbitt says: "It's okay to know you are already okay."

Just as I needed to learn to walk before I could run, I must learn to survive before I can thrive. If my body cannot live healthily and my heart doesn't know I'm perfectly okay, I won't thrive or help others thrive around me.

Survival Beliefs Start Young

Kids become aware of the fragile nature of basic survival at an early age. Living in survival mode can keep one from fully experiencing all life offers. This phenomenon can occur no matter how "good" you look on the outside or whether you grow up wealthy.

For example, I know some adults who, as kids, had food withheld even though their parents were multi-millionaires. I say this because at times there are life circumstances that appear to be "healthy" to others but which—in actual fact—are harmful to the individual. Such circumstances can trigger survival thinking, where the core challenge becomes getting your basic needs met. In this type of home, the child may develop **false beliefs** such as:

"If I do something wrong, then I can't eat."
"I am a criminal because I steal food in my home
or sneak out to get food to survive."
"I don't count as much as others."
"I'm a burden or a hassle to my family."
"I'm worthless."
"I don't belong, and I am not welcome in my home."

My Early Start with Survival

What is interesting about survival mode is that there are often unconscious belief systems—typically negative and self-defeating—working behind the scenes.

I formed my own core beliefs based on the parenting, environment, and situations I experienced. The formation of these core beliefs, part of my perceived "reality," started early, when I was ten years old. By seventeen they were firmly rooted, becoming an ingrained, subconscious part of my thinking, where I was not even aware that such beliefs were running my life.

Two examples of false beliefs I developed at an early age were:

"I am a mistake. I don't belong here."
"People can't be trusted."

If life had gone perfectly in my early years, I would have been equipped with many of the tools I needed to meet my basic needs, and with these tools, I could have learned how to thrive in childhood and laid the foundations to thrive in adulthood. However, I believe my parents were not equipped to teach me some of the love-based and practical tools I needed to create a solid foundation for my life. As a result, I ended up with developmental gaps that hindered my ability to survive which, in turn, reduced my ability to thrive.

Note: In my case, some of the most significant gaps were mental and emotional, and we will be looking more deeply at the role of these unconscious belief systems in chapter 21. Feel free to jump ahead, then come back to this section later if you need to!

Acceptance of Gaps without Blame

Before I could investigate the learning gaps from childhood, I had to accept that it was normal for any adult to have gaps in the first place. The fact that I didn't learn in childhood the necessary basics to survive and thrive in life, did not mean I was a failure. I wasn't to blame for my current circumstances any more than my parents were. People cannot give me what they don't already have.

Before even looking at my own developmental gaps, I had to become open to the idea of letting go of fault-finding and commit to just focusing on the actual gaps in my learning and where they originated. I was so preoccupied with placing blame on myself for not "having it together" that I had no opportunity to see the reality of my developmental gaps.

As soon as I let go of fault-finding, I invited a mental health counselor and other close, supportive friends into my life to acknowledge and process feelings, fears, and thoughts that came up around some of my unmet needs, false beliefs, and trauma from childhood and young adult years. Their support led to a tiny speck of acceptance for what happened or didn't happen. I could finally look at my past without blaming myself or others, no matter how justified I felt in my anger or blame. The entire process of curtailing blame leveled at myself or others, has taken years for me to learn and apply.

Beginning the healing process and committing to being at source in my own life opened me up emotionally and mentally to taking personal responsibility for my developmental gaps as a regulated adult. The term "being at source" to me means that I am taking full responsibility for my happiness and looking at what I can control with the forces and resources at my disposal versus expecting people, places, things, and circumstances outside of myself to change for me to be happy and thriving.

What Prompted Me to Change?

Once ready, I started noticing gaps in my development without self-judgment. One day when talking to friends, I realized that I didn't know how to balance my checkbook, and they did. Apparently, this was an expected skill to have in your mid-twenties. I somehow missed this lesson growing up. I also noticed that I had a lot of resistance to recording all of my expenses. I was more comfortable keeping my head in the sand and fantasizing that my finances were fine. I call this "living life in vagueness."

In addition to financial pressure, I had other challenges. They were the usual suspects:

- Not having a safe place to live
- Not having a clue about where to work or what career to build
- Not knowing how to build a career even when I could find one
- Not knowing how to calm myself down, which resulted in mental health issues such as daily panic attacks and post-traumatic stress responses (PTSD)
- Not knowing how to date or form a long-term mutually "healthy" relationship

I felt pressure to solve all these challenges at the same time. However, my list of life pressures seemed endless and repetitive. The pressures reinforced and fed on each other, leading to even more pressure in my life!

For example, in my early twenties, I started doing well. I found a job and a place to live, but then wound up in a relationship with a man because "Why not?" Then one area fell apart when I lost my job. Next, my housing situation went downhill, and then my boyfriend left me, leading to panic attacks, which impacted going to school or finding another job. Like a house of cards, everything around me collapsed.

It also took everything I had to mentally sit in a classroom and not run out screaming due to the post-traumatic stress disorder (PTSD) springing from my phobias. This limited my career options because I had to choose a college degree that was easier to complete but which did not meet the requirements for the career I really wanted. It takes a surprising amount of focus and grit to stay in a chair when your mind and body, flowing with adrenaline, are shouting at you to scramble to safety.

After experiencing several mental and emotional breakdowns, I finally reached a point where I accepted something had to change. I finally accepted I was missing critical information which led to gaps in my ability to cope and survive.

Finding and Filling in Developmental Gaps

Filling developmental gaps is like creating new grooves or pathways for the brain to follow. I know now that new life strategies and methods I learn today can fill gaps in my learning, helping me to replace old ones I had developed to cope in childhood. The survival skills of my youth were supplanted with newfound knowledge and strategies acquired by diving into deep-level research, even though I didn't view myself as particularly academically inclined. My research led me to mentors, books, programs, counselors, and a myriad of other sources as I set about filling my needs and developmental gaps in an abundant, healthy way.

For instance, I would start noticing people, often strangers, who appeared to have what I wanted in different areas of life. I was so desperate for help to fill my newfound developmental gaps that I would boldly ask them how they created the life they had. I didn't even know my true underlying needs at the time, but I knew the areas of my life where I experienced the deepest pain.

Most of the time, these "strangers," soon to be mentors, responded by first validating my true underlying needs and desires. Next, they shared different beliefs, strategies, and actions they had taken to reach their life goals, which included being happy and feeling peaceful and free most of the time. I began to learn, practice, and expand upon the skills I needed to survive and thrive.

Over time, I observed I was still trying to use old skills or strategies that were no longer working, and so, I opened up to learning new beliefs, skills, and strategies to fill both my visible and invisible needs in healthy ways.

Sample Developmental Stages from Erik Erikson

One of the tools I reference today is the list of developmental stages provided by Erik Erikson, a developmental psychologist and psychoanalyst.

Erikson's theory is that there are eight stages of development a person must go through to reach a reasonably happy and successful life. He believed that "successful completion of each stage results in a healthy personality and the acquisition of basic virtues. Basic virtues are characteristic strengths which the ego can use to resolve subsequent crises. Failure to complete a stage can result in a reduced ability to complete further stages and, therefore, a more unhealthy personality and sense of self. These stages, however, can be resolved successfully at a later time." (McLeod, 2020)

Figure 1: Erik Erikson's Stages of Psychosocial Development (McLeod 2018)

Stage	Psychosocial Crisis	Basic Virtue	Age
1.	Trust vs. Mistrust	Hope	0 - 1½
2.	Autonomy vs. Shame	Will	1½ - 3
3.	Initiative vs. Guilt	Purpose	3 - 5
4.	Industry vs. Inferiority	Competency	5 - 12
5.	Identity vs. Role Confusion	Fidelity	12 - 18
6.	Intimacy vs. Isolation	Love	18 - 40
7.	Generativity vs. Stagnation	Care	40 - 65
8.	Ego Integrity vs. Despair	Wisdom	65+

Overall, I believe Erikson's developmental stages are actually coping mechanisms or strategies that serve to fill real underlying needs. My most significant breakthrough came when I was able to find and clarify what precisely these underlying needs were. Clarifying these needs gave me a target, so to speak, that I could finally aim at.

Survival is Based on Meeting Your Needs

Each of us is born with instinctive needs that must be satisfied to stay alive and ultimately thrive. We are like growing flowers. In the dark, with little water or light, many of us wither away. So, what are the "needs" that must be satisfied to live and prosper? Should we ask Baby Yoda? Let's ask Abraham Maslow instead. Maslow was an American psychologist from the twentieth century who categorized lifetime needs as a hierarchy. From his perspective, lower survival level needs have to be satisfied, at least in part, before higher-level needs can be met.

Figure 2: Abraham Maslow's Hierarchy of Needs (McLeod 2020)

By looking at his hierarchy of needs above, we can see that Maslow placed physical needs as the foundation for life. He believed people have within themselves the power to learn and grow. Therefore, once their physical needs were satisfied, they could learn to meet their emotional and mental needs as well. Eventually, he thought, people would transcend into becoming the best "self" they could be.

Maslow apparently spent a lot of time researching why people do not live up to their full potential once their basic physical needs are met. He concluded that human beings also need to be connected to some bigger natural force or principle such as beauty, truth, and goodness. In turn, that connection would continue to inspire and motivate each person to be the best individual they could be in this world. His ideas have some similarities to Erikson's "virtues" discussed earlier.

When I first read Maslow's work in my early twenties, all my needs were jumbled up together in my mind—I felt frozen in fear that my life would always be painful and hopeless. I didn't know if the cause of my misery was my poor finances or my inability to form a relationship. I couldn't determine if I had legitimate physical health issues or was just basically insane (which was my suspicion). It was like asking, "What comes first, the chicken or the egg?" Looking back, I may have added my emotional needs to the basic needs at the pyramid's foundation, as you can see in the chart below. But again, this is a chicken and egg situation.

Figure 3: Maslow's Hierarchy of Needs + My Emotional Addition

In the last few years, I have shifted my belief; instead of a hierarchy of needs, which can be subjective and debatable, I see all my needs as equally important, whether visible and physical or invisible and emotional/mental. Here is how I view my needs today:

Figure 4: Visible and Invisible Needs

Visible Needs: Water, Food, Clothing, Hygiene, Shelter, Touch, Transportation

Invisible Needs: Security, Love, Validation

We'll be exploring my perspectives on human needs in more detail later. For now, let's break down the basics of my observations about needs and how they work together for a balanced life.

Visible vs. Invisible Needs

I am a huge fan of clarity. There is something powerful about writing things out in black and white (or sparkly pink if you prefer). It relieves confusion and gives my thoughts organization. It helps me realize that the large swirling mass of thought in my head, which at times feels overwhelming, is not endless. Today I know that filling each type of need demands a tailored thinking approach. That is why I break needs down on paper so I can address each and every need separately.

Organizing my needs in this manner led me to realize that there are two types of basic needs: visible and invisible.

Visible needs are physical and concrete. I can see, feel, hear, smell, and touch the objects that can fill my visible needs. For instance, if I feel hungry, I can fill that visible need with a visible solution: food. Visible needs include:

- **Physical needs:** These would include air to breathe, food to eat, clean water to drink, physical touch, and a means of going to the bathroom.
- **Financial needs:** These include money or assets that can support my physical requirements for eating, sleeping, and more. I can count my money and see the amount on my computer or record book. Likewise, I can price many of the physical belongings I own and sell them if I wish, should the need arise.
- **Relationship needs:** Included here is the instinct to form a family and keep the human race going. Although not everyone has a strong instinct to reproduce, a large number of us do. Relationships can be visible and physical. I can touch my spouse and hold a real baby. I can also experience visible relationships at a physical distance with phones, letters, email and more. I can listen and read messages from people.

In contrast, invisible needs cannot be seen, touched, smelled, or heard. Invisible needs come in the form of underlying emotional and or mental needs. Invisible needs (not in order) are:

- **Security:** This is the desire to experience a sense of emotional, mental, physical, and financial security. These feelings of security can be felt but are not concrete or the same for each of us. To me, this emotional type of security, when fully met, translates into the feeling and experience of abundance no matter what is happening in the material world around me.
- **Validation:** I feel validated when I know and accept on the deepest levels that I am okay and have always been perfectly all right. I am priceless just for breathing and being alive.
- **Unconditional Love:** This is the ability to realize "I am loved, lovable, and can love others no matter what."

Note: Relationships have both visible and invisible needs. I believe if both sets of needs are not met, many of us struggle to achieve healthy, happy, satisfying relationships. We will explore visible and invisible relationship needs in much greater detail later in the book.

Balancing Needs

As you have probably experienced, satisfying one need is often helpful but doesn't solve all the issues at hand. As I mentioned previously, there are many different types of needs that compete for my attention but juggling them is not always a piece of cake. For instance, I often experienced the thrill of learning how to meet and fill an unmet need but before I could finish congratulating myself on filling that one, another need would raise its head to capture my attention. I would fill my need for safe housing, and a need for a reliable car or nutritious food or money would pop up next. It was like being permanently immersed in a "Whack a Mole" game.

The next realization I had was that I would have to work on getting resources to fill each of my needs every day. I know now this is called **growing into a stable, regulated, mature adult**. As an adult, there is no vacation from bringing food home, particularly if I have kids. It's an everyday and often thankless job. Even if I am not the person earning the income in my household, I am still responsible for my part, such as shopping for food and preparing it.

It used to be so easy to invalidate myself for not balancing everything, but, in fact, successfully balancing my life is a skill that I could only learn and develop over decades. It was like learning how to drive a car. When I first learned how to drive, there was an incredible amount of information to take in. I had to:

- Learn how to unlock and get in the car
- Adjust my mirrors and seat
- Learn the gears such as drive and reverse
- Back out of my driveway in reverse without hitting people
- Stop at stop signs and lights
- Look for pedestrians and bicyclists at every turn
- Learn how to change lanes and merge onto highways
- Learn how to run the windshield wipers
- Become mindful of other people's driving to make sure I was safe on the road

Yikes! When I look back, I see I had to pay attention to everything as driving was brand new to me. Just like driving, learning to fill and balance my visible and invisible needs has taken many years to perfect. Frankly, I am still learning.

Accepting that survival is made up of filling many diverse needs that may have to be addressed at the same time, has helped me develop into a regulated adult instead of feeling like a panicked kid in an adult body.

Survival Needs Can Be Interrelated

It is important to realize that survival needs can be interrelated. Not only did I find I had multiple needs that I needed to juggle at the same time, but also, I discovered that one survival "problem" or "pressure" was often connected to another "problem" or "pressure."

I found this out by observing the circumstance around each crisis I experienced. For instance, I started learning about personal finance and money in my mid-twenties by recording what I was earning and what I was spending. I was shocked to see that I was spending more on gifts for others, such as taking people to dinner or covering their cash shortfalls, than I was on my own food. Also, I only paid my student loans when I had a surplus. As a result, I got further behind every month.

As you can see, just looking at my income and expenses served to teach me that my financial, food, physical health, and relationship needs were interrelated. First, I played the bigshot by buying gifts for others and paying their bills while my own bills were going into delinquency. I thought this codependent behavior was bringing me self-esteem and closeness to others. When I stopped overdoing it, while I lost a good friend and roommate, I gained genuine self-esteem by developing the integrity to pay my own way.

Second, clarifying my finances showed me I was not spending enough money on food. I was addicted to living on adrenaline and was perhaps on the edge of anorexia as I tried to control my anxiety and other emotions. Somehow, I falsely believed that minimizing food and living on adrenaline would keep me sharp enough to respond to dangers and keep me safe. I was in such a crazy state of mind at the time that I actually drank half a dozen cups of coffee to relax! On top of that, I thought taking others to lunch was a higher priority than eating. I would mainly eat at work because I felt eating took too much time. The less I ate the less hungry I was. Fortunately, since that time, I have made significant changes to my diet, and I am eternally happier for it.

Working to find clarity is what I still do every day as I make changes to improve my life.

Each set of needs I resolve helps resolve other needs. As I began "problem-solving" one crisis after another through trial and error, I discovered an organized process for moving into a truly balanced life all the way around. In the next chapter, I outline this dynamic survival process.

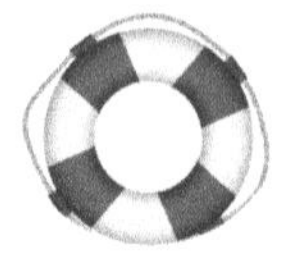

Chapter 2: Principles to Adopt for Your New Beginning

"Here comes the sun, doo-doo-doo-doo, here comes the sun,
And I say, it's all right."

- The Beatles

To me, beginning the process of survival and moving into thriving is a journey that starts with two steps: I remind myself of helpful principles then gather tools for the trip.

Principle #1: All is Well!

The first principle is that "life is basically good." No, seriously! **There is absolutely nothing that can or has already happened to me or anything I can do that can stand in the way of reaching a peaceful, abundant place in life, even if I'm on the edge of death.** I know this to be true because I have experienced a transformation in my own life—from hopelessness and escape to peace and clarity. The peace I enjoy today is hard-won but totally worth it. In fact, I have surpassed survival and live a thriving life today, which is happy, peaceful, and abundant.

How did I get here? Years ago, when I was going through deep mental and emotional issues, the leader of a support group I was attending asked me, "How good do you want it?" and he followed with, "That is your limitation." Assuming you want it good, the highest possibility in your reality is your only limitation. In essence, you decide what is possible.

It seems I wanted peace and happiness pretty badly because I have spent decades working hard on all fronts with countless friends, resources, and support systems to reach a place of daily peace and abundance. My journey started when I became willing to stop to get a clear sense of where I was at that moment.

Principle #2: Clarity is the Key

Before I was introduced to the concept of clarity, I spent 90 percent of the day feeling overwhelmed and in panic. The other 10 percent of the day, I found ways to escape through a relationship, playing guitar, or partying. After years of living this way, I learned that if I really wanted to learn how to survive and not be in fear that any second the other shoe was going to drop, I needed to get clarity by answering three questions:

1. Where was I right now in each area of my life (e.g., career, finances, or health)?
2. Ideally, where did I want to be in each area?
3. What were new and better strategies that I could learn to survive and thrive in each area?

I'm here to report, many years later, that I was not only able to learn how to survive the daily or sudden experiences of catastrophe but also joined the fellowship of those who thrive. In the process, I found that people who are thriving can live without constantly worrying if the other shoe will drop. Instead, they stay clear-headed and in the present moment most of the time. They even look forward to facing challenges that arise as a way to grow in all areas of their lives. They seem to handle smoothly any unexpected situations that come up in their lives and seem better and happier for it. All the people I see "making it happen" do so with supportive people at their sides. So, remember...

You are not alone!

Principle #3: I Can Only Change Myself

Focusing on myself and my own circumstances is one of the biggest lessons I have learned. I know now that I can only change myself. For many years, I focused on the opposite. I was trying to change others, thinking "if only my partner would change, then I'd be happy," or "if I can just get other people to do what I think they should do, everything will be perfect." Surprise! I found out others were thinking the same: if only I would change, they would be happy.

My ego always wants to be "right." Strengthening my ego somehow seemed to boost my self-esteem. But this was an empty promise. I could get the perfect degree, but that didn't mean my dream company would hire me.

I eventually learned that I had to take calculated risks and be willing to change my beliefs, actions, emotions, and circumstances without knowing how others would respond. Discovering this has led me to become more self-aware and focus on what I am doing and thinking instead of what others are doing and thinking.

After years of trying to change other people or a company's culture, I learned it just does not work. The more I tried, the more frustrated I became. I believe the people I thought I was "helping" found me arrogant and pushy. I was operating under the assumption that I knew what was best for everyone. I was in the habit of judging and finding fault with everyone. I felt a victim to other people's behavior, emotions, and beliefs most of the time. If they were mad or judged me or overlooked me for a promotion, either they were wrong or I was.

Somewhere along the line, I changed my point of view and started accepting others exactly as they were instead of trying to change them. As my perspective and values transformed, I had to leave some relationships because they were no longer a match; more often, they would leave before I did. I know now that the **Serenity Prayer for Codependency** matches my experience of what works:

"Grant me the serenity to accept people, places, things,
and circumstances as they are,
the power to change the one person I can and the
wisdom to know that one person is me."
- Anonymous

Principle #4: Just Start Somewhere

During some of the most painful and confusing times in my life, I picked up a priceless coping strategy which my friend Sheri Files later coined "**Just start somewhere!**" How does one eat a large plate of food? One bite at a time. As I started to separate things and focus on one aspect of my life at a time, I began to feel less overwhelmed. The daunting tasks in front of me seemed more doable.

I remember a time when I was graduating from college. I had to move out of the sorority housing, find a new home, and find a job to pay my rent. At the time, my savings were low, and I didn't have any prospects for steady employment. I was occupied with how to save money and feel relatively safe and secure until my income stabilized. I didn't know where I wanted to live or work.

I started by calling a couple of friends and asking them if I could stay at their homes for a couple of months until I could land a permanent job. Next, I signed up with five temporary employment agencies and started earning income. Then, the ad company I had interned with offered me a full-time job. Finally, a room came open in one of my friend's homes, and I started paying rent. I was "home." **It all started with a call to a friend.**

Tools for the Journey

There are two more preparation "tools" that have helped me on my journey to survive and thrive: first, **organization**, and second, **simplicity**.

Organization

I do not seem to be born with a natural sense of organization. In fact, I am one of those people who would keep my house disorganized to discourage guests. According to Marla Cilley, the FlyLady, organizational coach and author of "Sink Reflections," some of us follow the C.H.A.O.S. system. The acronym stands for "Can't have anyone over syndrome." (Cilley 2002, p. 13)

I don't know what caused C.H.A.O.S. to develop in my life, but I have chosen to learn more about organization and cleaning from the FlyLady and Marie Kondo. Being somewhat organized has helped me form a survival plan and kept my mind and energy consistently clear.

Here are a few of the organizational tools I have employed throughout my journey to survival and beyond:

- **Calendar** - I only have a digital calendar. The likelihood of accomplishing some task or learning something is much greater if I write it down. I depend on my calendar. What I don't schedule doesn't get my attention. (Binge-watching videos do instead!)
- **Record of my finances** - I have learned to track my income and expenses and create a spending plan for myself each

month based on an ideal spending plan. My system for recording finances and forming spending plans comes from the Jerrold Mundis book, How to Get Out of Debt, Stay Out of Debt, and Live Prosperously (Mundis, 2012).

- **Tracking my contacts** - For years, I have had systems to track the contact information for all my friends, relatives, and key working relationships. This has paid off personally and professionally.

  Note: Sending thank you notes after interviews and to express gratitude to key clients pays off big time!

- **Create a file system** - I have a filing system for all of my important papers, such as health records and projects. More and more of my files are now digital. If I think something is worth saving, then it is also worth finding. If I can find something quickly, it keeps my survival journey going smoothly.
- **Review and eliminate clutter and vagueness where possible** - This is an area I am still working on. I have improved over the years. However, I still have pockets of papers and unorganized photos I haven't dealt with yet. If I have too many papers, clothes, or stuff, my attention and focus are split in too many directions.

Overall, practicing organization helps me recapture precious, limited time in my life. It also provides a clear space that gives room physically and mentally for new ideas and projects to flow into and change my life. Being more clear and organized creates time and space for more ambitious and risky projects that could lead to thriving instead of just surviving. Finally, having less clutter reduces competition for attention. Attention is critical. And as many have found—that on which you focus grows.

Simplicity

The next "tool" I find invaluable is maintaining an attitude of simplicity and positivity.

"Life is very simple. We complicate everything."
-Don Miguel Ruiz

Keeping things simple involves breaking issues or projects down into their most basic pieces and then taking care of one small piece at a time. So, in dealing with survival, this breaks down into two questions:

What is the most basic need I have at this moment?
How am I going to go about getting this need met in the simplest way possible?

To simplify is to stop everything I'm doing and be in the moment—see what is really happening. Where is the pressure? What's going right? Where is the pain?

It's easy for any of us to say I WANT things this way or that and NEED to be here or there. However, when I break things down, things are simple, and when they are simple, they are manageable and more likely to be solved. Whether I'm having a tough or easy day, simplicity is waking up, eating, drinking water, using the restroom, staying warm, staying dry, staying clean, staying healthy, staying safe, staying sane, staying inspired and staying connected to others. There are many ways to do each of these tasks. One simple concept that helps me get up in the morning and face ANYTHING is choosing every day to believe:

Life is basically good!
I've **chosen** to believe this. It's another way I simplify life.
Other choices are:

Everything can be worked through and turned around!
Abundance and happiness are always an option!
I can make the best of any situation!

Now, when I say abundance is always possible, that means I can strive to fill a need, and I can win no matter what. I have adjusted my thinking so that "winning" now means I need to ask for what I need and accept whatever the outcome is. Personally, if I've done that, then I've won, even if, for example, the other person in a relationship walks away or turns down what I am asking for.

The bottom line is I can make the best of any situation I create or find myself in. When I am successful at *simply believing I can make the best of ANY situation*, I stand a chance at forming a foundation in my life that will allow deeper needs for meaning, family, and accomplishments to be discovered and met. I can tell you firsthand that by believing, knowing, and trusting on the deepest levels, I can make the best of ANY situation.

I have not just learned to survive but to thrive every day and be relatively happy no matter what the circumstances I find myself in, most of the time. And, for me, most of the time is pretty good. I believe each one of us may have a different definition of what "surviving" and "thriving" looks like. However, that looks for you, we need to get to clarity, which we will examine in the next chapter.

Chapter 3: The Clarity Process

So here we are! Are you ready to get started? Through facing survival challenges head-on and with much help from friends, therapists, and support programs, I have found my key to unlocking my ability to survive—and then thrive in life—is what I call the Clarity Process. After all the years of struggling to survive in different areas of my life and before moving into a thriving life, this is the process I use and apply to any issue that comes up in my life; it has worked for me over and over again on pretty much any challenge.

I have listed the steps below. I will cover steps 1 through 3 in detail below. Steps 4 through 10 are incorporated into an action plan in Part IV, so we will not cover them in detail here.

The Clarity Process for Facing Pressures

1. Identify the greatest pressures (e.g., do not have enough money for rent)
2. Record the facts (e.g., income and expenses, how late is rent)
3. Share and brainstorm with a trusted person(s) (Steps 3-5 and 7-10)

4. Draft possible options. (Include wild ideas! Or get outside professional help)
5. Commit to action items
6. Act on action items
7. Celebrate accomplishments and milestones with a trusted person(s)
8. Review how actions worked (or didn't)
9. Change direction as needed
10. Identify the next biggest pressure and repeat

Let's go into greater detail on these steps now.

Step 1: Identifying the Greatest Pressures

Determining "where the pressure is" is the first action I take when I find myself in any stressful situation. When I'm feeling desperate or overwhelmed, I STOP EVERYTHING as soon as possible. I pause and observe. I do a little inventory. Here are some questions I ask myself first to get grounded:

Am I standing or sitting?
Am I inside or outside?
What town or city am I in?
How do I feel physically? Healthy? Sick? Tired? Hungry? Thirsty?
Do I need to use the restroom?
Am I clear-headed?
How do I feel emotionally? e.g., Am I in fear? What am I afraid of?
How are my finances?
How are my relationships?
What is causing me the most pressure right now?
Do I have enough for today?

Switching into the Role of the Internal "Observer"

Are you used to asking yourself questions like the ones above? If I want to really get underneath my greatest "pressures," I often have to open myself up to obvious questions on visible issues, such as a financial challenge, as well as questions on emotional issues, such as a relationship challenge. Tough questions like the ones listed above can help me become open and willing to accept both the physical and emotional aspects of the pain and pressure I am feeling.

Emotional Pain is Real.

What is your emotional pain level right now on a 0 to 10 point scale? Nine times out of ten, when I look at a problem I am having around money, a job, a marriage or a housing crisis, the deepest pain I experience is emotional and mental. If I don't at least acknowledge this emotional pain, I'm not allowing all the pieces of the problem to be represented in the solution.

Note: Go to chapter 21 to learn more about false messages that contribute to emotional and mental pain.

Which Pressure First?

If I am overwhelmed by too many things, it can feel like pressure is building up inside me to the bursting point. One day while experiencing this, a friend asked me directly:

"Where is the pressure coming from right this moment?"

All of a sudden, this question broke my isolation. Now I had a witness who cared (even though she was a total stranger in a personal finance program). I was not alone with my own pain and fear anymore. It seemed to break the trance I had been in that reinforced hopelessness over and over in my life. I found myself directly facing my pressures for the first time in my life.

Some pressures were bigger, and others were smaller. At my new friend's prompting, I asked myself, "Which situation is causing me the 'most' emotional and physical stress?" That was the moment I realized the importance of **measuring the level of pain I was feeling about each pressing issue**. So, I have learned to identify not only where my pressures are, but also where they are coming from as well as how I feel when these pressures hook me like a fish. Now, when I'm feeling pressured, I ask myself:

"How does the pressure feel on a scale of 0 to 10?"
(0 being no pressure or pain at all and 10 being unbearable pressure and pain)

I tend to focus on the deepest and most painful pressures first, detaching myself to view them as if I am looking at someone else's life. This detached view supports me in acknowledging the pain and the circumstances I am attributing to that pain without allowing the discomfort to overwhelm me and cause me to freeze up. After going through this process a few times, I now know that I can handle two or three of my biggest pressures at a time. Sure, I may still have other challenges to address after I work through the first two or three, but most likely, the remaining challenges are less pressing.

Note: If you are in an **urgent state of panic right now** and your emotional/mental pain on a ten-point scale feels like a nine or ten, to the point where you are considering hurting yourself or others, **stop now and get help**. Call your local hospital, the police (911 in the United States), or counseling resources such as the Suicide Hotline (1-800-273-TALK (8255) in the United States) and ask for a well-check. **Don't wait. Get help immediately!**

Meanwhile, focus on the physical aspects of your surroundings at this moment. Notice the colors in your environment, feel the ground you are standing on or the couch on which you are sitting, rub your hands together, and most importantly - breathe. This process is called "orienting" and can help reduce anxiety in the present moment.

Examples of pressures both my friends and I experienced early on our survival paths:

- Not having a safe place to live or enough money
- Not being able to face the day without drinking alcohol
- Not having any trusted friends and feeling lonely
- Experiencing mental health challenges like post-traumatic stress
- Fear of not being able to take care of my children
- Scary health conditions, whether real or imagined
- No job or a stressful job
- Inability to form true partnerships with others

"Pressures" are a Natural Part of Life

"Fire removes low-growing underbrush, cleans the forest floor of debris, opens it up to sunlight, and nourishes the soil. Reducing this competition for nutrients allows established trees to grow stronger and healthier."

- Cal Fire (California Department of Forestry and Fire Protection, n.d.)

I finally accepted that in my life, "pressures" like fires are going to pop up now and then as a natural part of life. Before I realized this, it felt like I was enveloped by and dodging a constant stream of uncontrolled wildfires. I was constantly on alert, ready to jump into action, or run away, or just bury my head in the sand by escaping my issues through relationships, partying, or some other means. And whenever I peeked out of my hiding hole, I would see the fire was worse, so I would dive back and avoid my issues.

I used to believe that acknowledging and facing the survival issues in my life was "too hard" and "boring." I felt helpless to change anything. So why try? I didn't believe what life was handing me was fair. Everyone else had a better starting point. I felt like I was just barely keeping my head above water. Often, I had the mistaken idea that I deserved all the bad things happening in my life.

I know now that just as in nature, I need fires or pressures in my life as wake-up calls to give me the motivation to face what is happening. Today I can address an issue to the best of my ability and stay present during the Clarity Process most of the time. Instead of fighting the fires in my life, working "with" the fires helps me clear out the junk or old ideas that no longer work for me.

Facing my pressures provides necessary nutrients for me to grow. I always seem to grow more out of the tough lessons that include pain and suffering in life. When I started accepting that difficulties and pressures were a natural part of life, that they had to be embraced, and that they offered opportunities to learn, I discovered a great truth:

> Whenever I stop to find out the true nature of what is driving the pressure and pain in my life, I give myself the option to stop the downward spiral and turn things around right at that moment.

Getting clarity and acting to alleviate the pressures in my life has proven to be the *starting point* to surviving and a *foundation* for thriving in all areas of my life. This concept of clarity is also outlined in Jerrold Mundis's book (Mundis 2012). He explains the difference between living a life in vagueness versus living life in clarity. Jerrold Mundis applies this concept to money, but I've found the Clarity Process works in every area of my life.

Step 2: Record the Facts

This inventory process is metaphorically like counting and recording the number of apples I sell in a grocery store. Once I know how many apples I have, I can look at the apples' actual condition. How many of the apples are ripe, and which are starting to spoil? After all, I need to get some sense of when to buy new apples and when to discard spoiled apples. The more I learn about how quickly the apples sell or how many spoil, the better I can estimate how many I need to stock or when to lower prices before apples spoil.

How does learning to inventory apples in a store relate to my life? It helps me remember to stop at any moment and search for what is working or not working in my life. Today, I still track both what is working and what is not working and write them down when I need to.

> **Tip:** It helps to be as clear-headed as possible when acknowledging and writing down the most significant pressures you are facing in life now.

General Areas of My Life to Inventory

To start taking a life inventory, I break things down into four areas:

- **Emotional** - includes feelings, mental health, and spiritual health
- **Business** - includes finances, work, and education
- **Social** - relationships, marriage, family, friends, and communities
- **Physical** - health, nutrition, clothing, and safety

Writing down how you feel in each area of life can help you determine where to start the changes you need to survive and thrive.

Note: Go to "Part IV: What's Next in Your Plan?" **(or** Every-oneCounts.world) to find blank forms to evaluate where you are now in these four areas of your life. You are welcome to copy these or print these out from the website and have them sitting next to you as you are reading this.

Although writing an overall inventory of what needs to change in one's life can be useful, I have found the most vital and rewarding life areas to work on become clear by noticing the pain points in my life. As soon as I know where I am basically at, what the pressures are and how I feel, I can take the bold but necessary step to share with another person what those pressures are.

Step 3: Find a Trusted Person with Whom to Share

The next big step I embrace when dealing with a survival issue is sharing with a person I trust where I am, my biggest pressures, and the feelings I may be experiencing in connection with those pressures. Before I learned this vital tool, I used to think and act like a lone ranger. I saw myself as "out in the world doing the best I could to function and look good." I thought I was either above everyone or below everyone I met. I had internalized the attitude of others who felt that my going to counseling was a weakness and an admission that I was a failure and couldn't handle life by myself.

Underneath it all, I felt like an imposter most of the time. I felt embarrassed about my body, lack of accomplishments, unhealthy and juvenile behavior, and more. I used to judge myself harshly. I basically thought that sharing my struggles with others was a weakness. In my case, this was mainly my ego trying to run my life and make me look good while telling me I was a loser at the same time.

Well, it turns out that half of that was true. I couldn't "control" or "handle" my life very well. I was missing some key tools such as self-love and acceptance and didn't even know it. However, I soon learned that believing I was a failure—because I had to go to a counsellor—was a big fat lie. I know now that sharing with people I can trust who "have my back," is an incredible strength. Who knew! Mr. Roger's thinks so, too:

> "Anything that's human is mentionable, and anything that is mentionable can be more manageable. When we can talk about our feelings, they become less overwhelming, less upsetting, and less scary."
>
> - Mr. Rogers (Kris 2018)

What Changed my Thinking about Getting Outside Help?

I ended up feeling so much pain that I finally broke down and went for help. I stopped keeping secrets from everyone as well as myself. The first real support person I went to was a mental health counselor in our college medical center. I was hesitant as I had tried going to a therapist before to discuss my panic attacks but instead, had ended up with a person who seemed to blame me for causing problems for my mom (my mom was paying for my sessions at the time). So, I was afraid to try again; afraid of just ending up with more shame and guilt for not straightening out my own life.

When I finally broke down physically and mentally and started sharing some of the pressures and feelings of shame and pain with another counselor at the college, it felt like a huge weight fell off my shoulders. Contrary to my fears, the person I opened up to didn't run out screaming trying to get away or act like I didn't exist when I walked by them later. Instead, they smiled and welcomed me, validating where I was at with my feelings and mental state at that time.

Opening up to her about my symptoms and pain led to

solutions that, to my surprise, worked. For instance, she sent me to a biofeedback clinic for anxiety, which yielded almost immediate relaxation. Biofeedback was like a sophisticated lie detector test. They hooked my palms, forehead and fingertips to several sensors that turned my anxiety induced physical reactions to an audible sound that increased in pitch and frequency as my anxiety rose. When the therapist asked me about some traumatic event in my life, all the machines would start beeping. Through this, I was able to link my thoughts to the physical reactions in my body. In other words, I understood the mind-body connection and the importance of calming techniques such as meditation.

Working with this second counselor gave me the basic structure for working with any support person or friend on any issue. Here are a few of the best practices I learned when opening up to someone else about personal challenges:

- Pick a person who you feel has your best interests at heart and keeps what is discussed strictly confidential
- Share no more than three pressures to keep your meetings focused
- Share your feelings and fears
- Ask your friend to reflect back on what they believe are your issues to give you clarity

Note: Make sure your friend is there for you and not trying to either please or criticize you. They must offer their honest opinion even if it doesn't match your beliefs. Know that their opinion is a data point, but your judgment is the final decider. Your friend does not have to live with the decisions you make. You do!

- Write down where you think you are now with each issue
- Draft a plan using your own judgment and your friend's suggestions, including actions you can take before your next meeting to resolve issues

- Meet again after trying some of the action items from your plan to review how well your strategy is working

No matter what you and your support person meet about, make sure your friend supports you by keeping the focus on what you can do to change your own actions, beliefs, attitudes, circumstances, and emotions.

Note: The details of each pressure or circumstance are different, so I may choose different people to deal with different issues, though often the person or people are the same, namely trusted friends. Professionals are great, but even a friend who has no experience with an issue but is someone I can trust and know is in my corner, can help. I've found this to be true even if my friend is going through some of the same issues I am. "Two heads are better than one," as the saying goes.

Whether you choose to open up to someone else with your struggles for survival or not, I hope you can find ways to get clarity on the pressures in your present life. Procrastinating until the "right time" will likely only add fuel to the pressure you feel and make it tougher to put out fires later. You can pick up wherever you are. Anywhere is a good place to start.

Build a Dream Team!

A "dream team," a term I first heard at a presentation by Maryann Touitou and Dana Kobold of Red Rocks Community College, is a group of people who you select that can support you to not only survive but thrive. The key to selecting someone for your dream team is that the person truly has your best interests at heart. Such a person wants to see you succeed in every area of your life and does not feel threatened to see you grow and prosper but instead, feels enriched by your success.

One would think that our closest family members and friends

might fit into this team, but it doesn't always turn out that way. You may have a grandmother who says she wants you to succeed in college yet keeps calling you to take her to doctor appointments, cutting into the time you need to attend classes. Actions definitely speak louder than words.

Sometimes friends mean well, but as we start to flourish, they may become competitive and invalidate our progress. Some of our friends may appear stuck in the "scarcity" mentality, thinking there is a single pie out there that is shrinking, feeling threatened or envious of you as start to enjoy more pie or "the good life."

Some friends and family believe if you surpass their success in some way (e.g., earning more than your father or mother), you are breaking some kind of family code about them being at the top of the imaginary pecking order. What if you've been kind of the black sheep of the family but start turning things around? Your older sister may have been dependent upon you "failing." When you begin to flourish that may upset her sense of superiority and undermine her identity and self-validation as the "one who has it all together." Once someone thinks your success or capabilities are threatening their identity and worth, watch out. They could become saboteurs instead of supporters of your survival and thriving path.

Sometimes saying "no" to a particular team or family member is part of healing old, childhood traumas. I agree with Pete Walker, author of *Complex PTSD* (Walker 2013) who shared this opinion with me in a phone interview.

> "To get over trauma, you need a witness... We don't have trauma if we didn't come from a place where our parents (or others) treated us as if our pain was our fatal flaw. It (Believing that our pain is our fatal flaw) creates much shame around it (our pain). The way out of that shame is to find people, fellow survivors who know what that's like and have empathy rather than narcissistic contempt."
>
> -Pete Walker

I have carefully selected many of the members of my dream team; the people I choose can change over time, depending on my goals and how my needs change. I have selected some people to be on my dream team who work in the industries I want to work in. I have drawn on friends, relatives, counselors, program guides, professional mentors, spiritual advisors, accountability partners, teachers, a life partner/spouse, professional accounting and finance brokerage specialists, and many more. I may depend on one person for financial aid guidance at college and another person for mentoring me in a new field. It truly takes a village, and I love mine.

Here are some of the traits of the people I have added to my dream team:

- **Win-Win Thinker** – People who thrive by seeing me thrive as well as themselves. We admire and celebrate both of our successes
- **Gently honest** – They do not "people-please" to boost my ego but share their perspective on my strengths and weaknesses with me, especially as related to my goals. They ask before sharing to see if I am interested in feedback
- **Reliable** – They show up when they say they will, as best they can
- **Knowledgeable** – They have expertise in an area that I do not. (e.g., professor, accountant, counselor, job coach, athletic coach, etc.)
- **Accomplished** – They can mentor as they have already achieved the goal(s) I have or know how to help me achieve my goals
- **Practicing and Supporting Accountability** - I tell them what I will do and then check back with them to let them know if I completed my task. I refer to this as bookending or sandwiching a task
- **Welcoming** – They are excited to see me

- **Accessible** – They are people I spend time with regularly and/or who I have access to

Once I pick the people I would like on my dream team, I ask each person on the list if they are willing to support me in my goals by being on my dream team (some people just are on your team and always have been, and you know who they are!).

> **Tip:** Make sure you have each person's correct contact information, including email addresses.

Things Do Change

Clarity has helped me unlock solutions to *all* of my "issues" which before appeared like mysterious doors. Initially, I used the Clarity Process to solve issues such as paying my rent without stress and getting my income to exceed my expenses. Later, I used the Clarity Process to solve more complex issues such as how to get a job, build a career, or heal from post-traumatic stress. Solving these issues helped me with my work and college goals until I could progress to becoming financially self-supporting.

How Did this Change Me?

I turned around and stopped running from my fears and feelings of inadequacy and faced head-on what I thought was my enemy. When I looked at my issues directly, they turned from gigantic monsters into small kittens. The longer I avoided my issues, the more my fears and issues grew; the sooner I faced my issues in a clear, direct way, the quicker they shrank.

Pain as the Primary Teacher

As I faced, then solved, one issue after another, I reached a point where pain and fear were no longer my primary motivators. I was able to let go. Pain became my teacher and alerted me to areas of my life I could turn my attention to.

Every month, I scheduled time for the Clarity Process to unpack my pain and fear. This included recording, planning, and evaluating what was working and what was not. I felt hopeful and empowered instead of just plain hopeless and suffering as the result of giving up. Following the Clarity Process helped me understand how to have an abundant life, which included areas I thought were lost for good: how to be in a successful, how to have a loving relationship with a partner as well as how to form close, reliable, healthy, and fun friendships. In the next chapter, let's look at a real example of how I used the Clarity Process.

Chapter 4: The Clarity Process at Work

One of the best ways I learn something new is by sharing a real-life example of the principle at work. Here is a record of how I worked through some of my money problems using the clarity process.

Example of Financial Clarity

One of the first big pressures I faced was financial. At a conference for life improvement, I was sitting in a room after a meeting had ended when a friend walked in and sat next to me. As we were catching up, the next session got underway: personal finance. I was already curious about the topic, so my friend invited me to stay. I'm forever grateful I accepted the invitation. On that day, I opened up to getting clarity on my personal finances. The following is an example of how I applied the process.

Applying the Clarity Process:

1. *Identify the greatest pressures*

   As I sat at the conference, I realized that I was constantly worried about finances. It was a big issue for me at the time.

The more I heard and thought about my lack of money, the more the feeling of panic and scarcity welled up in me. I wanted to run out of the room but I forced myself to stay. It was one of the most uncomfortable situations I had ever been in. I just sat and listened.

2. *Record the facts (e.g., income and expenses, how late is rent)*

One of the first tools they talked about was recording our "numbers" every month and even every week. The speaker suggested that each of us record what our income and expenses were each week and then add them up at the end of the month. They suggested trying this for thirty days, then meeting with people willing to lend support and reviewing and forming an action plan.

I was in shock! Never before had I had the courage to look at the reality of my income and expenses. At this point, even though the speaker had shared a handout on spending categories to record, the best I could do was record my cash payments in my calendar and keep all my receipts. I was doubly shocked at the suggestion to share my financial reality with another person. I barely knew the friend who had invited me to stay, yet she said she was going to do it. A month later, as desperation and a new curiosity took over, I met with two women in a group for mutual support around finances. This experience was entirely different from anything I had ever done.

Note: Steps 3-5 and 7-10 of the Clarity Process were all done in the small "dream team" group of three people.

3. *Share with a trusted person(s)*

When I met the two other women, we took turns sharing our progress with record keeping. I shakily pulled out all my chicken scratch records of cash purchases in my calendar and all of my receipts for the month. These kind women sat with me for an hour, filling out the record-keeping sheet. Once we entered all records, we took a look at the results. My first observation was that my expenses were not as bad or scary as I thought they would be. But my second observation was that my spending was exceeding my income by around 10 percent.

The way I handled this shortfall was like a shell game. I paid my student loans late or not at all. The unpaid student loans were my slush fund. If I had extra money, I paid the creditors. If I didn't have it, I would not pay and avoid their letters. In fact, I rediscovered a pile of unopened envelopes from student loan companies when I started getting clarity. I felt terrified!

My newfound friends also pointed out that my grocery bill was low. I realized that I took money from one area, like my grocery category, and used that money to take people out to eat. I was acting like the bigshot to boost my ego. Meanwhile, my spending record showed me I was on the edge of anorexia, as I failed to cover my own nutritional needs. This realization came as somewhat of a shock.

4. *Draft possible options— including wild ideas!*

The next thing the women did was help me brainstorm options. Alone, I used to have tunnel vision and only think there was one option or, at best, a black and white option of two choices, usually equally stressful. The other two women were not in my shoes, so they could afford to get creative. I learned to look for at least three options for every challenge. This gave me choice.

Through their patient reflection on my life, I realized I

would have to spend more on food, which launched us into a discussion on nutrition. Also, I would have to stop paying for other people's lunches until I could afford my own. They gave me thirty more days to think about opening the unopened bills and told me to buy myself some clothes and go to a couple of movies. That was my first action plan. But the most crucial action item of the day was to draft an ideal spending plan within thirty days. That plan was to show my ideal income and expenses by category.

I can still feel the happiness and hopefulness I felt the first time I exceeded the goals of my ideal spending plan (which I falsely believed was a total pipe dream). In fact, the overall abundance in my life has increased exponentially since I began using the Clarity Process. I chose to say my "abundance" grew rather than my "money," as money has always been a reflection of what life brings me. These gifts can come in many ways, not always through an exchange of currency, but sometimes as gifts or opportunities. One such gift was getting a 70 percent discount on my MBA degree due to working at a college during that time.

One of the wild ideas I had when I first started the Clarity Process was to ask for a raise for a new job opportunity at the company where I worked. How bold was that to ask for a 30 percent increase in income for a position that had previously been filled by much more experienced people? Well, management rejected my proposal, but at least with clarity I knew that if I had accepted the position at the salary they were offering, I would have actually lost money due to more travel expenses on my part. Within a couple of years, I was offered 50 percent more pay to work at another company doing what I love—video editing and technical sales support versus selling outdated products. This trend continues.

5. *Commit to action items*

   We each committed to our individual plan of action. For the first time ever, I saw a clear, understandable structure for recording and planning my financial life. I also saw how to keep my momentum going through working in a team with clear accountability, support, and cheerleading. We adopted the practice of "bookending" or "sandwiching," where we would tell each other an action we were going to complete and then "bookend" or call one another to report taking that action when it was done.

   Overall, those in my financial support group all had similar problems. It was like the blind leading the blind. But as a result of our combined efforts, I felt highly motivated, hopeful and could see real change.

6. *Put your list into action*

   After I left the group meeting, I immediately started working on my action plan. I walked through a grocery store slowly and bought food I felt would be abundant. I even went to a clothing store and purchased some new simple clothing that fit! I found myself feeling more loved and alive with these simple acts. I felt relaxed knowing I had a plan, even if it was for just a month.

   The most challenging thing for me was to let go of giving people gifts or taking them to lunch in order to feel more important and worthy. But it was necessary since I was working in retail at the time and earning close to minimum wage. I literally felt a physical pull on my heart, letting go. I realized I had attached my identity to being a hero and rescuer and thought with such acts I could buy love and approval. But it had never really worked. Sure enough, when I stopped paying for a person's lunch, they quit the friendship. It was a big, painful lesson for me about what *not* to base a friendship on.

7. *Celebrate accomplishments and milestones with a trusted person*

   Thirty days after our first meeting, I again met with the two women. They helped me finish my ideal spending plan, as I had been too afraid to finish it on my own. Getting clarity almost seemed physically painful. I was terrified of giving up my fantasy of being rich and popular for the simple reality of being able to buy my first set of dishes and a vacuum cleaner. I had swallowed the red pill and left fantasy behind.

8. *Review how actions worked*

   At my second meeting with my two women friends, the feeling I had was one of relief and hope that things could be different. I logged which actions worked and which ones had not and identified areas that still needed work.

9. *Change direction when needed*

   At the second meeting, we also dove into my debts. I looked at the actual amount of student loans and devised a plan to proactively write to the agencies instead of reactively taking or dodging their calls. The main point was that I had clarity on what I could afford to pay. I let them know what I could afford and sent them a little money towards what I owed.

   At first, the debt collectors were still giving me a hard time, but I continued increasing my payments every month until I satisfied their minimum payments. However, occasionally, I would run out of money as I got too ambitious and overpaid the previous month's debt. I learned that I must keep a balance. Each month, I applied more money towards my debts, and eventually I paid all of my debts off without taking a huge chunk out of my monthly bills. Also, my creditors and the government tax collectors worked with me when I had an issue paying my taxes later. Clarity and communication were keys to getting my debts taken care of.

10. *Identify the next biggest pressure and repeat*

After my finances began to stabilize, I began doing vision work on my ideal career. This vision work has continued since then and has given me the privilege of experiencing multiple dream jobs since I began the Clarity Process.

I continue this work today by seeing the "pressures" as opportunities. Writing this field guide is part of that "dream work." I've benefited from so many other people's self-help books over the years that I decided if I ever had the chance to put something out there myself, I would take it, even if only one or two people benefited.

I have used this process repeatedly on my own and with various support people and professionals. I've used this "clarity" process for career, marriage, relationships, housing, mental health, investing, education, choosing a car, and in more areas than I can count.

Practical Tips for Surviving with Clarity

Drop the Self-Judgment

I have found that criticizing or judging myself and where I am in the moment is, ironically, the best way to stay stuck under high pressure. The illusion of being a failure is one of the greatest fuels for remaining in vagueness and escaping from my situation's reality. I recommend practicing the act of "dropping the judge" when it comes to yourself and others. Look instead for options to change your circumstances, regardless of their cause.

Be Open to Creative Possibilities

I have found that if I keep using the same strategies I have always used to "fix" my issues (e.g., in a relationship, job, etc.), I will experience the same results. I often felt consumed by a constant state of fear that the house of cards called my life would fall apart at any moment. If you keep trying the same thing over and over again, eventually, that house of cards will fall, and you'll have to pick up the pieces and build on a firmer foundation. To do so, I recommend staying open to new ideas and creative possibilities.

Notice Transformational Moments

Eureka! One of the other fun facts I have observed is that as I keep moving through and resolving each pressure, there comes a point when my pressures transform from simply trying to survive to luxury problems or questions on how to thrive. My challenges of scrambling to pay rent when a roommate moved out changed to the luxury problem of figuring out "where I should go on vacation?" So, when did that happen?

I could see my thinking becoming clearer and clearer in each area of my life I honestly faced and worked on. This clarity supported me in stabilizing one life area after another. The increased stability unlocked previously unknown pools of energy and resources inside and outside of myself, allowing me to identify and pursue other visions and dreams.

Today, I have incorporated the concept of "vision" work into my daily routine to find and pursue my passion in each area of life. The day I realized I could feel abundance, hope, happiness, and freedom no matter what my circumstances, was the day true feelings of lasting peace and prosperity started to blossom. Each time I alleviated a pressure, my anxiety dropped. By repeating the Clarity Process in various aspects of my life, surviving turned into thriving.

Realize You Can't Fail, No Matter What

When I realized my life and perspective had changed, I internalized the truth that I was a success just for breathing air, just as a newborn baby is priceless not because of their accomplishment but, simply, for being born.

An example of this is the day a friend sat with me voluntarily for hours to support me, like a midwife, to let go of the false idea that I was worthless. I thought I was failing at life because of things I had done or not done in the past and the lack of progress in my personal life and career and so I felt worthless. I learned that day to embrace the idea that I am priceless just for being alive. I had lost this insight which I am convinced I was born with.

When I know I am worthy just for being alive, I really can't fail. What I used to call failures are only learning opportunities. Some lessons may be more difficult, painful, and expensive than others, yet I know now that there is no such thing as failure for me. There are things I may not like that I did or said in the past or mistakes I made that affect my life or the lives of others, but I choose to believe today that *I can't do it wrong no matter what.* This belief is true for me even if a specific job, income stream, or relationship doesn't turn out the way I think it should, or I feel I've made a mistake. This belief holds true, particularly when I do my best to do what I believe is the right thing with the information and resources I have available at the time. The work of personally planting and caring for my dreams and needs has become its own reward; the harvest of my work has exceeded my expectations in all possible ways. So, I ask you now: If you knew you couldn't fail, what would you do?

Share What You Learn with Others

Over the years, I've had the honor and privilege of supporting other people on their challenging journeys. They have often taken great risks to trust me with their dream seedlings and "pressures" as I have trusted them with mine. I almost added this "principle of sharing what you know with others" as another step in the process because it has been so vital to my progress.

I learned about sharing my skills, knowledge, and support with others by observing people who seemed happy and thriving. I believe one hundred percent of the people I met for guidance were happy to share what they learned with me. In fact, they seemed to enjoy talking about their process and how they had achieved their dreams, whether professional or personal.

After sharing my experience, progress, and encouragement with others, I know that seeing them succeed in important areas of their lives motivates me to keep moving forward, take risks, create, and live life to the fullest! Giving another person a hand or pitching in on a team effort, feeds my thriving life in diverse and surprising ways!

What's Next?

The remaining sections in this book are best practices and strategies for specific areas, like finding housing when money is tight or learning to find love in all the right places. I learned many of these strategies in the process of moving from living on the edge of survival to a thriving and abundant life. You will also find tactics that have worked for me to fill both visible and invisible needs. I hope that practicing some of these suggested strategies will help you gain peace and abundance in one or more critical areas of your life.

As you read on, some of the definitions of needs and the tips I suggest may make sense, while others may not be the right fit. I experience the same when I read self-help books. That's why I like to embrace the ideas that make sense to me and leave the rest behind. I totally trust your process, no matter what. Just don't give up on yourself or the miracles before they happen. Everything eventually passes, and change is the only true constant in life. I can embrace and accept the change or fight it. It will happen either way.

The next section is dedicated to the physical side of human survival, where we focus on filling visible needs like physical security, hunger, thirst, shelter, staying warm and cool as well as transportation. I'll review my beliefs around personal finance to support visible needs as well as the practical role of relationships in physical survival. To effectively talk about physical survival, I will be switching into a physical survival mindset during this section.

Part II: Visible Survival

Chapter 5: Meeting Your Physical Needs

For me, visible survival is about meeting needs I have in the "real" or "material" world. Such needs support my physical life. I can visually see food, money, my spouse, my children, and my car. For me, visible needs break down into three areas: physical well-being, financial stability, and the practical side of fulfilling relationships. When I turn my attention to filling my visible/physical needs, my mental gears shift into the physical survival mindset. This mindset kicks in automatically when I am backed against a wall and my physical survival is at risk. That's the gear or "mindset" we are shifting to now in this section.

What is the Physical Survival Mindset?

I remember when I was in my first year of college at a large university. It was the early 1980's and I entered college like thousands of other students that fall. I moved into the dorm (a.k.a. residence hall) and had a roommate. We shared about 200 square feet of space. Everything seemed to be going well for the first three or four weeks. I went to class and parties. One of my parents paid the initial deposit to the school.

Then, something unexpected happened. The real bill came due, and my parents said they could not help. Circumstances had changed, and they were unable to send more money. My first thought was *"WTF! What the hell do I do now?"*

I look back and feel fortunate that in this circumstance, I was already living in the dorm on campus. If I had not been already there and going to those classes, I am not sure how my life would have evolved. Because I was in the college system, it seemed natural at the time to use the resources at hand to survive.

What happened? I did survive. I even earned my degree and live a thriving life today that is beyond my personal dreams and expectations of my 18-year-old self. I'll share more details later in this section on how I survived this moment and was able to graduate. But the main point I am making now is the survival mindset truly kicked in. Here is **my** *physical mindset*:

Start somewhere… anywhere… right around me.
Stay calm.
Get the facts and options.
Ask for and accept help.
Do the next right thing.
Never give up on survival.

I think most of us agree that physical needs for food, water, air, shelter, and sleep are considered visible or material needs that are essential to staying alive. As reflected on Maslow's lower levels of the hierarchy of needs, a person feels in the survival mode if they are hungry, especially if they do not have access to regular and sufficient quality food.

Where Physical Survival Beliefs Begin

I have observed that when children lack food, they develop a belief that there is not enough in the world for them. They start believing that food can be scarce, and they cannot trust that the world will provide what they need when they need it. So, scarcity belief can develop in childhood. This scarcity belief generates fears of survival, especially since a young child cannot fully support their own basic physical needs.

In contrast to Maslow's hierarchy, I like to view needs as circular. The physical needs of a newborn baby are shown here:

Figure 5: Visible Physical Needs

Water, Food, Clothing, Hygiene, Shelter, Touch, Transportation

Observing a baby's visible needs helps me understand every person's basic physical needs to survive since a baby cannot survive independently. As adults, we all carry old ideas about filling basic physical needs instinctively from our past. However, if we did not get our physical needs met fully as a child, we may have developed beliefs that make it harder for us to identify some of these unfulfilled needs as an adult. I grew up without a clear understanding of what was "normal." Hence, I leaned towards anorexia and actually drank coffee to calm down.

As shown in figure 5 above, a baby needs air to breathe, water to drink, nutritious food to eat. The baby needs shelter to avoid exposure and clothing to stay warm. The baby needs to have their diaper changed regularly to stay clean and prevent disease and premature death.

In addition to the obvious physical needs, the degree of physical touch and connection may vary from child to child and parent to parent. According to Tiffany Field, director of the Touch Research Institute at the University of Miami School of Medicine, "Positive touch stimulates pressure receptors under the skin, lowering the heart rate, slowing the breath, decreasing stress hormones and boosting the immune system. In other words, touch helps bodies stay healthy. Plus, it raises kids' spirits immeasurably; science has shown that positive touch lowers depression."

As a baby, we count on our parents or guardians to fulfill our basic physical needs. As an adult (and for many as a young adult), the tables turn, and we need to take over responsibility for providing not only for our own basic needs but for the needs of our children. So, what do I do if these visible needs are not met? I start by stopping and separating out whether the needs I'm lacking were missing in childhood and/or if my physical needs are not being met in the present.

Needs Not Being Met Now

To me, observing and finding healthy ways to meet unmet visible needs is relatively straightforward. It involves stopping and making a quick list of the areas I am struggling with. Want to see how well our needs are currently being met? Jump ahead to Form 4: Basic Life Inventory in Part IV and fill out the needs assessment. After you identify your needs that are most pressing, prioritize each need in order to fill the most urgent needs first. These needs relate again to immediate needs for food, water, clothing, hygiene, shelter, physical security, touch, transportation, finances, and relationships in the present.

Needs Not Met from Childhood

I find it much harder to locate and identify needs that were not met from childhood that I am still affected by. Quite often, I uncover these invisible needs for validation, unconditional love and security by asking myself what my deepest underlying desire is in the moment. Alternatively, I ask myself where my greatest emotional pain or pressure is coming from. Either strategy I use to raise my awareness of my unmet invisible needs has always led me to gaps in my emotional and mental development. As a result, I have struggled in my adult years with over dependence on other people, jobs, or pets to fill these invisible needs with limited success.

What I found has worked best for me is validating my own invisible needs, grieving for my unfilled needs, then re-parenting myself to learn how to fill these needs as a regulated adult. This way I do not rely on visible, physical solutions like buying a fancier house if I'm feeling worthless.

Note: Feel free to jump ahead to Part III: Invisible Survival: Mental and Emotional Needs if you believe that unmet childhood needs may be your primary challenge to survival, thriving and balancing in your life.

Meanwhile, I will focus on the visible or physical unmet needs you may be experiencing now in your life in this Part II of the book. I will elaborate more about the mindset that helped me survive physically and share practical strategies that I adopted because of this survival mindset. It is the survival mindset that really matters to me more than the specific strategies. The strategies illustrate the mindset in action. You may find other strategies that fit your circumstances better.

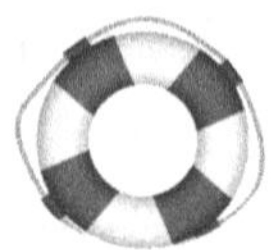

Chapter 6: Strategies for Physical Safety

When I was a kid, the concept of physical safety was pretty inconsistent. My brother, sister, and I lived in both the "safe" and "risky" worlds. In one parent's home, we ran in the streets. In fact, one time we hooked-up with friends, built torches out of branches and tightly woven fabric and explored the caves in the ditch near our home. Those "caves" were actually 4-foot concrete and subsurface galvanized steel pipes meant for the city's rain runoff. I'm super grateful we never went in there during a rainstorm. In the other parent's house, we literally couldn't leave the cul-de-sac until we were 20 years old (slight exaggeration). By some kind of grace, I eventually did learn to calculate dangerous risks more wisely, such as learning to scan my surroundings.

Staying Alert

Through trial and error, I started learning street smarts. Although I started out trusting everyone I met wanted my highest and best good, I found—many times the hard way—that I had to discern whether a situation, particularly with people and natural forces, was likely to be safe or harmful. An example of a harmful situation was one of my relatives driving downtown with their doors unlocked when someone yanked their back door open at a stoplight and grabbed their purse and luggage from the back seat.

Such incidents can be hard to get over. I have experienced PTSD and paranoia worrying about when the next person is going to attack me or try to steal something from me. Being alert to my surroundings does pay off. I know of a person, who was visiting the Colosseum in Rome, when he noticed a dozen or so young kids standing around, hiding one hand under a newspaper. Being alert, he caught on to the absurdity of small kids with newspapers, held tightly to his bag, and quickened his pace. Then he saw the kids swarming a woman with an open bag and shouted a warning to the woman. Heeding his warning, the woman managed to save her purse and belongings by reacting quickly.

As a result, I've learned awareness is important at all times, not just when you are monitoring your social network

Verbal Communication as the First Choice

My experience from way back in childhood is that communicating calmly instead of resorting to verbal or physical fights, is the most effective way to navigate tough situations. I regularly practice re-centering to a calm, regulated adult mindset to access an adult perspective in all situations, especially emergencies.

When I find myself with someone who is raging, I try to gauge, as quickly as I can, the other person's needs at that moment. I do this by asking the other person questions like: "There seems to be a misunderstanding. What do you really need? I want to help you if I can. What is happening?" I try to put myself in their shoes. How would I want someone to treat me if we switched places? I try to understand what must be going on in their lives that they feel they need to threaten me. Then, I think of what I really can do, even if it is referring the person to support people for help.

Prioritize Safety

I used to normalize dangerous situations. Today, when I find myself in a potentially unsafe situation—wherever, whenever and with whomever—I find a way to *get to safety* as soon as possible. Not only do I look for ways to get myself and others to safety in the most direct way possible, I also have improved my radar for spotting potentially dangerous situations so I can avoid them altogether. Part of this learning involved putting my own physical safety first so I can be there for others and not enable people to physically harm me or others I am caring for.

Physical Safety Trumps Feelings

I've also found that I need to shift from an empathetic point of view towards people's feelings in an emergency and focus more on my own and others' physical safety first. I used to worry about people's feelings when exposed to physically dangerous situations like sexual assault. A few times, in my teens and even earlier, I found myself more worried about the feelings of the person assaulting me than I was about my own physical safety. I felt responsible for the other person's happiness and was focused on whether they liked me or not, even when they were assaulting me. My typical response was to dissociate from my body during physical crises such as accidents and assaults.

I know now the needs I was addressing in some of these physical crises, with people using aggression or intimidation to get something from me, were actually unmet invisible needs for validation and love. This focus on trying to get "love" and "protection" from people who were unavailable and/or directing dangerous behavior at me, got in the way of taking care of myself physically. Now, I stop, time permitting, and think about what I can do to help myself or others.

Live Role-Playing Emergencies

I am one of those people who learns more by doing instead of talking. Over the years, I have appreciated the formal opportunities I have had to role-play emergency situations. For example, during these formal role-plays, I've asked questions such as: "what will I do if someone with a bomb walks in the front door of my office?" or, "what if someone opens fire or tries to assault me on the way to my car in the parking lot?" And from such roles plays I've learned if you can run, run. If you need to hide, hide. And if you need to fight, fight. Do what you can to take care of yourself.

Pause and Respond

I really appreciate the advice a cage fighter once shared with me about how to leverage the element of surprise in encounters with people threatening my physical safety:

> "If someone tries to attack you at a grocery store parking lot, and they are touching you before you can get away, try grabbing their collar and pushing them back and telling them to back the f**k off. They will likely be taken by surprise, particularly if you are smaller than they are. Then in the few moments of confusion, before they can figure out what is going on, you can run like h**l and call the police."
>
> - Anonymous Cagefighter/Firefighter

Fortunately, I have not had to use that tactic yet. However, many of us can probably relate to situations where we have faced physical and verbal intimidation while growing up at school.

Verbal Bullying Challenges

Many times, with strangers or people I've been close to, I've felt attacked verbally. At first, I did not know how to handle people's angry or blaming behavior. Years of therapy later, I've learned to ignore the person completely, observe silence, or repeat back broken-record responses such as the **S.T.O.P.** acronym (which I learned from this book's photographer, Laura Jaye years ago). **S.T.O.P** stands for:

- **S**o
- **T**hat's your opinion
- **O**h
- **P**erhaps

Here's another one that works for me a lot: "I can't argue with that." I try to do whatever it takes to ensure that I do not take the bait myself and react aggressively towards a person acting aggressively. If I do "lose it" myself, I get pulled into their world of anger and invalidation, and my judgment goes right out the window. I move into a fear-driven fight or flight "survival" response when I jump into the ring with a person acting with malice towards me, returning malice for malice.

It is particularly tempting to respond with anger and aggression, blaming others when I feel my anger is justified. It gives me a temporary false sense of superiority and bolsters my self-esteem proving myself "right" and them "wrong." But all it really proves is that I am in the grip of anger or fear and am a victim to the other person or circumstance at hand.

Accepting the other person's actions, beliefs, attitudes, and feelings exactly as I see them, instead of how I think they "should be," allows me to be present at the moment with the facts in front of me. Being present enables me to reflect on the best course of action with a clear, compassionate mindset. I know now I can be clear and compassionate with others even if I suffer injustice at the moment. *I do not have to "accept" abusive behavior.* Staying calm in a crisis helps everyone—myself included—to experience the best outcome available to everyone involved.

One of the most challenging situations I had to learn to navigate was knowing how to respond when someone was literally raging at me. I've observed when a person rages at me, they usually use a sharp, elevated tone as they blame me for triggering harm in them because of something I have or have not done, said or not said. One kind of rage takes the form of narcissistic behavior. Pete Walker, author of Complex PTSD, explains that people projecting narcissistic behavior "not only use their anger to make you afraid, even worse, they use their disgust to make you feel shame. That's just one of the biggest things we've got to overcome."

I used to try to reason or "fix" such situations. Sometimes I would use logic to point out what I thought the other person's problem or struggle was, but this whipped up their rage. In hindsight, I realized that while I thought I was being helpful, I was coming across as an expert or superior person by holding myself up as the one who is "healthy." I know now that if someone is raging at me, I need to immediately pause and accept that neither one of us is in a good place to be logical. Today, when I find myself around someone raging, I say, "I don't want to be in a conversation with blame and anger. I'm going to leave and take a break. I'll be back when our moods are better." Often, I give the other person a time frame when I will return, such as fifteen minutes, an hour, or the next day.

Rage or desperation in another person can be more powerful than I am. I often cannot talk myself out of these situations, even if I think I am logical, caring, and right. As one of my friends puts it: *"I can be right, or I can be happy. But I can't always be both at the same time."* I choose to be happy myself :)

Limiting or Eliminating Drugs and Alcohol In my Life

In my past, when I drank, especially to excess, my inhibitions were lowered, and I would find myself in dangerous situations I would normalize. I would then do things I would not do if I were sober. Even though when I drank, I was not responsible for the harm done to me by others, I would set myself up as a target by advertising that I am "not in my right mind."

I've observed that many safety issues can arise for individuals who like to party, drink to excess, or use drugs, as well as those who like to hang with them. If my judgment is impaired while under the influence, I'm more likely to follow other people's suggestions and "go along" with their ideas and desires. If I drink to excess and pass out somewhere, how much more likely is it that I will be robbed or harmed?

I try to keep in mind that if I encounter an assailant or robber, they may be drunk or high too. Being clear-headed helps me stay calm when I find myself facing a confrontation with someone. Being clear-headed can also help me use my judgment and not react violently or feel like a victim if something unexpected happens.

Non-Violent Communication - Being Calm and Cooperative vs. Being Aggressive

"Violence begets violence."
- Marshall B. Rosenberg, Ph.D.

Non-violent communication is a strategy you can apply to intense conversations and situations. Being calm and cooperative rather than getting verbally or physically abusive in a violent confrontation that is out of your control can help you regulate the encounter's intensity. Only defend yourself with violence if it is your only option to survive. To initiate non-violent dialog, first observe the other person's needs, sobriety, and state of mind, then use your observations to guide your options.

Being Aware of Your Own and Others' Needs

One of the most important aspects of being safe around people, especially at work, home, or on a playground is stopping when you sense conflict and viewing the other person as a human being. According to Marshall B. Rosenberg, Author of *Nonviolent Communication*, the number one factor to consider when experiencing a conflict with one or more people is to assess what the other person's needs are by asking questions and listening (Rosenberg, 2015).

Rosenberg says that listening to that person empathetically "without hearing blame or criticism" can also help you understand where the other person is really coming from and, most significantly, help you understand their needs. After understanding and listening to the other person's needs, share your own needs if the opportunity presents itself.

Here is a basic guideline in the form of the Nonviolent Communication logo that can serve as a guide to have the best communication possible in a difficult interaction:

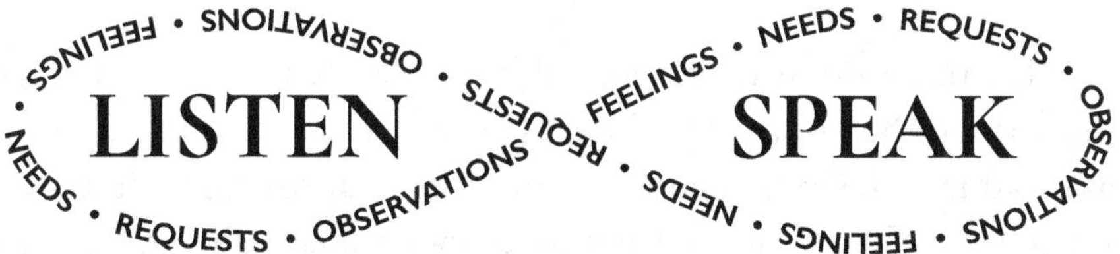

(The Center for Nonviolent Communication, n.d.)

Chapter 7: Physical Health

Many aspects of our health are within our control when we keep conscious of our body's needs. In this chapter, we'll discuss pre-emptive measures, small and large, to keep our bodies happy and healthy, no matter what our circumstance.

Food/Water

For me, water is the essence of life. I may be used to drinking juice or soda but having clean water to drink is as essential to my life as breathing air. I've trained myself over the years to drink primarily water. I'm still working on drinking enough water each day. Eating nutritious food is also vital to my survival. Have you ever been hungry? I've never forgotten the few times I've gone hungry.

To me, these needs are essential and must be provided for every human being. Having clean water to drink and bathe in and nutritious food to eat is a fundamental human right. We don't see some robins going around hiring other robins to find and bring them worms while the rest of the robins starve. It's one thing to have a vision of living with beauty and abundance; it's another thing when basic food and water becomes scarce for individuals, families, and communities. The United Nations includes nutritious food and clean water in two of their seventeen sustainable development goals designed to transform our world.

> "The Sustainable Development Goals are a call for action by all countries – poor, rich, and middle-income – to promote prosperity while protecting the planet. They recognize that ending poverty must go hand-in-hand with strategies that build economic growth and address a range of social needs including education, health, social protection, and job opportunities while tackling climate change and environmental protection."
>
> -un.org

UN Goal # 2 is Zero Hunger. (United Nations 2016)
UN Goal # 6 is Clean Water and Sanitation. (United Nations 2016)

Food Sources

Lack of food can generate a lot of fear and desperation. It is vital to stop and consider the consequences before trying anything illegal, such as stealing during such moments. Realistically though, if you get arrested, you will likely have a warmish place to stay, meals, and basic needs met for the duration of your imprisonment.

Try to think of the possible long-term effects of doing something illegal versus looking to other means. Some people get used to prison life after being in the system for a while; they no longer know how to get their needs met outside of jail. Once they are released, if they haven't devised a new strategy in advance to get their needs met, tasks, such as getting food or doing laundry, feel overwhelming and can trigger a reversion to old habits which no longer work. I observed this while volunteering for intervention work to people being released from prison.

Ideas for dealing with a hunger crisis.

Some of the first places to go if you are out of food:

- **Food banks** – Food banks have stores of donated food. Food is available to match the availability of appliances, such as a stove, microwave, refrigerator or no appliances. Food banks tend to make food available one to four times per month, depending on the bank's resources and your family's needs. My friend and I used a food bank in college.

    I currently volunteer at a food bank and a soup kitchen. I strongly recommend volunteering at a food bank or anywhere that serves food if you can. For me, it feels good, gives me hope, happiness, and purpose, and helps me keep perspective by truly knowing what is going on in my community. A side benefit of volunteering is that you can make contacts who may give you references for a job or school program.

- **Soup kitchens** – Soup kitchens or missions, also known as "bread lines" in the Great Depression, are set up in various areas of town or churches and generally serve some type of hot meal, anywhere from one to five days a week. Availability may depend on the weather as well. During deep winter months, more food lines may be available than during warmer summer months. You are welcome to dine any day. Volunteering at a soup kitchen has the extra perk that you often get to eat the food yourself or take home leftover food that would otherwise go to waste.

- **Churches** – Many churches will have food pantries, food deliveries, or grocery store gift cards to tide you over. Generally, you do not need to be a member of the church to receive aid. This aid works better as a stopgap for exceptions rather than as a reliable source for the long term.

- **Foraging** – I like to think like a bird. I love the saying, "early bird gets the worm." So I look around when I walk to the park for what plants I could eat in a pinch. You could forage for edible plants like clover and dandelion greens (there are many options), pick through trash cans, or ask for expired food from a grocery store.

  I may not need to forage for food today to survive, but just knowing about edible plants adds a measure of comfort and helps me realize how abundant the world really is around me. It helps me make better decisions knowing there is bountiful food available naturally. To get tips on what I can eat, I like working from a regional edible plant guidebook.

  Warning: There are inherent dangers in foraging local plants for food. Generally, food foraging for plants and weeds in town is prohibited—so many chemicals and pesticides are sprayed onto the plants that eating them could pose a severe health risk. Also, you may think you know a plant is edible only to find out that some or all of it is poisonous. Take care and be 100 percent sure that you have an edible plant in front of you before eating it. Make sure to wash the plants as thoroughly as possible if you try this food foraging method. ALWAYS ask private owners if you can have some of their fruit or garden items before taking them. I know of people who were shot at for stealing apples from a neighbor. It's not worth the risk.

- **Work for food** – Many people who are houseless or migrating from one place to another, hold up cardboard signs that say, "Will work for food." If you are holding such a sign, know that people will hire you and give you food if food is what you really want. Many people with resources hesitate to give money as they are afraid the money will be feeding alcohol or drug addiction instead of going towards necessities or food.

One tip that worked for me several times was to work in a restaurant, college dorm kitchen, or someone's home, and trade work for food and boarding. I worked in the college cafeteria twenty hours a week, which paid for my entire room and board including food. Plus, I earned a little extra for pocket change. I also lived with a single working mom and traded childcare and other chores around the house for room and board.

Help is Available

If you cannot get enough food to eat or find nutritious food, or your energy and morale are low, go to any local community service agency or church. There are also many 12-step programs, like Alcoholics Anonymous, where you can find support if you are struggling with an addiction.

I believe there are many people out there you can trust to give you guidance and direction for survival and thriving. Many people you run into have been in your shoes before. Seek out people who have been able to stabilize their lives. Holding fast to the belief that there is always a way up and out is one of the keys to surviving, stabilizing, innovating, and thriving.

Going to school or sending your kids to school, whether it is an elementary school, high school, or college, is one great way to get food as well as an education. Overall, regularly getting nutritious food can help you stabilize and have the energy and judgment to form a long-term survival plan.

> **Tip:** I was concerned early on that having too much food would lead to me becoming overweight. As a result, I made a decision, years ago, not to own a bathroom scale

I do not and never have owned a bathroom scale in my home.

This strategy has totally paid off for me. Every now and then, I am weighed at the doctor's office. Often, I ask not to be told my weight—like through pregnancy! Worked like a charm! I filter out messages from advertising or relatives telling me what I should look like physically. Instead, I focus on nutritious, abundant food, and regular, energizing exercise to care for my body, stay healthy, and be physically toned.

Bottom Line

To have the energy to go to school, work, or function in society on any level, you need to find a way to access regular, nutritious food for yourself and your family. Otherwise, your judgment may be impaired and you may fall into using negative or harmful coping strategies such as stealing, drinking alcohol, or doing drugs to substitute for calories, and generally just checking out instead of facing problems and stabilizing. Your problems won't go away if you check out. Taking appropriate action is the best way to change your circumstances and how you feel about them.

Emergency Preparation

Since this is a book on "survival," I recommend developing emergency supplies that will carry you and your family for at least 72 hours (three days) in any kind of emergency. I would include various medical supplies and blankets as well. Here is a suggested list of emergency supply items for a family of four from the Red Cross Backpack (American Red Cross 2021):

- **Heavy-duty, durable backpack** – Consider a backpack or at least a hydration pack to carry your supplies if you need to go mobile. The backpack needs to be durable and roomy enough for both essential and fun items. Look for a water-resistant backpack or wear a rain poncho over it if it rains.
- **Non-perishable food** – Start with canned or freeze-dried meals, jerky, dried fruit, nuts, peanut butter, oatmeal packets, tea bags, instant coffee, etc. I believe food takes many forms. However, non-perishable food is like a survival tool to me. It is portable, light, and remains unspoiled if you have to be on the go with your backpack and have limited access to refrigeration or stoves.
- **Water** – There are many ways to make sure you'll always have access to water. Purchase bottled, packet-sealed or large containers of water. You can also use hydration backpacks with water reservoirs, water purification tables or personal water filtration systems. I have a metal thermos that is tall and carries a lot of water. I like it because it is primarily metal and not plastic. However, we also store water in our home in water bricks in case of an emergency, such as an earthquake or a power outage.

  Note: If you find yourself desperate for drinking water, take some tips from Clint Emerson in his 100 Deadly Skills Survival Edition guidebook. Clint shows you how to get water in a rainforest by tapping bamboo and vines or how to rig a water bottle and aluminum can to get drinkable water when all you have around you is saltwater (Emerson 2016).
- **Tools** – Keep your backpack stocked with essential tools including LED flashlights, multi-tools, a knife, crank-powered

rechargeable flashlight/radio/cell-phone charger with weather band and solar panel, emergency whistles, wire saw, duct tape, and a fire extinguisher.

- **Knives** – I like Swiss Army knives and the Leatherman multi-tools. Multi-tool knives can be very convenient. Having a simple, small knife that you can carry around in a pocket or a purse can be useful as well. Ensure you leave them at home or check them in in your luggage if you're going on a flight. It's depressing to be stopped by security and told to either go back to check in your bag or lose your tool, especially if you've already checked in your bags.
- **Clothing** – Keep in mind the various weather conditions you might encounter and include pieces for warmth and protection such as emergency rain ponchos.
- **Additional items included in one of the Red Cross survival backpacks:**

  4 - Aluminized Rescue Blanket 52" x 84"
  8 - Hand Warmers
  4 - Dust-Protection Face Mask
  1 - Hand Sanitizer Bottle 50 ml.
  4 - Mesh Bag for Comfort Supplies
  4 - 4" Ivory Toothbrush 30 Tuft
  4 - Fluoride Toothpaste .6oz Tube
  4 - Disposable razor
  4 - Travel Shave Gel
  4 - Travel Tissues (15-Pack)
  4 - Washcloth
  4 - Hair Comb
  4 - Travel Bar Soap
  4 - Travel Shampoo/Body Wash
  4 - Travel Roll-on Deodorant
  4 - Hand and Body Lotion

1 - First Aid Supplies Zip Pouch
1 - First Aid Guidebook
1 - Nitrile Exam Gloves (2 per Bag)
6 - BZK Antiseptic Wipes
3 - Triple Antibiotic Ointment Packets
1 - 5" x 9" Trauma Pad
1 - 0.5" x 5 yards of First Aid Tape
1 - 2" Conforming Gauze Roll
1 - 2" x 4" Plastic Bandage
1 - 2" x 2" Sterile Gauze Pads
2 - 0.75" x 3" Plastic Bandages (5-Pack)
1 - 1" x 3" Plastic Bandages (5-Pack)
5 - Junior Adhesive Bandages
1 - 1.5 x 1.5 Patch Bandage
10 - 7/8" Spot Round Bandages
3 - Butterfly Wound Closures
1 - Aspirin Tablets (2-pack)
1 - Extra-strength Non-Aspirin (2-pack)
1 - Ibuprofen Tablets (2-pack)

- **Mylar/Aluminized Rescue Blankets** – Mylar rescue blankets help retain your body heat when the weather is cold as well as deflect sun when it is hot. Having several can make a big difference to survival. See mylar blankets in the clothing section for details.
- **Guidebooks** – Purchase a guidebook like this one! I own several interesting guidebooks for both physical survival and mental/emotional survival. For physical survival, look for books on survival in either urban or rural settings or both. Also, look for books on foraging plants for your specific region or hunting, gathering, and cooking in wilderness survival books.

  Note: I often purchase guidebooks I can access from my

cell phone. You may agree that the cell phone is now considered a survival tool as phones can store a whole library of resources and guidebooks and provide access to the web at any time. I recently purchased a solar phone charger from the Red Cross to ensure I can always charge my cell phone in case of an emergency.

Remember, no matter what:

You are not alone!
Start somewhere. Anywhere.

Sleep: The Great Restorer

Speaking of sleep, I can't imagine what it must be like to have trouble sleeping on a regular basis. When I can't sleep, which is seldom, it is usually because I am too excited about something that has captured my interest. I love lying in bed thinking about what I will do the next day. And then I fall asleep.

It has been years since I have struggled with insomnia. At one time in my life, sleeplessness was a big problem. One issue was that being alone at night in my bed felt like a vacation from my social phobias. I wanted to be awake, so I could "steal" time to relax, imagine, and fantasize about how great life could be. There was no pressure from people to perform or show up. It was my free time. Another issue was that I was afraid of facing the next day at work or school, primarily because, I was phobic in social settings.

Fears in the Night and Beyond

Although I enjoyed escaping by staying awake late at night, the point I started to nod off was terrifying to me. For some reason, I felt completely exposed and vulnerable. Mostly, I was afraid of an intruder. My eyesight was poor due to severe cataracts, so I was literally blind for most of my life. I also lived in many high-risk neighborhoods.

Eventually, my sleep improved. One of the biggest changes that helped was getting cataract surgery in my 40's. Suddenly, I could see 20/20 without corrective lenses, and my fears of not seeing someone or something coming at me evaporated with my improved eyesight. I wasn't planning for this positive change in my sense of security. It just happened as a result of the surgery.

Right around the time of my surgery, I also participated in some guided imagery coaching through a counselor named Marcia Beachy. These coaching sessions helped me unhook from old beliefs. The result was I was able to leave behind my fears of the dark, and I experienced more relaxation and rejuvenation due to the improved sleep patterns.

Let's look at some of the general benefits of getting restful sleep.

Benefits of Getting Good Sleep

Just like drinking enough water, getting good sleep has benefits that go beyond what you might expect. According to SCL Health (SCL Health, n.d.), which is a faith-based, nonprofit healthcare organization, some of the top benefits of getting high-quality sleep are:

- A boost to your immune system
- Stable body weight
- Strengthening of your heart
- Better mood
- Increased productivity
- Increased performance during exercise
- Improved memory

Missing sleep can be dangerous, literally! Sleep deprivation can cause car accidents. "According to a study from the AAA Foundation for Traffic Safety (AAA Foundation for Traffic Safety and Tefft

2016), you're twice as likely to get in a car accident when you're cruising on six to seven hours of sleep compared to if you get a full eight hours. If you sleep less than five hours a night, your chances of a crash quadruple! That's because your reaction time slows way down when your brain isn't fully rested."

SCL Health (SCL Health, n.d.) shows that "Sleep is good. And necessary." Dr. Roy Kohler, MD, who specializes in sleep medicine at SCL Health in Montana, "reaffirms the benefits of sleep, citing research that shows people who get less sleep tend to be heavier, eat more, have a higher BMI (body-mass index), and are more likely to be diabetic."

Dr. Kohler says that "Consistent sleep of seven hours a night is what's recommended for adults just for daytime functioning—being on task, being alert for the day and being able to concentrate and not be so moody and tired during the day."

Exercise

My relationship with exercise has varied over the years. For some reason, I was always drawn to moderate exercise with occasional bursts of intensity. As a kid, I enjoyed physical education most of the time. In seventh grade, I pushed myself to achieve the Presidential Physical Fitness Award in the U.S. I also played volleyball and ran track. My most consistent exercise has been walking for transportation and health, and I just plain love it.

My dad influenced my exercise development strongly. He participated in regular exercise as well. Most of his exercise had to do with moving around a lot on his jobs. He seemed to like exercising while accomplishing something else, like picking up trash. He and his wife and my other family members still do this. It's called "plogging," when you run or jog and pick up trash at the same time. They walk but go for quite a distance.

Since childhood, I've also enjoyed mountain climbing and hiking. As of this writing, I have climbed to the summit of at least fifteen Colorado mountains over 14,000 feet in elevation. Besides climbing and hiking, I do moderate aerobic and strength training exercises about three times a week and regularly practice yoga. Finally, I walk two or three times a day, thanks to my dog, Bruce!

Benefits of Exercise

I have found that regular, moderate exercise is vital to my physical, mental, and emotional well-being. Exercise helps me to:

- Keep my heart rate up and circulation moving
- Support my physical energy and endurance for other daily tasks
- Optimize my mobility at all ages
- Practice being in the present moment
- Strengthen the muscles around my joints for more stability
- Improve my sense of balance
- Gain physical, mental, and emotional strength
- Clear my mind, meditate and commune with nature
- Decrease the chances of pulling muscles and being out of commission for an extended time.

As my good friend, Jodi, a therapist, reminds me, "Exercise promotes chemicals in the brain that improve your mood and make you more relaxed. Specifically, the brain releases feel-good chemicals called endorphins throughout the body." The National Center for Biotechnology (Bremner 2006, 445-461) states, "Stress results in acute and chronic changes in neurochemical systems and specific brain regions, which result in long-term changes in brain *circuits* involved in the stress response." I believe exercise is one part of changing these brain pathways when needed.

Sometimes I Overdo It.

In my zest for fun and physical activity, I have torn a knee ligament during a motorcycle accident, nearly hyperextended my knee in a farming incident, and injured my jaw in a skateboarding accident. This may sound adventurous, but I was just trying to copy my brother and didn't have the talent developed yet. But hey, no broken bones yet!

Again, I have turned to self-help and coaching instructors for guidance in forming my exercise plan. Here is a basic exercise routine that I follow advised by Dr. Kenneth Cooper that I ran across in Marc David's book The Slow Down Diet (David 2015, 133):

> "Kenneth Cooper in The Antioxidant Revolution discovered that low- to moderate-intensity exercise for only thirty minutes three or four times per week was the best prescription for health, weight maintenance, and fitness."
>
> -Marc David

So, I try to find creative ways get to exercise: taking the stairs instead of elevators while staying at a hotel, parking farther away in the parking lot to walk more, taking Tai Chi lessons, dancing, rollerblading, hiking, strengthening exercises with hand weights and bands, yoga, house cleaning, yard work and using home exercise equipment. What are your favorite forms of exercise?

Cleanliness

> "When my brother and I were starting our first company, instead of getting an apartment, we just rented a small office, and we slept on the couch. We showered at the YMCA."
>
> - Elon Musk's 10 Rules for Success
> (Alpha Leaders and Musk 2020)

According to John Makohen (Makohen, n.d.), a freelance conversational copywriter with experience being homeless, staying clean physically and keeping your clothing clean is essential. One of the most important reasons for being clean—especially if you are homeless—is that it helps you blend into normal day-to-day society. If you do not keep yourself clean and carry all your belongings with you, you will look homeless and be treated less kindly. You may be asked to leave a public area while someone who does not look homeless will be allowed to stay.

Cleanliness is vital for health and wellness issues, particularly with the pandemics around us. So, where and how can you get clean when you are low on resources and living like a nomad? Many cities offer portable shower trucks designed explicitly for homeless individuals. Private and public agencies provide many of these portable showers. You can also clean up in public restrooms or campgrounds if you are legally camping there. Another idea is to create a shield with a drop cloth or cardboard box and spray yourself with water and soap. Swimming in the ocean or a lake can also be an option.

Another great tip from John Makohen (Makohen, n.d.) on staying clean is to pay for a gym membership. Gym memberships can run around $50 per month to use the facilities for cleaning yourself, working out, going to yoga classes, and more.

Strength of the Young

Speaking of gym memberships, the YMCA is an organization that not only provides a gym with showers but may also provide early learning for your kids and job training for yourself. Kevin Washington, the current president and CEO of YMCA of the USA at the time of this writing, believes that young people coming on board to lead our world can address many of the issues we face today (YMCA of the USA and Washington 2020).

> "This current generation of young people is not only the largest in our nation's history but also the most diverse. They value diversity, inclusion, and equity and care deeply about the welfare of others. They are the changemakers we need for the communities we want—communities where all people, no matter who they are or where they come from or what their current circumstances, get the support they need, when they need it, to reach their full potential."
>
> -Kevin Washington, President/CEO YMCA of the USA

Hopefully, the youth rising in the world today will also understand the role of money and work to build a solvent and abundant life as well as communities where everyone can "win" and thrive.

Body Temp - Clothing/Dry Space

Clothing is essential for survival. Finding the correct clothing for the weather is vital. If you become too cold, you risk getting hypothermia, becoming disoriented, and ultimately dying from exposure. On the other hand, too much heat could lead to heat exhaustion and, eventually, heat stroke, also leading to death.

Dressing for The Cold

You might recognize some of these (great) tips from our emergency preparation backpack section earlier in this chapter! If you find yourself in a situation where you are cold or know you are going to be extremely cold, follow the WikiHow suggestions on staying warm (wikiHow 2020):

- **Dress in layers.** Look for clothing like coats, even in the hot seasons. You can save it or use it as a pillow in the warmer months.
- **Add extra insulation.** If you do not have enough layers, try

to fill in your clothing with foam or newspaper for extra insulation.

- **Stay dry** – Keep yourself and your clothing and bedding as dry as possible. If your clothing or bedding gets wet, you will become cold and risk hypothermia. Once wet, it is almost impossible to get clothing or bedding dry in cold weather.
    - Store your cold-weather clothing, sleeping blanket, and bags in a plastic bag or waterproof container
    - Avoid sleeping on or near water that could spray or seep into your sleeping bag or clothing
    - Use large trash bags or rain ponchos to keep rain from soaking into your clothing
    - Keep your hair dry
    - Use umbrellas or large hats to ward off both the rain and sun
- **Use extra clothing for bedding or a pillow if necessary**
- **Wear multiple pairs of socks** – Get tall boots big enough to fit multiple layers of socks and cover a portion of your leg. If you are in a frigid environment, you need to protect your feet and toes from exposure. Losing toes due to frostbite or exposure can affect your quality of life and your work opportunities as well.
- **Gather and use plastic bags** – Again, WikiHow (wikiHow 2020) recommends gathering plastic bags and potentially using these plastic bags as liners to keep your feet dry.
- **Wear thick nitrile gloves to help with the cold** – You may also consider getting some inexpensive nitrile plastic gloves to wear under your other gloves. As Eastwood, the auto body and welding supply company notes (Eastwood and James R. 2015), "Since nitrile gloves are non-porous, they act as insulation by not letting any heat or moisture escape from your hands." Eastwood further notes that nitrile

gloves can protect you from chemical residue and viruses on objects you touch as long as you do not touch your eye or face.

- **Use a mylar aluminized emergency "space" blanket** - Having several of these blankets can make a big difference to survival. According to Practical Survival Blog, Mylar space blankets "are designed to minimize heat loss in an individual's body. This heat loss results from water evaporation, convection, or thermal radiation." In addition to maintaining your body heat, space blankets are water-resistant, so they can also be used as a temporary shelter.

  Space blankets can also protect you from the heat of the sun if you shelter under them with the reflective side facing the sun. Another benefit is that if you are lost in the wilderness and are in distress, you can lay one of the blankets out with the shiny, reflective side up. The blanket then serves as a visual beacon for search and rescue teams. The space blanket is an especially handy tool to pack as it takes up very little space.
- **Get a rain poncho or large plastic trash-sized bag** - It is vital to stay dry to stay warm. Rain ponchos and plastic trash bags are light and easy to pack into small spaces.

Dressing for The Heat

Dressing for the heat can be as crucial to life and health as dressing for the cold weather. According to Seattle Children's Hospital (Seattle Children's Hospital and Schmitt Pediatric Guidelines LLC 2021), there are three dangers to watch out for when exposed to the heat.

1. **Heat cramps** - These muscle cramps may occur in your legs or stomach. There is usually no fever, though spasms or tightness in the hands can indicate heat cramps. The main

solution is to hydrate. Once hydrated, these symptoms should subside.

2. **Heat exhaustion** – Symptoms of heat exhaustion include profuse sweating, nausea, pale skin, dizziness, fainting or weakness, and a low fever. Fevers are rare at this stage. Symptoms are primarily due to dehydration from sweating. **Note:** You run a high risk of developing heat stroke if your heat exhaustion goes untreated. In addition, if you have sweated profusely, not only do you need water to rehydrate but also salt to restore your blood pressure and prevent dizziness and confusion.
3. **Heatstroke** – During heat stroke, a person experiences hot, flushed skin with a fever reaching over 105 degrees F (40.5 degrees C). Fifty percent of the children studied with heatstroke didn't sweat. People experiencing heatstroke may be confused, in a shock-like state, or in a coma. **Note:** Heatstroke has a high probability of leading to death if not treated immediately.

As you can see, overheating without hydration or relief from the heat can be as life-threatening as exposure to extreme cold conditions. Although shelter and hydration are of utmost importance, the clothing you wear can help. Again, dressing in layers can help in the heat. It is essential to take off layers as you start to sweat, so that your clothing does not get soaked. This especially applies to thicker clothing, as thicker clothing can block your sweat from evaporating, preventing the body's natural cooling mechanism. Not only will you be unable to cool down but your soaked clothing will also cause you to feel cold as the temperature drops during the night.

Whatever clothing you choose, it must be loose for sweat to evaporate. Platinum Heritage (*7 Ways Bedouins Can Teach Us to Stay Cool in Summer and 1 From Us*, 2013) is an organization that runs safaris in the Dubai desert for tourists. Here is what they recommend to their clients:

> "After conducting numerous experiments including wearing loose white clothing, loose dark clothing, an army uniform, and shorts with no shirt, the scientists concluded that both black and white loose clothing was the most effective way to stay cool under the sun. While the white colors reflected the sun, the black was best at absorbing body heat."
>
> -Platinum Heritage ("7 Ways Bedouins Can Teach Us to Stay Cool in Summer and 1 From Us" 2013)

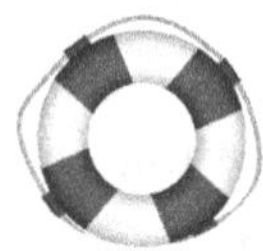

Chapter 8: Housing: A Safe Place to Stay

Feeling safe at home is another essential aspect of physical safety. Make sure to take that into account when choosing a place to live to minimize the danger in your home environment. I need my home to be a refuge and an oasis; otherwise, everything else in my life is at risk.

On numerous occasions, I have struggled to find any kind of housing, much less a safe, clean place to live. Here are some strategies I have used to find housing over the years in good times and bad.

Private Homes

Some of the safest and most welcoming places I have stayed have been in people's private homes. Ironically, this was not immediate family but friends' homes or rooms I found through advertisements.

Friends (Real)/Family

Staying with friends and family is also known as "couch surfing." It can be a relatively safe alternative to being homeless on the streets. I stayed on friends' couches after college for months while I regrouped to find a steady job. While I couch surfed, I made sure to be of service. I cleaned, did the dishes, and prepared meals. And I socialized and generally enjoyed time with my friends.

One of the homes I couch surfed at had five different people working and renting rooms. Within a few months, I landed a job and a room opened up, so I signed a lease and started paying rent. I lived in that home for a couple of years.

Room in Someone's Home

Renting a room in someone's home has pluses and minuses. On the plus side, it is less expensive than renting an apartment. There is also a more homelike feel as you cook together, eat together, and share responsibilities around the home, such as cleaning and yard work.

There are minuses as well. You are always aware that the "owner" of the home is in charge, and you feel that slight insecurity they could at any time "change their minds" about you staying. They may also have habits or values that are not a good match, so you may struggle to tolerate your living arrangement. You may become used to living in this home and put your own plans on hold. And often, the owner does not want you to have romantic partners visiting or staying over. That means you have to build your relationship outside the "home" you live in.

Trading Work for Rent and Board

Besides paying lower rent, I have been able to trade skills such as childcare or pet-sitting in place of rent. It can be a win-win situation that saves you money while you get back on your feet. Food can also be part of the deal. Not having to pay for food can add up to significant savings.

Living in someone else's home requires deep-level honesty, patience, and tolerance for everyone involved. This is not to say you have to put up with behavior you find unacceptable, but you do need to be trustworthy if others are to trust you around their children, pets, and belongings.

Local Community Housing Options

Homeless Shelter

I have never spent a night at a homeless shelter. What I know, I have discovered through research, volunteering, professional work, and discussions with people who have stayed at a one.

Homeless shelters vary in availability, safety, and quality from one area to another. On the minus side, shelters may attract people operating from a criminal mindset, which turns the shelter into a place of further stress. Wondering if others will steal from you or try to sell you drugs or alcohol makes it challenging to stay clean and sober if that is your goal.

Being in a shelter may limit your options to bring in a pet or use alcohol or drugs if you feel compelled. Shelters may also divide up families where the dad may have a separate living arrangement from the mom and kids. More than likely, the shelter will run out of room if you don't get there soon enough to sign up.

On the plus side, shelters protect you from rain, cold, and snow, which could lead to illness and death. Food is often available, as are basic sanitation facilities. As an additional plus, shelters often attract extra resources such as job counselors. Overall, a well-run shelter may be your best bet if you can get there early enough in the day to sign up. For instance, a shelter may beat staying in a violent home.

Youth Hostel

Youth hostels tend to be lower-cost facilities providing dorm-like and individual room options for travelers. The name can be a little deceiving as anyone of any age is welcome to stay. According to Hostels Worldwide (Hostels Worldwide, n.d.), there is a "worldwide network of Not-for-Profit Youth Hostel Associations," which "believe that exploration and travel lead to a better understanding of other cultures, and in turn, this creates a peaceful, smarter and more tolerant world." Whether you share their idealism or not, it's an excellent opportunity to find a relatively inexpensive place to stay.

After my first year in college, I stayed in a local youth hostel for about ten days as I sorted out summer jobs and found more permanent housing. There were about ten of us women in bunk beds in one room. We had access to bathrooms and common areas, such as a living room, and continental breakfast was offered as well. It was a simple time.

One of the biggest perks was meeting other women trying to stabilize their lives. I met one of my best lifelong friends in the youth hostel. We helped each other and were able to get cheaper housing after the youth hostel experience by pooling our resources. One of our female roommates knew how to cook whole chickens. We learned together as we spent our money on meager meals and shared the cost of newspapers to find jobs. In the end, we all found legal and safe jobs. Three women rented an inexpensive apartment together, and two women found a "deal" renting extra rooms in a fraternity house.

Fraternity, Sorority, and Other Organizational Lodgings

It is not just wealthy college students who live in the fraternities, sororities, and other exclusive type homes on college campuses. Other students and working individuals can also rent extra rooms when available due to a dip in membership.

In a fraternity, I shared an apartment with a female friend. We had our own entrance and bathroom but had to share the kitchen with a handful of guys. Half the house was filled with non-fraternity brothers. Later, when I lived in a sorority annex house, I had my own room and shared a common bath with several other men and women (some of them sorority members) who lived on the same floor I did.

Living in fraternities and sororities is not for the faint of heart. There is a lot of drinking, drug use, and occasions of extreme sexual misconduct, some of which may be criminal. Also, there can be theft. We all had locks on our kitchen cupboards of the sorority house. On several occasions, police were called. In one case, arson was suspected. But overall, the opportunity to live in these homes helped me financially and enabled me to build and maintain a basic working community.

Car Living

Car/Van

Many of us believe that living in our cars or vans is a last resort. We would only do it if we absolutely had to. Maybe I would do so in Silicon Valley, for instance, if I couldn't afford any other housing. Like me, you may have felt empathy for people who "have" to live out of their cars, especially in colder or hotter regions of the world.

People living in their vehicles have a whole set of unique issues such as finding a bathroom and shower, determining where to park legally, and deciding where is relatively safe. A major concern is living in fear that someone might break in while you are sleeping. Though I have only slept in a car during "camping" trips (where I feared bears) or in-between destinations on a long road trip, I have experienced how unsettling it can be to sleep in a car.

On the flip side, as I researched car and van living, I found an astonishing *number of people choosing car and van living as a lifestyle*. It's an affordable life of travel with far fewer routines. There are countless articles and videos on how to outfit your car or van for long term occupancy. If you are into an outdoor lifestyle of hiking, skiing, kayaking, rock climbing, and more, then living in your car or van may be for you.

I was inspired by the article, "How to Live Out of Your Car" in Outside magazine (Brinlee, Jr. 2016) in which author Chris Brinlee, Jr. shares tips from professional vehicle dwellers on how they make the most out of living on the road. According to Brinlee, for many vehicle dwellers who live on the road "their reasoning often comes down to these core symbiotic benefits: financial freedom, mobility, and simplicity."

According to Meghan Murphy of the HandUp blog (Murphy 2015), one of the biggest issues you face, if you are going to rely on your car or van as a home, is to make sure you have enough financial resources to continue to pay for your license, car registration, insurance, and tags. Many people neglect these important issues and eventually lose their vehicle and end up living on the streets. Living on the streets or down by waterfronts can be unsanitary and dangerous.

On Someone Else's Turf

Homeless Encampment

Homeless encampments may afford some benefits. However, it is difficult to find sanitation, and the encampment can be detrimental to physical and mental safety. According to an article from Our Calling (Our Calling, n.d.), a non-profit serving the homeless, encampments can be peaceful and are neither less nor more dangerous than any other neighborhood in a city. However, residents may face instability due to lack of policing or, worse, police action to raid the camp, bulldoze their tents and trash their belongings.

The long and the short of it is, if you are thinking of living in an encampment, you need to be ready to move, even in the middle of the night. Be prepared for traumatic criminal action without the possibility of getting help from the police. Also, be on the lookout for more recent efforts to provide alternative encampments, such as the tiny homes initiative of San Jose (Lauer 2020).

The main thing is to focus on connecting with resources, not just for housing but also for food, mental health, work, and education. Also, consider yourself as "houseless" and not "homeless" because home is wherever you are. Houselessness is simply a temporary condition that you can change by using resources available to you.

Sleeping in Public Places

HandUp blog (Murphy 2015) cites that sleeping in public places can be difficult. Although sleeping during the day is safer to guard against theft, it is difficult to find public places like park benches or sidewalks that allow sleeping in public. Enforcement for public sleeping and eating is becoming stricter as local governments enforce their loitering laws more aggressively.

Camper/Tent Legal Locations

Camper or tent living is similar to car living, though it may be tougher to find a place to pitch a tent. There may be more restrictions, but enforcement and laws vary. Some towns are more lenient to camping, even on sidewalks during the night, while others are not.

Some believe that it is unconstitutional for authorities to displace homeless people from sleeping in public places. The American Civil Liberties Union (ACLU) (ACLU 2017) has summarized multiple cases where it has been argued successfully that a total ban on sleeping in public places where no other options were available amounted to "cruel and unusual [punishment], since it effectively criminalized sleeping on any public property, despite sleeping being an unavoidable consequence of being human."

Airport and Subways

Not everyone trying to live at an airport has Tom Hanks' luck, as in the movie The Terminal (Movieclips Classic Trailers 2017) where an Eastern European traveler gets stuck at the airport and finds ways to earn a few bucks while living in the terminal. In practice, airports are becoming stricter due to threats of terrorism and are very aware of loitering or unattended bags. Also, airports are closed to non-travelers earlier in the evening than they used to be. So, although you may catch a break resting during the day at an airport, the chances may be small that you can stay at the airport at nighttime.

According to John Makohen (Makohen, n.d.), who has experienced homelessness first hand, a subway is an option if you have one in your area, providing a warmish place to sleep. The tickets are cheap, and you can even get away with jumping the turnstile every now and then. But be on the lookout for people, especially renegade teens, trying to harass the homeless. Be aware of your surroundings as much as possible when sleeping in public areas.

Under a Bridge/Sidewalk

John Makohen (Makohen, n.d.) also talks about living under a bridge or on a sidewalk. Living under a bridge may keep you dry but is dangerous as you are far more likely to be a target of theft or assault since there are no witnesses to report a crime. Also, the cold may lead to exposure and death.

Sidewalks and doorways may seem safe places to stay but, in reality, are not. You become open to a host of crimes when you fall asleep, ranging from theft to assault, with few people around at night to witness or help. You may want to consider sleeping more during the day than at night.

In many areas, it is illegal to sleep in public on benches, under trees, or on sidewalks. So, you will likely be asked to leave, making it hard to get good sleep. Also, the less "homeless" you look (dirty hair and clothing, belongings in sacks or suitcases, etc.), the less likely you will be asked to leave.

Government Housing Assistance

Public/Subsidized Housing

If you have low income and are subject to other risk factors, such as disabilities, you may be eligible for subsidized housing. Even in small towns, there is something akin to a "Department of Housing." Also, many other organizations provide subsidized housing. Look around and do some research in your area. Public housing can be helpful at the right time. The rent can be very reasonable, especially in expensive areas. As long as you know and can follow the "rules," you can stay, most likely for as long as you qualify financially. Often public housing is maintained better than private low-income housing.

I believe in using subsidized housing temporarily and not permanently. I've seen many friends become dependent on subsidized housing, avoiding earning more so they won't lose their subsidized housing. Although I appreciate the help that is available, I want to make sure my kids and I know how to become fully self-supporting but be willing to accept support when there is a need.

Many communities focus only on housing to support peoples' social and health challenges but do not assist with other resources individuals need to survive and thrive. Our Calling (Our Calling, n.d.) states that support ends once you get the keys to public housing. There is "no support, no food, no toilet paper, no rehabilitation, no counseling, no care. If someone is in a situation where they need housing, it's a symptom of much bigger life problems. I know too many people who have gotten housing and have died, become victims of sex trafficking, become victims of human trafficking, or have relapsed into deeper chaos – only after being relocated far away from support. The wrong kind of housing does not help."

If you're on the brink of a financial crisis and need to rebalance, consider talking with people working in the social services or state workforce centers or commissions to find out more about subsidized housing in your area. You may need to navigate rules, such as restrictions on drug use or pets, to get a place.

If you choose to move into public housing, try to see what you can do to keep yourself and your family safe. Keep an eye out for the programs that your housing agency offers and take advantage of every opportunity and resource you find. Each agency you visit for assistance can refer you to another agency that might help you re-stabilize your income and life. One housing director I talked with was exploring giving tuition vouchers to study at the local community college to tenants who paid rent on time.

Housing Vouchers

In some areas, besides standard public housing, there are vouchers available enabling you to live in homes or apartments owned by private owners or other governmental agencies.

Some housing vouchers are guarantees made by a local government to pay private property owners a percentage of all rent payments on behalf of someone with a low income. The advantage with housing vouchers is that it enables you to pick safer neighborhoods. Housing vouchers can be difficult to get, but they are worth a shot.

Housing vouchers help private rental property owners and landlords as well. They enable the owner to have guaranteed rental income, whether the tenant is working or not. We own a small home in a small town. When the economy tanked recently, we let our tenant know that if he needed to get housing vouchers to survive, we would make the physical changes necessary to qualify the home for the voucher program. It helps us, and it helps our tenants. It also helps the housing department, as they get more housing options for people who suddenly find themselves facing financial hardships.

Subsidized Home Ownership

Is this for real? Is it possible for someone to buy a home when their income is low? Believe it or not, it is.

In the United States, many loan programs exist to help people purchase a home, *particularly in rural areas* with less than 35,000 people. Homes need to meet specific physical standards, but the loan often includes extra funds to bring the house up to code if it lacks something. The process is to appraise the property as it currently stands and create a second appraisal based on the proposed repairs. Many of these loans come with only a 1% or so interest rate. Note that you may need a good credit score to qualify.

Example of Subsidized Mortgage Payment Program

If you are renting a home for $1000/month, consider the cost of purchasing a $150,000 house instead. Sound steep? Let's do the math:

Mortgage: $150,000 at 1% interest for 30 years = $482.00 per month! You need to add taxes, which we estimate in some areas would be $50 per month, and home insurance of $150 per month, so you can own a home for $682 out of pocket per month. Much cheaper than rent!

Although it may be harder to find work in a rural area, the payoff may be worth it as you improve the quality of your life. Besides, if you are retired or living on disability insurance, a rural home may be a wonderful alternative to trying to scrounge out a life in an urban area.

The programs may change over time, but the idea is to keep

looking! Don't give up before your housing miracle happens. Consider a simpler and slower pace of life as a survival tactic.

Facing Evictions or Foreclosures

> "What we have always tried to do from the beginning is to find some common ground with the landlords and the renters."
>
> -Ken McElroy, Real-Estate Investor,
> Author and Entrepreneur

A Word About Eviction and Foreclosure

I remember going through foreclosure during the 2008 housing market crash. Looking back, I ask myself, "Was the foreclosure good news or bad news? Who knows?" I know now, it worked out better than I could have imagined, though, in hindsight, there may have been more things I could have tried to save my home and the ensuing seven years of low credit scores. Again, who knows?

On the surface, it may have looked like bad news at the time. But in retrospect, I think my ego felt more pain from the loss of the home than my family did. The foreclosure was on a house we had lived in before, but which, at that time, we were renting to someone else. When our renter left, we lost the income and couldn't rent it fast enough to keep up with the mortgage.

As it was, we were having to pay more on the property than the rent was bringing in. So, all in all, when we lost the tenant, the house was lost too. In our case, I believe we had overextended ourselves with too much debt relative to our income. We had two rentals and another vacant lot we were paying on that was undeveloped but we hoped would be the foundation for our dream home later. At the time, our current and future livelihood was hinging on everything going really well with a ton of good luck.

Being overextended financially was a setup for us to experience financial difficulties as there was not enough room in our spending plan to adjust to unexpected occurrences. Not only did we experience an economic downturn and a real estate crash, but we also had tenants who were unable to pay rent in either of our rentals, while we had lost our primary income due to a layoff.

As a result, I learned valuable lessons that might help you in the event of an eviction or if faced with the possibility of foreclosure.

To tenants and homeowners at risk of losing their "home":

- My home is there to serve myself and my family. We are not there to serve it.
- My income has to exceed my expenses. If the home is costing us more than we can afford, we need to let go of the home and look for alternatives. True security and abundance have come to me from following this basic principle. Your income needs to exceed your spending.
- My true home is wherever my loved ones are, even if we live in what seems like a shell of what we used to own or rent.
- My identity is not my home or any material belongings, whether renting or owning a home. Instead, my home serves as a haven and provides both emotional and physical security and abundance. That feeling of emotional and physical security and abundance can be created elsewhere in humbler settings, even if just for a while as we re-stabilize.
- A home is a secured asset. Letting it go back to the bank, in the worst-case scenario, is part of the "deal."
- Even if you let the bank repossess the home, be ready for a tax bill on the loan amount the bank wrote off, as in some countries, the amount of loan forgiven is seen as a capital gain.
- Only take on secured debt. A secured debt is a loan backed up by a physical or material object. Home and car loans are typical secured loans. With a secured loan, you can give back

the material object (the home), which will clear your debt to that lender as long as the object's value exceeds what you owe on it. If you are "underwater" and your material object is not valued more than your loan, then you may end up responsible for the difference.

- Avoid unsecured debt if you can. Credit card loans, for instance, are unsecured loans. If you purchase a couch on a credit card and don't pay off the bill when due, the card issuer can charge you fees and lower your credit rating, but they will not come to your home and repossess your couch. So this type of debt can snowball. As my small business professor used to say, "Never buy a short-term asset with a long-term loan." In other words, don't buy groceries with credit cards. Once you eat your bread, the debt lives on and on and on and on.
- Lose the battle (current home); win the war (solvency). To me, solvency means I can find a home, whether renting or buying, that matches my income and family's immediate needs instead of letting most of my income go to a home that "looks good." My family eventually sold every property we had in 2008 and rented for a while. We rose again brighter than ever, like a phoenix rising out of the ashes.
- With financial stability, you can rise again. I did. I bought a fixer-upper a year or two later, even though I had a poor credit rating. The home was smaller and needed tons of work. But we fixed it up and paid it off—with help from family—and now we have a haven when we need it if things go south again.
- If you want to save your home and it is possible for you to do so, try everything you can. Negotiate with the lender, take on renters to help pay the loan and combine family members to economize.

- Remember, if you own a home, do the math. Often your mortgage may be less than rent in your area, especially if you can get help from other family members or boarders during tough times. Other times, rent may be less than mortgage.
- Remember, you might be a rental property owner yourself someday. Treat your landlord and owner the way you would like to be treated if the tables were turned.

To landlords and mortgage holders:

- Think of the long term. Where do you want to be one year from now? Five years from now? Do you trust people living in your home to take care of it? Are you afraid they will start a meth lab? If you trust them, talk with them and share your concerns and issues. Look for win-win solutions.
- It may be easier to try to work out issues with current tenants who are super reliable and take care of the home than to find new tenants during a financial downturn. Each side may need to push past their comfort zone to share realities and make it through economic down cycles.
- If in crisis, consider selling your home to your tenants with owner financing. We paid 7.5% interest on our owner-financed home when we didn't have the credit to get a conventional home loan. Our mortgage payment was still way cheaper than the rental rates in the area! We tightened our belts, paid extra on the monthly principle and didn't get a second mortgage. Today, that home is paid off and serves as a rental.

If you offer your renter the option to purchase the home through owner financing, you will have a motivated renter; people I've seen will pull all the stops to make payments on their own home vs. trying to make rent.

Note: My experience is that owner financing often carries a higher interest rate than bank financing. I'm sure our landlord/ financer was happy to be earning 7.5% annually on the money we were borrowing from them. You still need to do thorough credit checks, and you may need to set money aside to repossess the home if the new owners are not able to pay.

- Offer to trade work on the home or property or hire your tenants for other work during an economic crisis. We are doing that now. We trade some rent for improvements on our property. I have also hired our tenant to fix antique chairs and do other odd jobs.
- Be a resource. Does your tenant need a job? Do you know anyone who is hiring? You can't solve everything, but you are a resource for them, which in turn helps you. To me, this is win-win thinking.
- Is your tenant unable to stay in the area due to a lack of work for the foreseeable future? Take time to work out a plan together so that neither of you is just frozen-in-action due to fear. I would guess most tenants do not want to have huge unpaid rental debt together with late fees that may never get paid. Brainstorm together to figure out the realities of the local market. If they need to move, what can you do to help? Be of service as a resource while staying clear of taking on their issues yourself. Who knows, maybe they know a tenant who is staying who would like to rent from you. This happens all the time. People like working with people who want a win-win outcome.
- If you face foreclosure yourself, turn some of these same tools around with your lender. Again, the home is ultimately an asset. So, ask yourself honestly: Is your property taking you down financially? Are you feeding your rental properties money every month, like we used to, because they cost more than the income they provide? If so, keeping that rental may

just deplete the resources your family needs to survive, so it can rise another day to thrive.

To everyone impacted by a real estate crisis this moment:

- I believe we are all on the same side of the ring, trying to work things out despite our ego-involvement and economic downturns. By using win-win thinking to try to work things out for the best of everyone involved, we stand a chance of everyone landing on their feet at the end of the day.
- Think of the "barn-raising" lessons from the past. In the old days, when people migrated to a new area, they would help each other construct a barn since the job was too much for one family to complete on their own. Everyone ended up with a barn, and everyone helped build each barn. The point is, if we help each other, we all win.
- I have found it necessary to be ready to pause, breathe and observe what is happening. Only then can I take the best actions available to me, such as leaving or asking more questions when things get heated or elevated emotionally. If I do not stop to pause, observe, and wait to act until calm, I will automatically get hooked into drama with people who might not be conscious and willing to work with me.
- Not everyone is capable of looking for win-win solutions. For example, banks may be inflexible and unwilling to get creative on win-win solutions. Things always change. Building relationships and keeping the door open are real options for all sides, including banks, in my opinion.
- Not sure whether to keep your home or leave? Consider Kenny Rogers' advice from his song "The Gambler" (Kenny and Genius Lyrics, n.d.):

"The secret to survivin' is knowin' what to throw away and knowin' what to keep... You've gotta know when to hold'em

[keep your home] *and know when to fold'em* [let go of your home]. *Know when to walk away and know when to run."*

- Get creative with your solutions. List out at least fifty things you can do to remedy your home and financial situation. Once you get past twenty, it will really get creative.
- As Stephen Covey, author of the *Seven Habits of Highly Effective People* says, look for "win/win" solutions in every situation. (Covey 1989, p. 309)
- One of my friends used to tell me, **"You can't do it wrong."** This concept tags onto the idea that I can't fail. I firmly believe if I pause and think about the next best thing to do, I can't do it wrong, even if I learn more later and change my strategy. Believing I can't do it wrong frees me up to act out of hope and possibility versus fear.
- Don't gamble with your honesty and integrity. This includes all parties—predatory lenders or landlords bent on short-term gain and tenants skipping paying rent when they can. Put yourself in other peoples' shoes when making your financial housing decisions.

  I don't personally believe that cheating people by taking advantage of others' misfortunes without even trying to work with them leads to long-term abundance. Cheating others in a financial crisis only leads to emptiness. Many people end up like Smaug sitting on his gold pile in *The Lord of the Rings*, all alone. Instead, helping others succeed, especially in bad times, benefits everyone involved, including yourself. I also consider that at any time, the tables could turn on me, when in an economic downturn, for instance, misfortune comes my way, and it has; another reason to treat others as I would want others to treat me.
- If you decide that you have to let go of your home, whether you rent it, own it, lease it to others, or finance it, take time

to stop and grieve. I thanked my home for the service it provided my family and me when we lost it to foreclosure. We moved into a crazy, unfinished place and then moved three more times before buying our fixer-upper through owner-financing and selling our land to fund the upgrades. We were in a whirlwind for a year or two after the foreclosure. But again, it worked out better than we could have imagined.

- Have fun if you possibly can. If you have kids, help them see it as an adventure and that events like this can happen in life. Show them that the family is what matters, not the assets you do or do not own.
- Please take your photographs with you when you leave home! I worked in real estate between 2005 and 2008 and worked on several dozen foreclosures. It is heartbreaking to see what people leave behind. Some leave photos that could be important memories to reflect on later.
- If you have to leave your home, pause a moment to take stock. You may be leaving behind red flags pointing to other areas of your life that may need attention. For example, if you leave behind a garage full of empty beer cans, consider if you are leaning on alcohol too much.

Take Time to Learn the Lessons

Misadventures happen, but I've grown through every one. They are the cost of going through the college of life. I'm here to talk about it from a place of abundance. That's what matters to me. I didn't give up, no matter what.

Negotiate! Negotiate! Negotiate!

Remember to negotiate if you need to. Practice asking for what you need and offer what you can that does not compromise your own or someone else's dignity, integrity, security, or freedom. Learning, practicing, and applying the skill of negotiation can help in almost all areas of life.

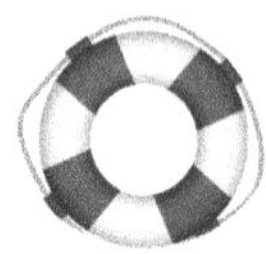

Chapter 9: Financial Well-Being

"Your money or your life!" - Jack Benny

In the past, people were responsible for growing and providing much of their own food, sewing many of their own clothes, and building their own homes. The community often shared in these tasks. Today, many of our needs are met by earning money, enabling us to pay for our basic needs. Many of us are far removed from our ancestors' skills of growing our own food and instead rely on grocery stores and restaurants. So today, our survival depends on our ability to survive financially.

I believe money is a means, not an end in itself. Earning an income helps pay for food, clothing, transportation, and housing. Money in and of itself is otherwise worthless. I can't eat cash or coins. I can't drive a digital number to school like a car. So, money for me is more of a tool for trade. I could also trade physical objects of similar value with someone who could fix my car instead of paying cash. And believe me, I will and do trade real goods and services with people when I need to survive. Hoarding gold and sitting on it like Smaug in The Hobbit, the Desolation of Smaug (Movieclips Coming Soon, 2013) will do nothing for me in the long run.

My personal goal is to earn enough income and create savings that provide for my family's basic needs and create reasonable security. Exploring and meeting other people through travel and education is something we also save for, which enhances our overall happiness and quality of life.

My family believes in giving back, investing in others and their business ventures, and volunteering our time in service. Your financial and basic needs will likely be unique to you.

What is Your Financial Goal?

Do you have a clear picture of your financial dreams and specific goals to achieve those dreams? If you don't have clear goals or are unsure, read on.

In life, there are decisions we make and associations we place on money and finances. Many people tie their identity to their net worth (what they have minus what they owe). Many such people will do just about anything to keep and increase their net worth, status, and social standing no matter who they have to step on or whose ideas they steal and credit as their own. There are many more who have never in their lives been able to build a positive balance. They are still working hard every month just to stay ahead of the rent and car breakdowns.

Almost all of us, with no access to significant financial wealth, believe that winning the lottery or having more money than we know what to do with would be the answer to our problems. However, famous and financially successful actor Jim Carrey says, "I think everybody should get rich and famous and do everything they dreamed of so they can see that it's not the answer." (Maharishi International University and Carrey 2014)

If having plenty of money isn't the answer, then what is? One theory offered by Eckhart Tolle (Tolle 2004, 66) is to strive to be present and clear with where you are right now. Tolle suggests balancing the horizontal part of your life – including the finances, work, family, savings, and pleasure, with the vertical side of life, being present wherever you are right now and accepting that reality to move forward. Appreciate your body, the trees, the flowers, and the ground that supports you. Stay out of your mind, go outside in the fresh air, and just absorb the beauty and abundance surrounding you.

My personal experience is that clarity and being present has been the key to financial abundance. When I was younger and my life was simpler, I reached a place of relative financial security using the clarity principles. But then family concerns came along and my economic life fell into a state of turmoil for eight years. It took me a while to regroup. Fortunately, I was able to regain a deep sense of financial security by re-applying the principles of clarity to money. The last thirteen years have felt much more abundant and prosperous. However, when things are challenging and I am in need, I look at how I can generate quick cash.

Quick Cash

Here are a few strategies I've used to get cash quickly, legally, and safely:

- **Sell something I own** – I have found that when times are tough, my well-being and sense of abundance are more important than any material object.
- **Ask a friend or family member for a secured loan** – A loan is secure when some type of collateral backs it up. For instance, if you need $100 to take your nursing exam, borrow it from a friend or relative and give them your leather jacket or a few pieces of jewelry or a TV to hold until you can pay them back. They may think you are crazy but secured borrowing like this helps you and them. If something happens and you

cannot pay them back, they can keep or sell your items, and you are free from that obligation. It also keeps you on notice when borrowing money and motivates you to avoid getting too deeply in debt. For more on secured borrowing read *How to Get Out of Debt, Stay Out of Debt, and Live Prosperously* by Jerrold Mundis (Mundis 2012).

- **Ask for a gift** – I have had pride in handling things independently, but sometimes asking someone for a direct gift without guilt-tripping or pressuring them may end up helping you and the other person. When I have a little extra, I feel good helping people in need and giving to causes I care about. I do believe we are in this together.
- **Stick with legal and healthy means to raise quick cash** – I have chosen NOT to sell my body, drugs or soul for quick cash. Just as there is a way to make it in life without incurring unsecured debt (like credit card debt), so too is there a way to make it with dignity without harming yourself or anyone else.

Pause and Consider Options

If you've already been selling your body or drugs, or selling alcohol to minors, or pursuing other illegal means of getting cash, consider that there may be other methods for survival which are both legal and healthy. It's true! You may believe you have no alternatives. I have talked with a few people who have used illegal methods to make money, and they told me it was easy to get addicted to the high income they received. But at what cost?

One of the biggest reasons I had difficulty changing old strategies that were no longer working to new, more effective win-win strategies, was that I judged myself and felt deep shame for engaging in destructive habits for so long. But now, I have developed a new habit of dropping the judge. I do not judge myself or anyone else when I examine any area of my life that doesn't seem to be working anymore. I ask myself whether changing the behavior or coping mechanism will benefit me and those around me. If so, I process letting go of the old "norm" and walk confidently toward a new "norm."

I tell myself I did the best I could with the information I had at the time. I made the old choices, and so did everyone else around me. As a friend once said, "I didn't know what I didn't know." Today, as soon as I realize I'm losing my dignity or need to change a norm for some reason, I take responsibility to research how to make that change effectively and then go to it!

It's ultimately your choice what you do. I'd rather clean toilets any day than give the most precious parts of myself to people who do not appreciate or cherish them. I also do not want to contribute to others' physical, mental, and emotional bankruptcy by selling them drugs or supporting their alcoholic habit.

If you are purchasing these services or products yourself, think about whether they truly help you or just give you a short-term escape. Ask yourself, when you have a moment of clarity, are you genuinely available to yourself and others or are you checking out? Could your emotional and mental escape possibly be due to fears of poverty, hopelessness, or even self-hate?

Look at the money you are spending on destructive habits. Do the math. Ask yourself what the true mental, emotional, and physical costs of participating in these purchases are? Sometimes I find if I pause and think about the real harm involved before I jump into addictive behavior, it can help me get perspective back and think of healthy, win-win solutions. If I cannot think of any ideas myself, then finding other individuals, like counsellors and social workers, to help me develop ideas and make a plan for change, is the next best action.

Identify Any Addictions That May Be Sabotaging Your Survival or Thriving Life

If your experience is anything like mine and my friends', working through addictions can make a key difference between barely surviving and enjoying a rich, relatively sane, and thriving life. I've observed many people feeling trapped in addictions to sex, gambling, food, alcohol, drugs, or money itself. Eventually, they seem to realize there will never be enough to fill the empty hole inside. I learned from being an intervention specialist that if you're experiencing an addiction you cannot control, you need to **stop and get help to be released from the prison of your addiction now.**

Start anywhere. There are free services everywhere you can utilize while you are getting back on your feet. These services include twelve-step programs, your local community mental health center, departments for social services, economic assistance, the Salvation Army, or local missions.

Start volunteering today to help someone else no matter what shape you're in. Just make sure your "gifts" are healthy for yourself and others. **Remember, you are not alone.** Countless people have gone before you and emerged from deep addictions and dependencies and are better for it.

Other Quick Work

Besides generating instant cash, you can look for work that pays you quickly or within a few days. I mowed lawns a little when I was young. I also made myself available for light cleaning work and babysitting. Ultimately, when I'm in a financial pinch, I become open to any type of legal, healthy work that pays weekly or daily until I re-stabilize with a more regular income. Family, friends, and neighbors can be great resources for quick work.

There are many types of jobs that we can do for others. I hire neighbors to mow my lawn and shovel my snow. I've also hired others to fix furniture, help me organize and clean my home before a move, provide content for a website, and more. The opportunities are endless for quick legal ways to generate cash.

Along these lines, if you're staying in a shelter, offer to help clean or serve others somehow. That could easily lead to referrals from the staff for more stable work outside. Hardly anyone does this. The action will set you apart and show your willingness to be of service.

Temp Jobs

Finding a temp job is one of my favorite all-time best ways to re-stabilize. Some agencies provide part-time and full-time temporary positions for individuals. Sure, some of these jobs could include dressing up in a foam guitar and dancing on the street corner, but that can be a lot of fun too! Think of the healthy exercise you can get while earning money.

The upside of temp jobs is that they often start within a day or two of applying. I have personally been through times where I needed to re-stabilize. I signed up with five temp agencies and checked in with each every day. Fortunately, I lived in an urban area where there were lots of temporary jobs available. And I could get local and regional bus passes and reach every one of the jobs on time.

Many of the positions are also temp-to-perm (temporary to permanent) positions. Temp-to-perm means you start work as a temp, but if you show up on time, pass a drug test, and do a great job at the company, employers may hire you as a permanent, full-time employee. Earning a permanent position is one of the benefits of working for temporary agencies.

Another advantage is gaining the opportunity to test out the employer and the work environment. The employer can test working with you as well before making a long-term commitment. There were times when I walked into a job thinking, "This is the perfect job," only to quit with the realization that the place would be highly stressful to work in day-after-day. I'm glad I got to try these jobs before working there full-time. Other positions or companies that were not even on my radar ended up teaching me what it is like to work for genuinely inspiring companies who excel with their clients, employees, and products. Working for a well-organized, honest, solvent, and caring organization is a beautiful experience to carry forward in life.

Taking some time to work a temporary job can also really open your eyes to basic needs or wants you would like in an ideal work environment. It is a fun way to experiment while stabilizing your housing and other areas of life and work.

As I noted earlier, when I graduated from college and needed to earn quick cash to pay for rent and food, I could not find any permanent job offers. So, I signed up with four temporary employment agencies and landed work within days. I ended up spending two to three months working temporary jobs until the company I interned with hired me full-time. Not only did I earn vital money to survive, but also, I learned what type of company and leadership I liked best and what kind of company or work wasn't a match. All that glitters is not gold.

Chapter 10: Balancing Income and Job Satisfaction

"They deem me mad because I will not sell my days for gold; and I deem them mad because they think my days have a price."

-Kahlil Gibran

How Do I Weigh Income Versus Happiness in My Work?

The first few times I got actual money in exchange for work, I was excited. I felt like a whole new world opened up to me. I mowed a lawn and got money. I babysat a neighbor's child and got money. I really experienced that feeling of semi-elation during my first "real" job at 14 years old as a general maid in a Victorian Hotel my dad owned because I was receiving weekly paychecks and I could see how work could enhance the quality of my life. Later, some jobs became less glamorous, and I felt they were serving as a barrier to my overall life happiness. Since then, I've had several "dream jobs" including writing this book for you!

Whether you have found your dream job or are working a temporary job until you find steady employment, consider the following when deciding which position to accept to balance your income and happiness needs:

- **Does the income meet or exceed your expenses in your spending plan (a.k.a. budget)?**
  Suppose the money you have coming in is less than the money you have going out. In that case, you will have to find ways to earn extra income. I've experienced that if I allow my expenses to exceed my income, I become more likely to fall into the trap of using debt, like credit cards. In my early 20's, I made the mistake of taking work that didn't cover my expenses simply to have a job. I ended up robbing Peter to pay Paul by not paying one bill in order to pay another. This launched me into a juggling act with my bills that started to snowball into a financial crisis.

  For years, I've noticed whether people bring in a higher or a lower income, many may still live beyond their means. Even with a higher income, if you spend more than you earn, you are just losing money by accepting work that doesn't cover all your expenses. You can adjust your expenses as well, but the habit of spending just a little more than you make is an important habit to break. I'm glad I had the support and clarity to do this in my own life.
- **Ability to enjoy, or at least tolerate, the type of work**
  The longer a job lasts, the more critical it is that I enjoy, or at least tolerate, the kind of work I am doing. For this reason, I try to keep enjoyable work at the forefront of my mind when selecting a full or part-time job. If you cannot stand getting up in the morning to go to work, for example, how likely is it that you may be late too often and eventually lose that job anyway? What if you need to earn a degree to get your dream

job? If your short-term job isn't at least bearable or, preferably, enjoyable, then that job has the potential to zap the energy out of you and take away what you need to succeed in school.

- **Guard against becoming dependent on a higher income**
I like to strive for an "abundant and adjustable" income versus a "higher" income. As a single mom, I experienced a 30 percent decrease in my income one year. This type of income drop can feel devastating. In my case, it was not as devastating because I was using a spending plan. I planned conservatively and ensured that I could make adjustments and live within my means if my income went down.

One of the most significant issues with being dependent on a higher income is that some of my spending categories ended up looking like needs instead of wants. European vacations are a want, not a need for me. Flexible spending plans fuel my finances today. When I have a higher income, I can spend more and save more. When I have a lower income, I can adjust my spending to meet that income. Being solvent with my finances, where my income exceeds my expenses and all my basic needs are met, ensures I have a feeling of abundance no matter my income.

It's easier for me to see addiction to higher income in others than myself. Years ago, one of my friends struggled financially and was earning three to four times my income at the time. She was stressed because she was having trouble affording her daughter's private horse-riding lessons along with the feed, hay, and boarding for the horse. Expenses for riding competitions were also taking a toll. My friend ended up spending 10 percent more than her income brought in meeting her daughter's horse-riding goals and her own ego's desire to compete at the shows with other rider's moms. After a few years, she accrued significant debt. When the debt pressure became unbearable, she stopped trying her same old strategies, got clarity, and turned things around financially. She now lives in prosperity and abundance by maintaining clarity with her finances and making changes to balance her income and expenses.

- **Pick an abundant career you love vs. a high-paying job you hate**
  It's one thing to become overly dependent on a high-paying job I love and quite another thing to work at a job I can't stand because "it looks good" to others. What's even crazier is getting addicted to a high income from a job I can't stand. To me, this feels like a serious trap. Deciding to switch to a job you like may be easier to do when younger, but I have witnessed older people choosing to re-start their careers and watched their lives, like my own, blossom.

I Cannot Do It Wrong

I've gone back and forth on career choices. Early on in my career, I gave in to social pressures to go into a stable career like law, business, medicine, nursing, or computer programming. I believed if I followed a high prestige career, I would gain everything I needed to be "successful" and "financially stable." So, I ended up pursuing a business degree in college instead of one I was passionate about, such as 3D animation, architecture, or human services.

When I started working in the sales and marketing fields, I debated whether I was "selling out." So, while I earned my income in advertising and sales, I used all the money I could spare to pay for 3D animation software and video editing systems. Then, I landed my "dream job" as a multimedia specialist, editing videos all day and providing technical support to sales reps. I really enjoyed working as a multimedia specialist, but guess what? I found I missed working with people and helping them identify and fill their needs.

Combining Paths Can Be Powerful

Eventually, I surprised myself by going back to sales, marketing, and business development. Today I combine the best of all my previous paths, and I know that I didn't take any "wrong" turns and gained from all my work experience. I have learned to enjoy some sales and marketing tasks by funneling my creativity into developing products—like this book and our web-based app—to help others with clear decisions. In my case, the careers I've had, dove-tailed nicely into doing what I love today and provide the overall benefits my family and I need. This type of examination takes time and introspection. There was no way for me to know this until I started somewhere and kept following the breadcrumbs and clues. I have never wavered from pursuing my passion for finding true happiness.

So, consider these other points when choosing your career path:

- **Is it you or your ego picking your career?**
  Being dependent on living a lifestyle so my ego can be satisfied can cause delays when readjusting my career. If I am obsessed with earning the highest income or looking good to others, I hesitate to change my job if new possibilities do not provide a high enough income. Free from the obsession, I would make the change and really add to my happiness and those close to me.

  Suppose you have two car payments, a mortgage, and private school tuition that demand a higher income. In that case, it may be challenging for you or your family to imagine change, such as downsizing if you get laid off or pursuing a teaching profession because you'd prefer it to working as an attorney.

  I've often witnessed my own and other people's egos standing in the way of finding significant abundant work due to fear of losing a lifestyle. I had another friend who earned a law degree and incurred considerable student debt. She went into practicing the law, and although she was making a good income, she found she couldn't stand it. Eventually, she earned her teaching certificate and is now happily teaching fifth grade. She didn't let the debt stop her and is successfully paying down her law degree loans. I believe I limit my options for a happy career and life when I rely too much on a higher income.

I know today money is supposed to support my life and not tie me down to a standard of living so I can impress anyone. True abundance, for me, needs to follow the principles of solvency. Discovering and following my work passion regardless of income is also part of the puzzle. If I feel drawn to be a stockbroker and my career pays a higher income than the average, so be it. I can be of service either way.

- **Relying on one income when you have two earners can be a game-changer**

It is wonderful to have two incomes supporting the family. However, if your spending plan requires both incomes to meet day-to-day financial obligations, you may consider changing your family spending plan to rely on one income only.

Sounds radical?

I have found that as long as one income can financially support the family adequately, using the other income for entrepreneurial or support roles (such as child rearing, cooking and cleaning), can be an excellent investment in a family. I have experienced some tremendous gains in financial and overall family abundance by committing to one spouse maintaining a reasonably stable job with family insurance and benefits. At the same time, the other person focuses on more risky ventures.

When we've been able to free up one partner's time for riskier ventures, it opened the door to starting new businesses, creating new products, writing a book like this, and pursuing a 100 percent commission-based real estate broker job. We're using this strategy right now. At the time of this writing, my husband has a "day" job in a resilient industry that allows us to use my time to take calculated risks like writing this book and developing a web-based app. Here are some benefits for placing your dependence on a single income when two incomes are available:

- The second income earner can go for bigger, riskier returns. There may be some losses along the way, but the family benefits incredibly when these calculated, financially risky (yet legal) jobs and products make home runs!
- If there are two incomes, you can assign the second income to an aggressive saving plan to guard against losing one of the incomes for a significant period, such as a downturn in the economy or a pandemic.
- A family can also direct the second-income earner's time and funds to learn new skills to help the family stay solvent and competitive when the traditional industry changes quickly. With the speed of technological changes today, it is more than likely that one or both industries could go through significant changes. Keeping one person's skills ahead of the curve can help keep the household stable during economic downturns.
- Earmarking a large percentage of a second income towards investments can significantly improve a couple's retirement goals and overall family prosperity.

I find it's essential to remain flexible with family careers. So, I thank my partner for working together to take more significant risks with investments, startups, writing this book, and more by having one person work a steady job to "keep the lights on" while the other person scrambles to pursue a high return opportunity. I've seen this work masterfully as long as one partner is not too stressed in the stable income job. It's also important to our family to switch roles now and then until the family reaches a point of financial independence.

Be Aware of Job Stagnation.

I try to make sure the momentum I build with each job contributes to my overall professional goals and day-to-day happiness. Once I start a job, I have found that it is easy to get comfortable in that position and stop seeking professional development or moving towards my larger professional goals. I go into a sort of automatic pilot mode.

The danger of landing and staying in a job that is not a clear fit for me is that I become used to the routines and imagined security of a known position. When this happens, I risk spending a lot of time and energy doing a job that takes more energy than it gives back and only gets me so far towards my goals. It's like putting a ladder against a wall, climbing it to the top, only to discover I've propped it against the "wrong" wall.

Wrong" to me means a career that doesn't feed me financially, creatively, or authentically. So, make sure, whenever possible, that every job fits into your overall career and financial plan. Again, it could be that having enough money right now with a temporary, legal position to keep a roof over your head is the most important and immediate goal to get stabilized. That need is real and valid. But keep your overall goals and what you want to accomplish in mind as you work that job and look for your next opportunity.

One final note: if you feel trapped in the comfort zone and momentum of a particular job that doesn't match your goals well, you run the risk of getting caught up in the politics, unfairness, and the day-to-day issues of the job, which can lead to unhappiness. You risk losing sight of your "real" career as you become dependent on the current position's known security. Don't lose sight of your abundant vision by focusing too much on any one job.

Matching Your Values

What criteria do you look for when you seek out a job or business opportunity? Does it match your values? Here are several values and benefits I look for when I seek out jobs and income opportunities:

- **I look for energized, honest, committed, and hard-working people wherever I go** – If you go to work and no one says hello to you, especially after you say hello, consider another job unless it is only a one-week job through a temp agency. Some of the most satisfying jobs I've had, including temp jobs, have not necessarily included my ideal work tasks. Instead, they have all had cooperative, positive, hard-working people as workmates. Another significant factor is working with people who do not take themselves too seriously, even if their jobs are serious.
- **The ability to work on "my own," if need be, can be powerful too** – If you thrive working on your own and want the bare minimum human contact necessary to accomplish your goals, then look for a job that offers an independent work opportunity. If you prefer to work alone, there is less need to look for energized people to work with. Instead, you can put more focus on seeking an environment that fits your work style. I'm currently writing this book on my own for hours at a time. That's the environment I need to be effective at completing this type of work.

- **Competitive or non-competitive jobs?** I can't say all the jobs I've ever had were non-competitive since I've worked in many sales positions. However, the competition seemed relatively friendly, and it drove each of us to excel within our craft and with our clients. We joked around with one another as we honed our expertise in our respective fields. I have noticed I can get a lot of satisfaction in almost any job if I and those around me maintain consistent, positive, win-win attitudes.
- **Find and follow your passion** – For as long as I can remember, I have been obsessed with careers, many of which I liked! Even as a young person, my practice has been to set aside some time to figure out my real passion and set my professional development goals. I sought out books on the subject. *What Color is Your Parachute* by Richard Nelson Bolles and *Do What You Love, the Money Will Follow* by Marsha Sinetar are excellent resources for finding your passion. I hope you don't miss the opportunity to go for the gold by finding and following your career passion(s). Seeing and doing what I love professionally, in my case, has been priceless.

  Most of us spend a lot of time at work. Conservatively, I suspect I will have spent around 100,000 hours working in my lifetime, which equates to 12,500 days over about 50 years. Thank goodness for short ladders in some areas! What I know now is that each moment is a precious gift. So, I want to constructively use this time working on something that contributes to my passion. Time, like land, are both resources we cannot create more of.
- **Enjoy where you are today** – I've adopted the motto "Enjoy the journey. You're in for a ride!" Since careers tend to be a process rather than a destination, I have found it valuable to truly enjoy every job I have ever had and appreciate and leverage everything I learn from each one.

As I said, I started my work career as a babysitter, lawnmower, and general maid in a hotel, cleaning bathrooms and baseboards. Then I graduated to cooking, waitressing, office work, advertising, sales, animation, digital video production, recruiting, and business development.

Later, I co-founded and became the CEO of a small internet company. After that, I went back to temporary office work while pregnant, then became a full-time mom—raising kids, cooking, and cleaning the home. While I continued to raise my kids, I jumped into real estate for a few years. Then, I landed a recruiter job in a community college when the real estate market tanked in 2008. At the community college, I learned about suicide intervention techniques and career/academic coaching. I finally went back to being a stay-at-home mom, caring for my husband, teens, and our household. But while staying at home, I continue to pursue opportunities, such as writing this book.

Practical Tips

Start Your Own Small Business

> "There's opportunities in real estate and to start an online business... you start small and take small steps but you start. Don't be paralyzed by fear, because a lot of people are right now. You can look in your own backyard and go '... what is needed and wanted that is not happening?' And if you can answer that question, just start small."
>
> -Kim Kiyosaki, Rich Dad Channel

The first "business" I had was during sixth grade. I made earrings and jewelry out of pumpkin and apple seeds for myself. A few girls saw these at school and asked me to make earrings for them as well. I earned a little bit of money and gained a lot of experience.

Since then, probably one-third of my work has been on a contract basis or as a small business owner. Working for myself has advantages and disadvantages. As I write this book, I'm working for myself again. I feel that building, running, and growing my own businesses is likely the best "job" security I will find in the long run, though my job may feel insecure in the short-term. I feel more secure because I've had the experience of earning a good living by offering someone a service and getting paid for it. For this reason, I know now I can earn income in any economic condition, even if I need to change my lifestyle temporarily to survive financially. If times get tough, I can pick up one or more of my skills and package an offering to sell to others, even if it is housecleaning or coaching people on their career via video conferencing.

I embraced the concept of self-employment when as a real estate broker I sat in the closing room on my first real estate sale. That day, I "got" the connection that my income was tied to my own efforts. I provided a service and was compensated for my role in the transaction. Working as a real estate professional helped me solidify the reality that the "customer or client" is the person signing my paycheck. That is easy to forget when working in someone else's business. If you are interested in starting your own business or feel you need to create a business to survive, begin by looking at your skills and determining how you can help others.

Sometimes I like having a job at another person's company or organization because I don't have to think about taxes and health insurance and make payroll for myself and others. However, my experience is that I earned more income from a 100 percent commission job as a real estate broker than I ever had at any position where I was an employee for someone else. Granted, my sales job took a huge number of hours. I was constantly answering my phone and had to be available during holidays and weekends when prospective clients were free to look at properties. But I loved it. The real estate brokerage job helped me support my family and get us through some rough economic times.

Every now and then, however, it helps to get a day job with a company. For instance, when the real estate market collapsed in 2008, I was fortunate to find a job at a local community college because I wanted to stay in my hometown to offer a stable home for my kids. So, I leveraged my sales experience to get a job as a recruiter at the local college. This career decision unexpectedly led to an exciting career, helping hundreds of students find their passion and accomplish their life and career goals while also resolving mental and emotional issues.

The Bartering Chip and Wild Ideas to Earn Income

No matter what the economy has looked like in my lifetime, I've noticed that people everywhere need services and products. With your own skillset, you can barter with others! You may have to trade carpentry for rent or even chickens, but it works!

Here are some other wild ideas to earn income creatively. With the newer technologies available, such as online video conferencing, why not take your dog-grooming skills and hold a live class for your clients on how to clip dog nails? Why not help people make decisions or learn to paint if you have experience painting?

Practical Planning, Decision-Making, Executing, and Managing

Years ago, I read an excellent book called The E-Myth Revisited by Michael E. Gerber (Gerber 2004). Even if you are thinking of starting a bakery business at the farmers' market, you may benefit from reading *E-Myth Revisited.* This book breaks down the three different skill sets needed to successfully and profitably build an entrepreneurial venture. The skill sets break down to working as a technician (subject matter expert/craftsperson), manager, and entrepreneur. Even if you have a sole proprietorship and work on your own, you need these three skill-sets to succeed. Countless other tips, such as planning for your business to grow large even if you want to run a solo enterprise, are sprinkled throughout the book.

Another tip I learned is that if I start a business, I must be prepared to wait a year or two for it to become profitable. Ideally, if I can save six to eighteen months of expenses saved away before I start, all the better. However, sometimes we do not have the luxury of waiting for our savings to build or the best timing before we can start. Then I focus on one thing: having my income exceed my expenses in my business and personal spending plans, even if I have to simplify my life for a while. Incurring any unsecured debt—for example on credit cards—to build or run a business is not a way of life for me.

What Would I Do Today in a Pinch?

While writing, I've been asking myself, "What would I do today if I suddenly lost everything I've worked for (money, close family, home, etc.)?" I would talk with a friend or other family member I trust. I would ask to live in their home or garage in exchange for helping them with cooking, cleaning, babysitting, lawn maintenance, or any other legal, dignified skill I could offer. I would then get with one or two friends to brainstorm what my ideal life would look like and start slowly working towards that vision.

I might volunteer at a soup kitchen or food pantry to secure food for myself and my family and network for part or full-time jobs. I might take on small jobs to buy a laptop, a cell phone with Wi-Fi, and at least one nice set of clothes from the thrift store. Then, I would start an online business using my web design, career, academic advising, or other skills, working out of my home, library, and coffee shops. For my own happiness, perspective, and sanity, I would also find ways to support others struggling even more than I am.

Notice how I focus on an abundant ideal life and work steadily towards that goal. I find that as long as I can keep my mind and body clear, keep my basic prayer and meditation routines going, and connect with support people and friends, **I not only can survive but thrive in any circumstance that comes up.**

Pivot When You Need to and When You Want to

"Human beings are comfort creatures.
We become uncomfortable with change.
That's our true work: to work on our inner state of balance…
so we can respond rather than react."

-Katherine Robertson-Pilling,
Strategic creativity coach, author
and founder of *The Wheel of Creativity*

Be ready to pivot when you need to change strategies for new income streams or because you've uncovered a new passion you want to go for. As I mentioned previously, to survive financially, I've experienced five different industry changes that have led me to adapt to newer industries. As a technical staff recruiter, for instance, we lost around 50 percent of our business in one year when the internet broke out. I had to scramble that year!

Retrain as Part of the Natural Flow

I had to change careers quickly when each of the following five industries "tanked":

- Traditional film and video markets, when digital cameras overran classic film
- Recruiting industry, when online job sites like Monster.com took over much of recruiting
- Dotcom bust in 2001

- Real estate market crash in 2008
- Higher education, when online learning began to take market share from traditional schools.

Are you in a field that is sinking right now, even temporarily? Consider retraining. Think big. Think creatively and get clarity on which careers are growing.

An example of a growing field is project management. According to an article from the Project Management Institute ("Project Management Job Growth and Talent Gap 2017– 2027" 2017, 1), "Across the globe, there's a widening gap between employers' need for skilled project management workers and the availability of professionals to fill those roles." I was a member of this excellent organization for a short while—influential people helping one another and their organizations grow and succeed. Project management is a field that covers any industry. Take time to look at job descriptions closely. You may find you are already a natural at a relatively abundant career like project management.

What about product management as well? The change in one word, "product" instead of "project," can make a huge difference in your day-to-day quality of life. Do you like working with people and have a flair for shepherding products into the market and landing them successfully? If you do, there are opportunities in product management. According to Productboard.com (Product Board and Schrock 2019), "The increase in demand that we are seeing for product management roles in the US outpaces the average increase in demand for other roles in the US by 5x."

Do you like working with people? This skill alone is worth gold. Hopefully, you can mine it! Don't forget, an enthusiastic counselor, coach, workforce advisor, or other dream team member can help you take interest tests or brainstorm ideas about the best fit for your skills and passions in an up-and-coming field.

I now just count on change. I embrace the changes and look

for new opportunities somewhere in my own backyard as shown in the book Acres of Diamonds by Russell H. Conwell. (Conwell and Project Gutenberg 2008). No matter my circumstances, I've learned to keep offering support to other people who are even in less fortunate circumstances.

What I've Learned About Work Overall?

IT'S ALL GOOD! Every job I've had has helped me in some way. And it's still helping me in some ways. I make it a point to enjoy whatever I am doing while doing it and try to have the best relationship with everyone involved. My respect for being a full-time wife and mother expanded greatly when I tried it. I never considered that a "real job" in the past.

I know now they are all real jobs, and they all matter. I needed everyone to get me to where I am today, becoming one of the consistently happiest people I know.

And remember, if the job isn't "perfect"—and most jobs aren't—you can do something for a short amount of time that might kill you if you tried to do it forever. Enjoy wherever you are and try to honor it as a real job, even if it is cleaning toilets. I've done it and still do it in my own home. It's a gift to have a working toilet to clean. According to the World Health Organization (World Health Organization 2019), **"2.0 billion people still do not have basic sanitation facilities in the world such as toilets or latrines."** Worldometers.info shows the world population today, May 17, 2021, is 7.866 billion ("Current World Population" 2021). Cleaning the toilet in my own or anyone's home is a gift and a privilege.

Paper-Based, Legal Tools

Do not underestimate the importance of having access to your legal documents. Any job or school you may want to attend is going to require identification. Often people have either lost or allowed these documents to lapse. It is challenging to apply for social services, like food stamps, if you do not have official identification, such as your birth certificate. Also, driving with a legal driver's license opens up all sorts of job possibilities. You also need a driver's license if you have a mobile lifestyle living out of your vehicle for part or all of your life.

Some of the most common documents you need on hand, according to Unpakt Blog ("10 Personal Documents You Need to Take With You When Moving" 2015):

- Driver's license or legal identification card
- Passport, if you have one
- Birth certificate
- Last two years of tax returns
- Recent utility bill (to prove residency in an area for schools, etc.)
- Social security card
- Title for your vehicles
- School transcripts
- Marriage certificates and divorce decrees
- Vaccination and medical records

Note: Documents needed will vary by country. These are just a few examples.

Internal Satisfaction

Give Financially to Others, Especially When it Feels Like You Can't

Giving support and time to help others "succeed" more than myself is a paradox, but it works. One way to give back to others is to do so directly. When I first started getting clear about my relationship with money, someone recommended that I give a small percentage of money to others. There were all these suggestions as to how much to give to various camps.

At the beginning of my financial learning path and when the worst challenges were occurring, what I came up with was to get a roll of coins (even penny rolls will do) and start giving them to causes and people at meetings. Maybe I would put a coin in someone's parking meter and not get found out. Maybe I would put a penny in a donation bin while everyone else put in a hundred times more. I began to realize that my penny was just as valuable as the other person's dollar.

I also give back to others by offering my time and sharing my learning, skills, and experience. I often share what I've learned with others for free, as countless others have done so for me. Somehow, when I support you, and I see you thrive, it increases my sense of a thriving life. It can be totally free!

The Good Life - Some Notes on Abundance

I can't tell you all these years later how this principle of giving to others added to my abundance. However, I can tell you I began this journey to support myself years ago and find myself today in a place where I have abundance beyond my expectations in all areas of life.

Giving Back Fuels My Feeling of Abundance

Giving back and paying it forward helps me feel peace, fulfillment, and abundance. I don't know how much of my current prosperity and abundance are directly due to giving money, time, experience, or gifts to others. Still, I do know that almost nothing gives me more pleasure and satisfaction today than giving to others.

Abundance is an Ever-Expanding Pie Not Tied to My Net Worth

I know that the pie of abundance is an ever-expanding pie with plenty for everyone, not a shrinking pie where we have to fight each other for the crumbs. I also know now that this feeling of abundance, which often shows up in the form of peace and happiness, is available to me no matter what my income or material circumstances. I don't believe I have to "earn" my abundance. I can find it where I am right now. I can then build abundance for myself and others from that basic appreciation of what I have, even if it is having lungs that allow me to breathe.

My belief in health, happiness, prosperity, and abundance for all through helping one another, is the primary reality I choose to live in today.

I have learned that there will always be people out there with more or less money than myself. I choose to connect with the people who seem genuinely happy no matter what their circumstances. Out there, at every single income level, happy people show up.

My Current Pursuits

As I mentioned earlier, I am currently writing this book and working on other books as well, and my husband and I are planning to launch a web app business to help people make decisions based on their values. Additionally, I just finished about 200-300 hours of video editing for my husband's affordable online programming course called Full Stack Grow (Alai 2020). He developed this course to help others learn basic programming to stand up a web-app, including the webserver and database. Learning programming, testing, and documentation best practices in this course enables any individual or team to develop web-based apps cheaply, thus democratizing the web app development process. What a fun ride it's been!

But my journey doesn't end here.

My volunteer work has been a steady stream throughout my life as well. I'm currently volunteering as a prep cook in a soup kitchen once a week and picking up trash where I see it (a.k.a. "plogging"). I can see where all these jobs, both paid and unpaid, were fun and satisfying at one time or another. They also taught me many skills along the way, and I learned a lot about myself. Ultimately, they all led me here! I love where I'm at now, working on my own businesses. My career and life are more than good today. Abundance and prosperity come to mind.

My husband and I are both working hard to see if we can be part of the solution in this world and ultimately feel more peaceful, free, and happy because of our efforts. Our main goal is to provide tools to people like you to survive, thrive, and feel the abundance available on the planet while at the same time caring for the Earth. The abundance we are experiencing right now is both financial and physical, as well as emotional and mental. This perspective allows us to be in a great position to help others to live more abundant, peaceful lives and hopefully pass the gifts of abundance they receive on to still more people.

It usually takes some courage for me to change direction in my life, but I've found it's just part of the natural process of surviving and thriving. I agree with what my friend and coach, Katherine Robertson, says about change:

"Reach for the stars and take baby steps. It's a sign of wisdom to recalculate your goals in terms of what is actually feasible without judgments."

-Katherine Robertson-Pilling,
Strategic creativity coach, author
and founder of *The Wheel of Creativity*

Another friend and mentor used to remind me almost daily to "Drop the Judge" towards myself and others as I make changes in my life.

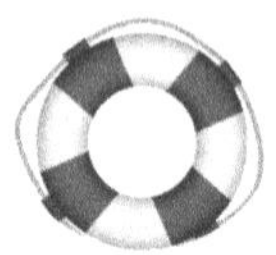

Chapter 11: Education

When I first started writing this section, I wanted to call it "School" instead of "Education." However, the word "school" brings to mind an actual institution of some kind where theoretically you gain learning. Yet, going to school doesn't always seem to result in deep learning for me, at least when trying to learn valuable lessons for surviving in the world. I really like the broader definition of education, which points to any person, teacher, situation, institution, or circumstance that contributes to my overall learning. Why? Because I have found that the toughest challenges in my life have ended up being my biggest teachers. In this section, I'll focus on how to gain an education to survive in life.

I see two types of education that have helped me grow: formal and informal.

Formal Education

Many of us have had the good fortune of receiving some formal education, at least at the primary levels (ages 6 to 11). I remember going to kindergarten in the U.S. when I was five years old. It was strange but engaging at the same time. Even though we didn't learn much academically in the first year, I learned to follow directions and get along with a larger group of kids than just my younger brother and baby sister.

Why did I go to school? I went because everyone in my area went to school, and it was the law. But attending school is not the "norm" everywhere in the world. According to data from the UNESCO Institute for Statistics (UIS), about 263 million children, adolescents, and youth worldwide (or one in every five) are out (of) school – a figure that has barely changed over the past five years" (United Nations Education, Scientific and Cultural Organization 2018).

So, one out of five children or youth did not attend school in 2016. Does this matter? What real benefit does a formal education give a person? Here is how the United Nations answered these questions in 2017:

- **What is the goal here?** Ensure inclusive and quality education for all and promote lifelong learning.
- **Why does education matter?**
- Education enables upward socioeconomic mobility and is a key to escaping poverty. When people can earn a quality education, **they can break from the cycle of poverty**.
- Education helps reduce inequalities and promotes gender equality.
- **Education empowers people everywhere to live more healthy and sustainable lives.**
- Education is also crucial to fostering tolerance between people and contributes to more peaceful societies."

Let's look briefly at a U.S. example of how peoples' income and unemployment rate can vary based on how much formal education they have attained (U.S. Bureau of Labor Statistics 2021):

Figure 6: Earnings and Unemployment rates by Educational Attainment, 2020

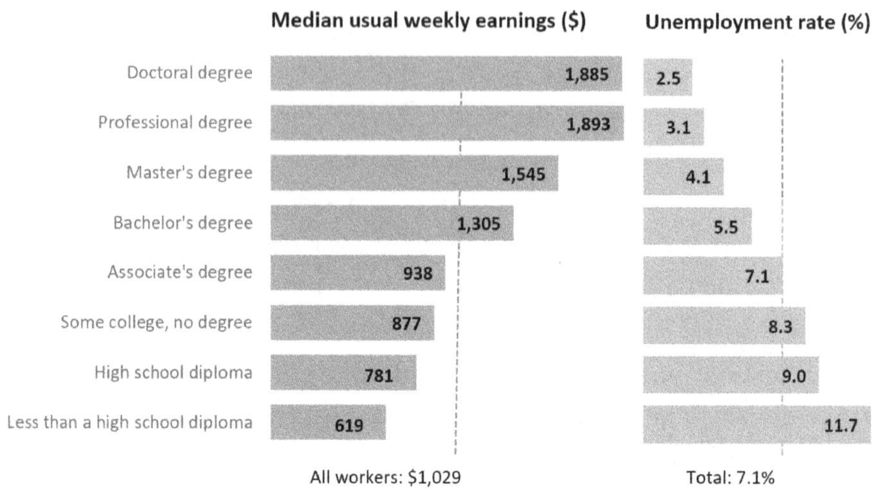

Looking at the left, or income, side of the chart above, it seems that the higher the level of formal education the higher the income. Then looking at the unemployment chart on the right, we see that the higher the level of formal education the lower the rate of unemployment. This information shows me that earning a formal education is valuable to achieving a sustainable income and staying above the poverty line.

Many groups around the world experience issues of inequality regarding access to effective formal education. According to the United Nations (United Nations Sustainable Development, n.d.), "Women and girls are one of these groups. About one-third of countries in the developing regions have not achieved gender parity in primary education. These disadvantages in education also translate into lack of access to skills and limited opportunities in the labor market for young women."

However, in this field guide, I am more concerned about your personal access to formal education. I have found that the specific degree I pursue and the income I wish to have needs to connect to and support my vision. I have personally known many Ph.D. graduates teaching in colleges that earn a lot less than a software engineer with a bachelor's or master's degree. You may not need to earn a master's degree in engineering if your passion is to be an electrician. I try to remember that income is only one measure of success. When determining which formal education to earn, the main consideration will be to evaluate which career advances you towards your personal vision, passion, and goals.

The only specific financial goal I do recommend is to make sure that when you plan your next career or mission in life, the income you anticipate earning from this new field outweighs your training cost. As mentioned earlier, earning a law degree with a large student loan but failing to practice law because you discover you dislike the profession may get you farther away from abundance and closer to the poverty line. If you find that your chosen, formal educational path is not engaging or you are not excelling in coursework, consider stopping and pivoting to a new career. Speak with a career advisor or take a little break. Sometimes working for a while, even in a basic job, can help clarify the direction you want your education to take.

There are countless ways to find a good fit for a career. For example, years ago, one of my friends took the newspaper and circled all the jobs that interested her. Through this exercise, she realized that her passion lay in helping professions rather than in business-minded careers.

So, we have seen data showing that formal education is essential to a person's overall life prospects and financial success. But what about all those people who dropped out of school and "made it" anyway?

Informal Education

"I have never let school interfere with my education."
-Mark Twain

Some people refer to "informal education" as the "School of Hard Knocks." Such a school provides education from living life and following the examples of other people who you admire. Note that you can also gain knowledge in an area by researching it yourself. There are countless self-help books and videos on how to learn different trades. You can take extra time at your job to learn new skills to help you improve your income and possibly gain a greater sense of meaning and accomplishment.

Additionally, you can leverage yourself into a totally new career by gaining skills you learn on-the-job from one or more jobs or careers. As I mentioned before, one book that can help you find your passion is What Color is Your Parachute by Richard Nelson Bolles (Bolles 2020). In his book, Bolles outlines countless ways to get the knowledge and experience you need to pursue your passion or a better-paying job.

One of the ways to understand informal school is to imagine working on a farm. Think about all the skills one learns growing up on a farm. First, you learn the discipline to wake up early and do chores. If you don't feed the chickens, they'll literally starve, then you'll starve or lose income. The cows and other animals also need to be fed. You will need to prepare the ground for planting crops while considering the seasons and weather cycles. You have to raise and harvest crops, take them to the market, and negotiate on prices.

When you are on a farm, you have to be creative and inventive in solving any technical or food issues that come up. You may be isolated and may not be able to run to the local hardware store in a pinch. Maintaining your equipment is imperative to your operations on the farm. Basically, you may need to be resourceful and able to approach any situation and fix it with a stick of baling wire and a few smashed aluminum cans.

On a farm, you are the one responsible for maintaining your own health, other people's health, and the animals' health. Yes, today, many of us in the world have good access to standard healthcare, including doctors, dentists, and veterinarians for our pets. But on a farm, you are still generally 20-40 minutes away from some of those health resources. So, I believe one needs basic medical supplies on hand and, more commonly, the ability to feed yourself and your family as part of your health care plan.

You need a cellar/basement with extra canned food and supplies to last you at least a month to account for any weather that could affect your access to grocery stores or your livelihood any given year. Building silos and haystacks to hold extra food for the livestock is also vital.

And to top it all off, you have to have a day job every now and then to support your farm. To summarize, farm life teaches you how to get up on time, work hard, take care of animals, take care of people, take care of yourself, handle money, negotiate, have patience, solve problems creatively, and much, much more.

When I was a recruiter for skilled welders and heavy equipment operators, the employers would tell me to look hard for job applicants who had farming backgrounds. Employees with farming backgrounds know how to get things done, and if they don't know how to do something, they will find a way to make it happen if possible. They will work hard, show up, and pass a drug test. They know how to hunt, fish, clean game, and store the food they need to survive. How many of us city dwellers still have these skills? We do not all have the opportunity or the interest to grow up or live on farms. However, we can take general skills we learn informally in one environment and apply them to another.

Here are some quick ideas on how to gain informal education:

- **Apprenticeships** – Assist someone who has mastered a craft or skill. Apprenticeships can include anything from woodworking, electrician work, hair artistry to manufacturing; the list goes on. You can also find formal apprenticeships through trade associations, local workforce offices, or technical schools. You may also earn certificates in specialist fields.
- **Internships** – Internships are common for technical, business, counseling, or other professional careers. You can either find these internships yourself or work through your school or local work center to find an internship that matches what you are trying to learn. Some technical internships, such as computer programming, might actually pay enough to cover much of your college expenses. Other internships may be short on pay but offer excellent industry experience and contacts. My internship in the advertising industry was on a volunteer basis but led to an actual job offer from the ad agency after my final year at college.
- **Informational interviews** – The way it works is to ask either a friend, relative or stranger if they would be willing to meet you for 10-15 minutes to answer some questions in their field. Send them a few questions to start the conversation when you meet:
    - What is your average day like in this field?
    - What do you like best or least about this career?
    - What types of people excel in this field, and what are their strongest skills?
    - If you had to do it over, would you still go into this field?
    - Do you think this field has a future?
    - Do you know anyone else who can share their experience with me in this field?

  - Would it be possible for me to shadow you (follow you around) at your job for a day?

Note: Always send a thank you note!

I have learned a lot through this process and been inspired by these individuals.

- **Job shadows** – Schedule a half to two-day job shadow with people you know, including people you have already conducted informational interviews with. You can frequently find professionals online willing to schedule a job shadow as well. Job shadows have helped me get a natural feel for what this person's average day is like. Again, you can initiate job shadow opportunities yourself or get referrals from a job or career counselor, teacher, or other professional to learn more about a particular career.
- **Join industry associations** – Industry associations are groups that generally meet monthly in-person or online. Go to learn, be inspired by speakers, and network. I have truly benefited from participating in industry associations.

  Participating in a local trade association paid off for me. When I was younger, I wanted to get into computer graphics and animation. I went to a trade show being held by our local SIGGRAPH computer graphics group. I volunteered to hand out badges in exchange for free admission to the conference. I ended up sitting next to a gentleman who was working in Robert Waxman's company. I had never heard of this company, but I did learn that they had a computer graphics department that sold video editing and animation software. He pointed out his wife to me, who was the lead computer graphics sales rep at the time.

  A few months later, I was laid-off from Griff Advertising, an award-winning medical advertising firm, because they were low on funds and between clients. So, I applied to work at Robert Waxman's in their retail store selling film, camera bags, and photo finishing services. Instead of completely freaking out about losing my job, I leveraged the contacts I had built through networking at trade shows to create a list of companies I could work for, and I began applying. Within a year, I was given the opportunity to have the position as the computer graphics sales lead, the exact position the man's wife had occupied, as she had quit and moved on.

- **On-the-job training** – I have often landed one job in a company, doing something I know how to do, then asked for opportunities to learn about another area in the company. I have found it vital that I give each job the respect and appreciation it deserves before moving on to another. I was told early on by David Keeler, a manager at Robert Waxman's in Colorado, "The best way to get to the next job is to do the absolute best job you can at the job you have right now." He taught us to treat our current job seriously and take pride in our efforts and accomplishments.

  Having said this, I believe it is important not to treat the job I am hired for as only a steppingstone to the next job. I can dream and plan another career, but until I am cleaning out my desk or locker from the job I have right now, I need to treat that job with respect and gratitude, no matter how lowly it appears to me or others.

  So, if you do the best job you can right now in the job you have and learn more about other areas of the company as opportunities present themselves, I don't think you can help but advance in that or another company. David Keeler started in the warehouse stacking boxes and ended up as the vice president of the company. He loved learning, finding solutions, and opportunities for himself, his employees, and the company to grow and prosper. Thank you, Mr. Keeler!

- **Ask someone to teach you what they know** - If you find any job you are interested in, you can ask someone who is already doing that dream job if you can hang out with them or be their assistant and learn what they know. Shadowing or following someone around is one of the most potent tools I've found to make it happen. Now, they may tell you to get a formal education since some careers, like those in the medical field, require certifications to practice. Nonetheless, having the ability to just "hang out and learn" with someone like a friend or a parent in a particular business can really give you a leg up.

> **Tip:** *Use every opportunity to stay in touch with people and grow your network.*

Personal Thank You to Dad

At this moment, I want to formally and publicly thank my dad for the hours and hours he spent taking all of us kids to work with him, as well as the Lions Club, Jaycees, Kiwanis, Chamber of Commerce, and other sundry places. Following him around helped me learn how to navigate between being of service and networking, all while learning best practices. We learned how to help ourselves work, grow towards prosperity and abundance, and contribute to the overall prosperity and abundance of our communities and world, including people in need. Thank you, Dad!

Summary

My story's moral is that both formal and informal education played vital roles in finding and achieving my career passion.

Formal education helped me get a foothold on what to do globally and offered me the credibility to apply to potential employers and clients and start a trusting conversation and working relationship. However, I embraced countless informal learning strategies that have had a high, if not higher, impact on achieving my goals and dreams. The combination of formal and informal education can be most powerful.

Work vs. School

Many people have to decide between working full-time or going to school. On the one hand, work brings in regular income and a sense of ease for you and your family. On the other hand, without education—trade or academic, depending on your interests—it can be hard to find work that matches your natural interests and highest potential ability. Also, some jobs do not pay enough to support you and your family abundantly. If you can relate to this, you may want to start looking at ways to grow and improve your work happiness and prospects.

Why is loving the work I do and appreciating my career so vital to me? Because earning income takes up a large percentage of my life. According to Payscale.com, "On average, people now spend approximately 13 years and two months of their lives at work. If you often put in overtime, you can factor in an additional year and two months. The average worker spends nearly a quarter of their time on the job during a typical 50-year stint of employment" (HuffPost and Campbell 2017).

For some people, one job isn't enough. Some people end up getting two or more jobs to make ends meet or have financial abundance. Working more than one job can take well over 40 hours per week. On the flip side, I've worked some jobs where I earned excellent income, which helped support my family, but I had to work over 60 hours a week. Plus, when I calculated the actual hourly rate, it was the same as working one and a half jobs; the income was simply not as good as I thought for that one "job."

Taking time to weigh work vs. school

How happy are you with your job? If you're not excited or aligned with your current career, you may want to stop and consider expanding your education. As recommended earlier, if you're on the fence about whether to get a job or go back to school, you can try job shadowing or interviewing someone in a career that interests you.

Let's talk about this.

I worked for several years with college students, unemployed workers, people on parole, and friends and family to help them with their vision, career, and academic paths. One fact stands out to me from my experience: **the people, myself included, who took the time to stop the clock and really look at the type of work available out there, and to find their passion, ended up the happiest with incomes that best matched their needs.**

People who gathered their courage to do informational interviews and job shadows with friends and strangers got even closer to finding their passion since they could see and feel what that type of work was really like on a day-to-day basis. Job shadows can also provide valuable insight into the industry and help you change directions if needed.

For example, I wanted to go into project management for a construction firm. I loved construction and woodworking. In 8th grade, I even took a construction course and loved every part of it, from designing plans to building small and larger-scale homes. At college, my dream had been to switch from business to civil and environmental engineering. I was afraid and stuck in marketing and advertising. So, having started work in marketing and sales after college, I did informational interviews with several construction firms. I was excited about the possibility of entering the construction field by leveraging my project management skills. When I got out into the field to do my informational interviews, the people at construction firms gave me warnings. Generally, they discouraged me by talking about how difficult it was to succeed and how it would be hard for me to enter the field. Some of these firms declined to even meet with me.

In contrast, one firm, ProLogis, which I had discounted because I thought it was way too good for me, had not one but three people meet me, all of whom were polite, curious, and doing their best to answer all my questions. And they encouraged me to pursue my dreams of working in construction. In my opinion, that company had it all. Instead of treating me like a waste of their time, everyone in that room treated me respectfully and positively. I felt like an important person rather than an underemployed retail sales rep.

But at the time, I didn't feel like I was qualified to apply to their company. Looking back, I could have possibly leveraged my sales background or even receptionist skills into a job at that company. I'll bet in time they would have supported me in gaining the education I needed to succeed in the project management, or even engineering fields, as long as I could perform the work. Thank you, ProLogis, for treating me like I mattered and inspiring me to be what I could be in this world.

If I hadn't knocked on that one extra door at ProLogis, I would have just accepted that my chances of becoming a construction project manager were nil. Maybe I would have followed advice from people in the other construction companies to go into a medical safety job or spend years perfecting the art of installing door trim. After all, that's just the way the industry was at the time. So, thanks to the informational interview process, I realized that I couldn't transfer my project management skills directly into that career path with most firms and would have to start from scratch. Based on where I was at during that time, this became a "no go" career. Therefore, I continued looking for work instead of gaining more education in this field. Later, I took my love for project management into the software, education, and business development tracks.

When is "No" Better Than "Yes"?

Sometimes not getting hired by a particular company or not getting accepted into a specific academic program is as good as hearing a "yes." I've found this to be true, especially if I can get to a "yes" or "no" on a career before investing time and money in a certification or degree I later regret.

I know one person in school who initially planned to become a computer programmer and switched careers after doing job shadows into architectural landscaping. He found he loved working and being outdoors instead of being stuck in an office. I had another friend who earned a degree in psychology but realized she didn't want to go into the field after graduation. She ended up burdened with debt, and her quality of life suffered in the short term since she had not taken the time to research her passion and get a feel for the day-to-day work involved. Eventually, she went into geology and loved it. Her experience was another example of why it is essential to get a sense of whether you want to go into a field before accumulating lots of debt to earn an advanced education. See the section on picking an abundant career for more details.

Work + School Together

Today's online education environment and flexible scheduling allows the possibility of earning a degree or gaining an education while working part-time or full-time.

When I was younger, I watched my own mom, who was single at the time, earn a master's degree while we lived in a single-wide trailer with limited resources. She set a powerful example of finding one's passion, setting goals, and getting support (including yoga). Her model started me on a journey towards several fulfilling dream careers. These careers have all provided me financial abundance and, more importantly, day-to-day enjoyment of work and life.

Non-Degree and Technical Programs

Are you considering changing careers but do not want to spend tons of money and time doing it? A great way to find and develop a job is to take a few courses online and just start doing the work you love to see if it is a match before investing in the field. Think big, think creatively, and think outside the box. As a video producer in Denver once told me, "Your imagination is your limit."

What does this mean? Want to be a 3D Animator? Well, you can spend a lot of time and money achieving this goal with formal education, OR you can take a low-cost course in 3D animation from online schools like edx.com or Udemy.com and see if you really like the work based on the course content. Maybe you will discover that you don't like it and try illustration or screenwriting classes instead.

But, if you do find you like the 3D animation course, then you can start planning to purchase at least a minimally viable computer animation system and load it up with tons of free or low-cost software that will allow you to create 3D worlds and characters to your heart's content. You can even produce your own 3D animated short films and videos in your own home today for a fraction of the cost of getting a formal education in animation. The result? You start posting your animations online in a few months instead of years. You can build a portfolio that showcases your work. You can start selling your animation services and your videos to other companies and earn an income doing what you love! Your clients may hire you as an employee or buy rights to distribute your animation as entertainment. Of course, you'll want to do a spending plan to see what this will cost. All and all, it is possible to become a 3D animator while you keep your lawn-mowing job to pay the rent. Plenty of people started with a day job to support their passions while they learn. You can too!

Volunteering

Volunteering, I have found, provides numerous and surprising benefits to myself and other people. Have you been out of work for a while? While you're waiting for work, why not volunteer to get back into the swing of things by being of service. Volunteering is also an excellent way to find out if you like a particular field. I remember volunteering at an ad agency for a year during my senior year of college. After a year, they hired me, and I loved getting to know the business.

There is nothing like the appreciation you often receive as a volunteer. If you are trying to get into the job market and volunteer, you may meet people who have paid work available or know someone else who has work available. If the people you are volunteering with notice you pitching in and showing up regularly in a cheerful, hard-working manner, many will help you in your search for other work. Volunteer coordinators can be an excellent source for references on a job or college application as well.

Even though there are many benefits to volunteering that we haven't even touched on, the biggest, most unexpected benefit could be your own surprise at the feeling you get when you see the lights turn on in someone else's eyes because you were there to help them. And even if you don't interact directly with the people or animals or trees who benefit from your volunteer work, you may find yourself leaving the volunteer location at the end of the shift energized, happy, empowered, and fulfilled.

I believe in volunteering even when I am struggling financially UNLESS the volunteering takes away from the actual time, I need to earn income to support myself and my family. I need to take care of myself first, then my family. It's like being on an airplane and putting on your oxygen mask before you put on your child's mask. If you don't survive, you won't be around to help anyone.

Take care of the goose that lays the golden eggs. That's you!

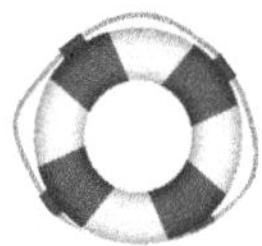

Chapter 12: Transportation

How do you get from point A to point B? Transportation is another fun, creative activity to brainstorm, particularly when it comes to prosperity and abundance.

I've personally used many forms of transportation both in rural and urban areas. I've also witnessed the difference with people I have worked with who have made choices to own or not to own a car. Frankly, where transportation is concerned, you'll likely have more insight than I do on the options that best suit your location, resources, and circumstances.

Here are some thoughts I can offer that may be helpful.

Your Most Basic Needs for Transportation

The primary purpose of any type of transportation is to get from Point A to Point B. Many factors weigh in when deciding the best form of transportation for each journey. When I consider which form of transportation to use, I prioritize what is more important to me. For instance, if the cost is more important, I might walk or take the bus or carpool. If time is more important, I may drive.

Transportation Example #1: 10-Mile Distance
Prioritizing COST and TIME

Let's say you just graduated from high school, and you want to find a job in a nearby city, 10 miles away, and your options are to get a car, ride the bus or walk to get to that job every day. Because you have recently graduated, you want to conserve your money and get to the job quickly.

In this example, the bus is the best option due to the cost of owning a car. Commuting with a car in this scenario would cost 25% of your monthly income when you calculate fuel, parking, maintenance, insurance, tolls, etc. Look at the table below (Figure 7) and notice how this graduate rates each transportation option against their needs. The ratings are on a 5-point scale, indicating how likely it is that the choice at the top (e.g., car) will satisfy the need or value on the left (e.g., be affordable): one being very unlikely, and five being highly likely.

Figure 7: Decision Matrix Transportation Bus

	Car	**Bus**	**Walk**
Affordable	2	4	5
Time saved	5	4	1
Relaxation	3	4	2
TOTAL	**10**	**12**	**8**

What Happens When We Overextend Ourselves for a Car?

Many of the college students I worked with purchased a car, even though car ownership consumed 30 to 40 percent of their income. If anything went wrong, such as financial aid not coming in on time, they were in trouble. This type of living on the edge, primarily due to car ownership, ended up creating more turmoil than convenience in their lives. If the car turned out to be a lemon or broke down, the debt became greater. However, when you can afford to own and run a car, the payoffs of owning a car are greater than taking a bus or cycling. Let's look at another example.

Transportation Example #2: 5-Mile Distance
Prioritizing TIME and RELAXATION

Let's say it's a year later, and you have landed a new job at a company closer to your home where your income has just doubled. (It happens!) However, your hours may vary, and this could make the bus ride to your job much longer, if not impossible.

Now, owning a car is a lot more affordable since the car costs something like 10 percent of your income, including fuel, parking, maintenance, insurance, and tolls. It is also more convenient and flexible than taking the bus in the suburban area where you work. Driving a car will likely save you time commuting to and from work versus taking the bus. The distance is still too long for walking and getting to work on time with a 5-mile walk could be stressful, especially in the snow. However, if you worked less than a mile away, walking starts to look more attractive. Let's see how the best option changes in figure 9.

Figure 8: Decision Matrix Transportation Car

	Car	**Bus**	**Walk**
Relaxation	5	3	3
Time saved	5	4	2
Affordable	4	5	5
TOTAL	**14**	**12**	**10**

As you can see, the best choice or ratings changed as your needs and resources changed. If this type of thinking is valid, why do so many people buy a car when they struggle financially and alternative, affordable options exist? Often it is because the purpose of a car is not just transportation.

Am I Buying Transportation or Something Else?

I suspect there are numerous reasons why some people believe they really "need" or "have to" have a car to survive. One of my friends, for example, needs to own a car because she cannot carry excessive weight like kitty litter or photo equipment. For others, when we break down their actual needs, the car is often serving their need for security or status or independence instead of just a straight need to get from A to B.

It might be tempting to invalidate or disqualify these other needs when facing financial challenges, but I believe these needs are equally important. The question I have, though, is if owning and operating a car, when another form of transportation is a better match in my current circumstances, the best way to get my other needs met? Is buying and operating a car when facing difficult financial circumstances like going to the hardware store for milk? You might luck out and find something like sunflower seeds for a snack, but that's not where you'll find an abundant, nourishing supply of milk.

Buying and operating a vehicle when you feel broke may end up making you dependent on it. As you try to keep the car on the road, you end up serving the car instead of yourself, taking away resources you could use to secure housing, get new clothing for job interviews, or take classes that can improve your job prospects. The list goes on.

There are many occasions, especially in college, where I found owning a car siphoned-off money that I could have used for other visible and invisible needs. So, for many of my college years I didn't own a car, since I realized this would not be the best way for me to achieve my vital needs at the time. Instead, I found that focusing my resources on counseling, job research, stable housing, and professional clothing, gave me the strength and clarity to be truly financially independent. I was able to live without a car while I couch surfed after college graduation, even though my temp jobs were over 20 miles away. Relying on the bus at that time, helped me become financially, mentally, and emotionally grounded enough to start taking some calculated risks after only a few short months of work, which led to more abundance and prosperity in all my life areas.

Car as a Shelter Too

You may be buying a car, even if you have few financial resources, as a possible backup place to live if things get tough. If this is the case, add the car to your list of potential housing options. Plenty of people outfit their cars to live in as a choice. According to the Outside Magazine (Brinlee, Jr. 2016), "Increasing numbers of people are willingly giving up their apartments for a home on the road—or, at the very least, adapting their lives to be more mobile. Their reasoning often comes down to these core symbiotic benefits: **financial freedom, mobility,** and **simplicity**."

You are not alone! You are in good company, even if you live in your vehicle temporarily. Just get the right gear for your environment and remember "safety first."

A Word About Pollution and Peace of Mind

Even if you can easily afford to own and operate a car, there may be reasons for taking the bus or walking.

Let's look at a few of the benefits of taking the bus:

- Costs less
- Decreases pollution

- Potentially meet a friend or a possible life mate
- Opportunity to catch up on reading, sleeping, gaming, and more
- Opportunity to get ahead on work or catch up with a friend on the phone
- Less fear of being involved in an accident as the driver of a car

And benefits of walking:

- Fresh air!
- Physical, mental, emotional, and spiritual renewal
- Opportunity to reflect and appreciate the beauty of nature
- Might meet your soulmate or befriend your neighbors
- It's FREE!

Alternate Transportation

You may be in an area or a position where you can bicycle, ride a subway or take a ferry to work. Take time to look at all your options with as much objectivity as possible. The point is to look at your **true underlying transportation needs**. Then, evaluate if you can meet your other transportation needs without owning a vehicle.

Even when faced with the simple decision of whether or not to purchase a car, it helps me to sleep on it and consult with someone on my dream team who has my best interests in mind and heart, especially if a car takes up a large percentage of my financial resources. These techniques keep my insecurities at bay.

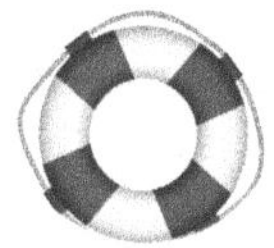

Chapter 13: Relationships

On relationships, there is so much ground to cover, that I could write several full-length books and movies.

I mentioned the importance of relationships with supporters like case managers, workforce advisors, and other dream team members. I also mentioned the value of "networking" and getting to know individuals and people in the fields you are pursuing. In my personal experience, however, I have found my survival is not so much dependent on the quantity as the quality of the relationships I have at a particular time. The quality of a relationship, including the roles I am playing in those relationships, can make a huge difference in my survival and sanity, financial solvency, peace of mind, and happiness. Recognizing, developing, participating in, and growing healthy relationships can support my survival and ability to thrive.

Relationships Can Make or Break My Physical Survival

So why am I talking about relationships in this section of the book dedicated to visible physical survival? I include it because relationships have profoundly affected my physical life. They have influenced who I trust, who I live with, who I work with, who I date, and much more.

Many of you have likely experienced a breakup, which led to depression, which led to lower-income and major rearrangements in your living situation. Have you ever stopped pursuing your dreams because someone you trusted told you that you weren't smart? I know how that feels. Have you ever thought your life was over because someone didn't see your spark and value? It can be hard to cope if I base my self-esteem or inherent value on what someone else thinks or says about me.

Some of us may hide out in addiction to escape the feelings that come up in negative encounters. However, I found out later in life that people I was in a relationship with were not "causing" me to drink alcohol or stop studying for an important exam. Instead, it was the beliefs in my own head about those people and the imaginary power I gave them which affected my grades, career, housing situation, and more.

My Beliefs Shape My Relationships Which Shape My Physical World

I originally learned how to act in relationships from my family, where I learned ways to relate to others that have proven incredibly supportive and even lifesaving at times. There were also qualities in the family relationships that I later consciously decided hurt my chances of survival, especially of having an abundant, thriving, peaceful life.

Old Beliefs That Lead to Less Supportive Relationships

I used to believe, for instance, that I couldn't trust anyone, not even myself. I also thought that the world was a scary, unpredictable, lonely place where I would always have to scrape by to make it. It felt like my lot in life was to suffer. I believed I was on my own and chose not to share my problems or traumatic experiences with anyone else. Maybe it was pride. Either way, it led me to some relationships that were painful and kept me on the brink of survival physically, mentally, emotionally, and spiritually.

I also thought deep down that I was an imposter and less worthy than other people. At other times, I thought I was superior to others, even if just morally. I know now these were all "false" beliefs for me. We'll review this concept more in the Validation Chapter in Part III.

The bottom line now is **these false beliefs were driving my internal relationship-seeking radar**. In my teens and early adult life, some of the people I attracted into my life who "looked good" to my internal radar, ended up being "bad" for me. Sometimes, I may have been an unhealthy or "bad" influence on others as well. This uncalibrated internal radar led me into relationships with people who drank excessively and had sex without committing to a relationship. I also got into dangerous housing environments loaded with people addicted to drugs and violence. And yes, there was community and mutual support and good things there too.

More than once, I would get involved with a man who appeared charming and strong. At first, he seemed to worship me and came across as a friend I could depend on. All this helped me feel more secure in myself and the world. But often, a short time after I would start to rely on that man, he would turn around and criticize me. This same pattern often repeated itself with female friends as well. The **biggest issue I could see in this reality, was that we were all blaming one another for our unhappiness**.

The false belief in this instance was that "people can't be trusted" or "there's something wrong with me." How about this one: "If they really get to know me, they won't like me"? Whenever a partner would criticize or blame me for the relationship's main issues, I would have a false belief: "There is something wrong with me. I just don't measure up". I kept finding relationships that tested and validated these false beliefs.

Adjusting My Beliefs or "Radar" For Healthier Relationships

It was the painful consequences of my dependence on people who were unavailable to form true lasting friendships that eventually drove me to question my beliefs and adjust my radar. What a gift in disguise!

One of the first beliefs I had to change was that I could change other people or their actions, beliefs, emotions, opinions of me, or the world. If they are determined to paint me as a villain in their lives, there is nothing I could do about it. Looking back, I crossed major boundaries trying to change others' opinions of me and attempting to convince them to love and support me when they couldn't even love and support themselves. Fear seemed to rule us all. **So, I learned I could change myself—my beliefs, actions, attitudes, and emotions. This is all I have control over.** I also learned how to stop chasing unavailable people and recognize what healthy looks like for me (more on this soon).

Second, I realized that just like small streams of water created the Grand Canyon, every second I spent using anger (justified or not), judgment, criticism, and blame towards a spouse or anyone, contributed to the erosion of both the relationship and the well-being of the other person. I'm officially truly sorry to anyone I judged, blamed, or tried to change in any way. That was my "stuff." It was unconscious. **I didn't know what I didn't know. I know today that I can be a regulated adult if I want to.**

Relationships Help Fill Visible Needs Today

These days, 99 percent of my relationships and interactions support growth and success for both me and those with whom I interact. Over the years, internalizing and applying the lessons

I have learned to identify and build win-win relationships, has contributed enormously to meeting my housing, food, education, transportation, health, and other visible physical needs. The fear I endured most of my life, that the physical and material abundance I had or would have would fail to materialize or dissolve once I had it, is now mostly gone.

Every material gift I enjoy today was made possible with the partnership of someone else. Now, my husband and I still drive older cars than our neighbors. But as of the time of this writing, we are debt-free. We sit at our table and enjoy the same wonderful meal we would if our home were a cottage or a mansion. The enjoyment and sense of security is all thanks to developing win-win relationships with people such as family, friends, employers, co-workers, psychological and spiritual leaders, peers, hairstylists, local grocery store workers, companies, writers, YouTubers, dog groomers, educators, yoga and meditation instructors, mail carriers, trash collectors, and many more people who we share abundance and prosperity with every day.

How Did I Switch My Radar to Win-Win Relationships?

Looking back, I first learned to distinguish a healthier relationship from a less healthy one by following this simple pro-versus-con type of exercise.

Exercise: Right/Left Comparison

Here are the steps in the right/left comparison process for relationships:

1. Get out a piece of paper.
2. On the right-hand side of the page, write the heading "Do Want."
3. On the left-hand side of the page, add the heading "Don't Want."

4. Writing what you don't want on the left-hand side and adding the corresponding text for what you do want on the right-hand side (e.g., don't want a person who blames me for their problems, do want someone who takes responsibility for their own problems.)

Here is a sample relationship list:

Figure 9: Personal Romantic Relationship Guide

Don't Want	Do Want
Anger	Kindness
Lying	Honesty
Conditional love	Unconditional love
Criticism	Acceptance of who we both are
Blaming	Personal responsibility
Vagueness around money	Clarity around money
Polygamy	Monogamy
Revulsion for one another	Admiration for one another
Ax in the trunk of their car*	Ask me questions to get to know me better*

*Real items on a friend's list!

Notice how I listed that I didn't want to build or expand relationships with people using anger, blame, and criticism on the left side. In contrast, on the right side, I listed people who practice unconditional love, acceptance, and who take personal responsibility for their circumstances and feelings.

Note: If I did do or say something that contributed to negative circumstances for another person, I need to repair the harm from my side. Following the golden rule helps me:

"Do unto others as you would have them
do unto you" (Matt. 7:12)

This list concept is only one out of hundreds of exercises and resources I have used to change my radar and to remind myself that what is good for me, really *is* good for me and what is bad for me, really *is* bad for me. The list helps me tell myself what my true relationship values are. Only then, can I recognize whether others have matching values or not.

Thankfully, I have, for the most part, successfully recalibrated my relationship-seeking radar. Throughout life, however, I work at accepting that we are all human. We all miss the mark or make mistakes by deviating from our own ideals. I believe that, along with everyone else on the planet, I will not be able to do win-win things all the time, especially when I am tired. I will do my best, as I know everyone else does too. Sometimes I make thoughtless comments about others and later have to go back and apologize. Other times, when someone says or does something, I am triggered, take things personally, and make matters worse.

Regardless of how imperfect my relationships are, I am forever grateful that I took countless hours over the years to research and experiment and learn how to change my beliefs and radar so I could have healthy relationships. My basic beliefs mirror Pope Francis' point of view with human interactions (Pope Francis 2020, 53):

> "There are only two kinds of people: those who care for someone who is hurting and those who pass by; those who bend down to help and those who look the other way and hurry off."
> -Pope Francis

According to Pope Francis, as he recalls the Parable of the Good Samaritan, each of us has the robber, the wounded victim, the passer-by, and the good Samaritan inside. I try to follow the good

Samaritan's example: to help those suffering unless I am suffering myself and need help. These two roles help me stay out of my internal robber and passer-by tendencies.

Note: The victim, in this case, refers to a mindset where I believe the world is doing things to me, that I'm not responsible, and that I am powerless to change anything. This is not to be confused with being an actual victim of physical and emotional violence.

One other paradox I've discovered is, if I ask another person for help, **I may be helping them more than they are helping me**. Although I'd rather be in the position of helping someone else (when they ask for it!) than needing help myself, the person helping me when I'm suffering feels empowered, and answers come to them that even surprise themselves. And when the helper and the one being helped grow and thrive as a result of working together, they both become empowered to help more people around them.

Today, I create healthy and safe environments for myself and those around me, an idea shared by Heather Forbes in her *Dare to Love Yourself: Affirmational Phrases* CD (Heather 2016). Heather Forbes also talks about taking care of our bodies as they are our oldest friends. Even the best relationships won't help me if I become lax on self-care, or my health starts going downhill for natural reasons. I need to act on medical and physical health needs too! Relationships that support mutual self-care are genuinely interdependent and can yield wonderful results.

Chapter 14: Did I Meet All My Physical Needs in the End?

Yes, I did!

Fulfilled visible needs help support my invisible, mental, and emotional needs and vice versa.

Just look at my food improvements, for example. Almost immediately after changing my diet, I felt my energy and focus blossoming. As my physical digestion issues and panic attacks began to subside, my mental and emotional well-being improved dramatically. Although it has taken years for my physical and mental issues to straighten out, I can see now how improvement in the fulfillment of both visible and invisible needs has resulted in me rating 95 percent happiness for all the areas of my life.

I can't say how much of my happiness today is due to visible physical and financial changes and how much was due to learning to use invisible tools such as meditation. The one practice that seemed to bridge both was biofeedback treatment, which helped immensely with my anxiety and panic attacks. The success of biofeedback treatment, for example, helped me realize that by combining visible physical tools with invisible psychological tools, I could truly transform my life and the lives of those around me.

In Part III (the next section) I focus on how I identified and began filling three primary invisible needs: security, validation, and unconditional love. Part III also shows how filling these invisible needs with appropriate solutions works hand-in-hand with the tools I've shared so far. Together, these tools have provided me with the most healthy, happy, abundant, prosperous, peaceful, and loving life I could ever imagine. So, let's take a look at what the invisible needs are next and how to get these needs met in healthy ways.

Part III: Invisible Survival: Mental and Emotional Needs

"Pain is only bearable if we know it will end, not if we deny it exists."

- Viktor Frankl

In the previous section, we saw how vital finding the correct tools for our physical needs is. For example, food is the solution for hunger. I used to believe my physical needs for food, shelter, clothing, money, and relationships were my main survival concerns in the world. If I managed my physical life well and lined up money, food, and shelter, I'd be happy, peaceful, and fulfilled. It didn't work. I found that I could survive physically in the world with the strategies I have already outlined, yet I still felt miserable. So, what was missing?

Food is Not Enough!

At one time or another, most of us have experienced having all our basic needs for food, shelter, clothing, air and water, and at least temporary physical safety met. **But honestly, is it enough?** I think of all the people around the world that are hungry or starving for food. I want to help them, as you may too. However, if filling basic physical needs is all there is, why do we see so many people, including wildly famous and wealthy people dying of addictions or loneliness? Why are some wealthy people suffering from extreme unhappiness and a sense of lack? Even with tons and tons of money, many people still suffer from mental and emotional turmoil and feel hopeless and inadequate.

Why visible needs are not enough to survive is a much bigger question than this little field guide can cover, but I will do my best to share my experiences about **identifying and filling invisible needs,**

including finding a sense of security, validation, and unconditional love.

Letting Go of The Scarcity Mindset Is Vital

I choose to believe that an abundant, prosperous, happy, joyous, and free mindset is available to me at any time and under any circumstance.

I have observed that an abundant mindset (one that views and experiences abundance in all areas of life) cannot coexist with the scarcity mindset (one that views and experiences lack in all areas of life). Many of us recognize whether we or those around us are leaning more towards the abundant or scarcity mindset. In my case, I had to shift from an entrenched mindset of scarcity, where I was consumed with worry about material security and which I assumed was reality, to a mindset of peace and contentment.

But what is this word "peace" I am speaking of?

Peace!

The deepest underlying need I have ever really had is to experience a life of **peace** and **contentment**, which includes **happiness, prosperity, abundance, connection, and freedom every day**.

My world of "peace" is like a place where I enter a beautiful, lush, protected forest that leads out to a field with abundant grain, followed by the beach where the waves of relaxation ebb back and forth across my mind. This place of peace is available to me anywhere, any time, and in any situation. It is a place where I can meet all my "visible" physical needs and "invisible" internal needs, such as feeling loveable, safe, and okay. Peace is the natural outcome of pausing and taking time to embrace and fulfill my invisible internal needs. Identifying with this sense of mental and emotional peace is my most immediate goal in any difficult or confusing situation.

I would even argue that satisfying these emotional needs first, gives me an overall sense of peace in any situation. So, fixing a visible need, like a financial crisis, will bring me some sense of security and ease. However, experiencing internal, mental, and emotional peace first, offers me a firm foundation and a clear mind to fix my financial crisis in a lasting way. This idea of finding inner mental and emotional peace first in any situation, has led me to true abundance. I have learned to access this peace when I need it. I believe this sense of peace is available to me 24 hours a day, 7 days per week, and 365 days a year, if I want it and am willing to work for it.

Just like love, there are a lot of "wrong places" to look for peace. I have found peace myself by becoming extremely clear on my needs for **security, validation, and love-based needs** and then finding direct, healthy ways to fill those needs.

Our current mission, then, should you choose to accept it, is to learn about the process of finding inner and outer peace. Let's get started, shall we?

Chapter 15: The Three Invisible Needs

Here we are! One of my favorite places to be, though, for years, this was the last place I wanted to be! We can now identify and ponder the three primary emotional and mental needs I've found to be the core of my life which, when added together, equal PEACE! These needs are **security, validation, and love.** Collectively, I refer to these as invisible needs.

Figure 10: Needs/Peace Equation

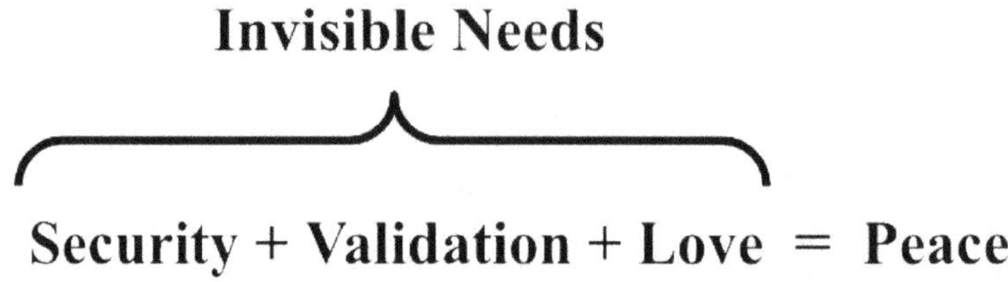

Invisible needs encompass the needs we cannot see or feel physically, even though emotions and thoughts are real in their own way.

Finding healthy, direct, internal ways to satisfy these three invisible mental/emotional needs has delivered lasting peace and happiness to myself and countless other people.

Hard to believe? I have discovered that finding reliable ways to meet these three needs is the first step to take in any situation. Taking this step has taken me way past survival, not only into a place of peace but also into thriving beyond my wildest imagination in all areas of my life.

Let's look at these three invisible needs from the point of view of a newborn baby.

Figure 11: Invisible Needs

Security, Validation & Love

In addition to the physical needs, babies also have **three invisible needs:** they need to know they are valued, safe, and loved to survive and thrive. This model I call the "Circle of Needs."

Unfortunately, in my opinion, society tends to overlook fulfilling these three invisible needs and instead focuses on the physical needs for food, shelter, safety, and clothing. Fulfilling these invisible needs is seen as "nice to have" or as "luxuries." To some families, acknowledging these invisible needs is tantamount to admitting weakness.

But if feeling secure, validated, and loved is a luxury, why do some people who can afford to buy any luxury turn to drugs, sex, alcohol addiction, or suicide to fill their invisible needs? To me, this shows our humanity and our need to find direct ways to serve our invisible needs. We have to recognize invisible needs as natural, instinctual, and valid.

Filling "Invisible" Needs Are Vital to Survive and Thrive

Invisible needs encompass the needs we cannot see or feel physically, even though emotions and thoughts seem and are quite real in their own way.

In my opinion, Maslow (as referenced in chapter 1) also clearly identified invisible needs on the higher levels of his hierarchy—needs such as **safety, love, esteem, and self-actualization,** in the diagram below. But, in my experience, some of these **emotional needs**, which include security, validation, and unconditional love should be added as a base layer to Maslow's hierarchy. This layer then forms a foundation of the basic needs of a person. I've shown this as a purple layer in a modified Maslow hierarchy below:

Figure 12: Maslow's Hierarchy of Needs + My Emotional Addition

Self-actualization
desire to become the most that one can be
Esteem
respect, self-esteem, status, recognition, strength, freedom
Love and belonging
friendship, intimacy, family, sense of connection
Safety needs
personal security, employment, resources, health, property
Physiological needs
air, water, food, shelter, sleep, clothing, reproduction
Emotional needs
validation, emotional security, unconditional love
Basic needs

Essentially, emotional needs do not only become essential "after" all the other physical safety and financial needs are met. **In my experience, finding a way to lovingly, safely, and legally get emotional and mental invisible needs met is *vital to physical survival!*** And while babies may not consciously understand this, they still need this to have a solid foundation.

Note: For those of you who may feel lacking in this department, there is always time to re-parent ourselves and learn to fill our invisible needs directly.

So yes, food and financial solvency can make a massive impact on my mental and emotional state. However, **the way I fill the three invisible needs of security, validation, and unconditional love dictates how I think and experience mental and emotional survival in the present**. AND these needs are not as validated in society as our physical needs for food, shelter, physical safety, and clothing.

Survival Requires You to Meet Both Invisible and Visible Needs

I started this book by addressing the physical, more visible needs since they often *seem* more pressing day-to-day. What I am emphasizing, however, is that your visible needs can only be truly met when supported by filling your invisible needs. Neglecting to fulfill your emotional, security, validation, and love needs is like leaving the flour out of the cake mix.

Furthermore, filling the invisible emotional and mental needs, like self-validation, supports physical needs, like pursuing a fulfilling job. Similarly, serving the visible needs, such as eating nutritious food, supports invisible needs like sanity and peace of mind. Satisfying the invisible and visible needs is similar to the question, "What came first, the chicken or the egg?" Who knows? The chicken lays the eggs, and the egg hatches the chicken. They are both equally needed and valuable.

Using the Correct Tool to Fill Each Need Leads to Peace and Abundance

I used to believe experiencing peace, harmony, and abundance daily, both physically and mentally, was a matter of luck. I felt it was all right for others to experience it, but it would never happen for me. I know now that no matter what the unmet needs are, either physical or emotional, I can apply the same basic survival process to fulfill them all. The tools are different, but the process is the same: I can use the same process to identify all my needs and find the right tools to meet them.

When I started sorting out which tool and resource worked to fill each of my physical, mental and emotional needs, things really started to turn around, and my life began expanding in all areas. The hardest lesson I learned and continue to have to reinforce is this:

It takes invisible tools to fulfill invisible needs.

What I've found on the "streets" of my mental and emotional health journey is that just the way visible needs, like hunger, require visible tools and solutions, like nutritious food, invisible needs, like validation, require invisible tools and solutions. These invisible tools relate to your thoughts, beliefs, emotions, and spirit.

Discovering invisible tools to fill my invisible needs and thus providing myself consistent peace can be challenging. In my case, filling the invisible needs of security, validation, and unconditional love begins with conscious observations of what I really need. I then replace unconscious automatic thoughts with consciously chosen healthy thoughts, beliefs, and choices to fill my invisible needs. We will go more into this in chapter 21.

The Train Wreck of Trying to Fill Invisible Needs with Visible Tools

Most of my deepest emotional issues have stemmed from trying to fill invisible needs with visible tools

When I try to use a visible physical tool like money to fill my invisible need for validation, security or love, **I always get into trouble**. Have you ever thought that a relationship (visible solution) would bring you that feeling of being lovable (invisible need)? Then, the person leaves you, and you end up feeling like moldy bread instead? Or perhaps you've made a ton of money (visible tool), and after a short feeling of joy or a "high," you end up feeling even worse, like it's still not enough? Maybe because you think subconsciously or consciously that you will never be enough? The payout of unlimited cash wasn't able to prove to you that you are okay. Johnny Lee describes this concept when he sings, "Looking for love in all the wrong places." I see it as going to the hardware store for milk.

Going to The Hardware Store for Milk

I have found that looking in all the "wrong" places for security, validation, and love, has been the cause of 99.9 percent of the stress and crisis in my adult life! When I eat too much ice cream or cake to "feel good," I end up sad in the end, which shows me I am attempting to use excess food to satisfy my internal needs for self-worth and comfort. In reality, overeating (visible tool) does not fill my invisible inner need for validation but instead sabotages my self-esteem.

Using the Wrong Tool for the Job

Another analogy is using a pair of pliers to pound in a nail. It doesn't work very well at all. I would often use the same tool repeatedly to satisfy many of my internal needs for validation. An example was working two or three jobs at a time, sometimes within the same career, and pushing myself to work 70 to 80 hours a week. No matter how much I worked or how great the results were, it couldn't satisfy my need for validation since my need for validation is an inside job, even though some try to convince us that it is an outside job.

Bait and Not the Nourishment

Advertisers prey on our invisible needs. If you drink our cola, you'll be energetic and popular. If you buy our luxury car, you'll be admired and get your validation. If you drink our beer, you'll be gorgeous, confident, popular, and get all the love you could ever want.

In truth, a tiny fraction of these internal needs can be met by these products and then only for a short time. The elation of driving off the car lot with an expensive vehicle may only last a few days. You could end up having buyer's remorse because you are now living for your car payment, and now that girl you were after is dating some guy who drives a 20-year-old Toyota. So, if you are like me, you could end up feeling worse off afterward.

In reality, I don't have any judgment against luxury cars. I just think they fall short of really filling the internal needs for validation and attracting true love in the long run. What do beer, a luxury car, and cola actually deliver? **I believe they deliver the bait—which is never enough—instead of real nourishment for our invisible needs.** This bait sets up a craving for more of the external, visible solution, whatever it is, even though it doesn't work.

Let's look at another example. I started my career in advertising. While working in advertising, I found that most advertising is trying to tell us if we use this or that we'll get our three invisible needs met. What other need could straight sugar mixed with water fill? I've found most of these products to be like modern-day snake oil, which does not fully satisfy true internal, invisible needs. These physical solutions never seem to meet the true invisible needs inside me.

When they ultimately fail to deliver the security, validation, and love that they say they will, it's at that moment that I feel even sharper pain from the unmet invisible needs for love, security, and validation. I unconsciously go back to an even stronger false belief that I'm not enough or lovable. So, what would I do when I unconsciously felt pain and realized a visible tool had failed to fill my invisible need? I'd go back for even more money, cola or relationships to fill my need to know I am okay and loved. My friend, Jodi, captured it well: "After all, advertisements say it works for everyone else, why not for me?"

I tried the same solution over and over again, expecting different results.
Definition of Insanity!

If you are tired of nothing ever working out, take time now to journal the thoughts in your head and the invisible survival needs you struggle to fill. This way, you can become conscious of real solutions for these invisible needs as we go forward. How can you tell the difference between an invisible and emotional need not being met and a visible physical need not being met? Let's start by hunting down what is bothering us the most (a.k.a. our deepest emotional pain points).

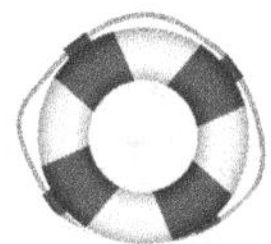

Chapter 16: Digging Deeper into Emotional Pain

"Success through the eyes of one once defeated is true VICTORY."
- Jim Cramer, of CNBC's "MADD Money"

For most of my life, **emotional and mental pain seemed to be the primary symptoms of anything going wrong.** The pain I experienced usually revolved around an incident with people or challenging circumstances that would arise in my life. I would essentially feel mental and emotional pain, and then my mind would unconsciously grab the first and most convenient reason for the feelings, whether the connection was real or not.

An example of me attaching my feelings in an unrealistic way to what someone else did, is when I panicked in a college Calculus class and wanted to run out of a classroom in embarrassment. Two people, sitting next to me, were whispering in a foreign language and my mind immediately jumped to the conclusion that they were talking about how badly I looked or smelled. My feelings of anxiety had likely nothing to do with the incident. These other students were probably talking about the homework or what movie to go to later.

The emotional and mental pain I experienced seemed so

overwhelming at times that I physically felt it was hard to breathe. I simply could not get a grip on what was happening. Everything seemed to blend: my thoughts, the facts, and my feelings. Often, I would perceive the situation as an insurmountable crisis, and it triggered a fight or flight response.

I first started feeling intense, emotional, mental pain when I was around sixteen. I had survived physical and mental trauma and was feeling the deepest pain I could imagine. I honestly didn't think I could live through the pain. Unconsciously, my mind started coming up with "reasons" why my life was a nightmare and that I should end it. Underneath it all, I subconsciously started believing that I was a subhuman freak, and I was at fault for everything that was going wrong around me. I punished myself emotionally and mentally, feeling I deserved the strictest consequences.

Looking back, with a lot of help from counseling and support groups, I realized this negative, subconscious belief that I was a subhuman freak, along with symptoms of high anxiety, began to manifest a year or so after an incident that happened when I was sixteen. These "false" beliefs that there was something wrong with me played out in the form of PTSD, panic, and phobic episodes. The panic attacks I suffered affected me physically, which affected my peace of mind in public.

As a result, I spent most of my time trying to manage my anxieties by blaming myself or others while hiding my problems and trying to "cure" my pain by escaping through overwork, relationships, and fixing other people's problems. You can find more examples of how I escaped later in this chapter. I call these examples my escape hatches.

Meanwhile, I judged and punished myself and other people in my mind. This, in turn, added tons more mental and emotional pain to an already heavy load. Did that pain suck? You bet! However, I know that if I had not become conscious of the level of pain I was in and occasionally had a clear and present mind, I would never have learned how to find and embrace a peaceful, abundant life.

Eliminating Emotional Pain Was the First Big Motivator in My Life

All I could think of from seventeen to about twenty-four was dissolving the emotional, mental pain of being an embarrassment and a burden on society. However, I know now, thanks to one of my mentors, that:

Pain is the dirt that must be moved to get to the gold: a happy, peaceful, and abundant life.

Now I see pain, especially **emotional or mental distress, as a signal in my life rather than a problem** in itself. I naturally want to alleviate these difficult emotions when they crop up. Still, I've also learned to respect these painful emotions as a messenger and catalyst for the most significant changes and transformations in my life. Whether emotional, mental or physical, pain delivers a message to me:

"Something is up! Pay attention to yourself.
Something needs to change."

- My internal pain voice

Acknowledging and investigating these painful feelings or "messengers" has been my gateway to developing happiness and true freedom.

My most significant challenges to reaching peace and abundance? My thoughts and old beliefs.

> "One of the greatest addictions, or the great addiction, is the addiction to compulsive thinking. So, the key, then, to becoming free of those unconscious mind patterns is to practice stepping out of compulsive thought activity."
>
> \- Eckhart Tolle.

Early on, I tried to manage the pain in all sorts of ways, not all of which were healthy for me. Mental issues and false beliefs about myself led to many of my physical issues until I was twenty-four. The panic attacks I suffered affected me physically, which affected my peace of mind in public. By my early twenties, however, I started investigating both of these issues on a deeper level, and as my investigation grew steadily over the years, I uncovered more clues.

The significant discovery I made about pain, especially emotional pain, is that it is rarely "caused" by what I think is causing it. I believed that the real reason for my pain was all "out there" —i.e., outside of me. For example, I thought men were not attracted to me physically because many left once we started dating. In hindsight, I think we were looking for different outcomes based on incompatible needs, values, communication styles, goals and more.

I have been shockingly surprised to find that the false beliefs, assumptions, and interpretations I was applying to myself, the world, and the universe caused almost all of my mental distress.

It's a Jungle in Here!

Many people experience adventure, terror, and happiness in the physical world through games or a rich fantasy life. But for me, the greatest dramas and adventures have played out in my own mind. I've seen my mind as a huge dense jungle, where I run and duck behind trees now and then to avoid threats which come in the form of emotional and mental arrows flying my way.

Most of the time, my underlying thoughts have been unconscious and presented themselves as "reality." When I finally reached the point of deepest pain, where I didn't think I could go on without isolating in Antarctica, I started facing the feelings and mental twists in my head. Here are some of the thoughts and feelings I heard when I began to listen to my fears:

- "What the f**k!!!"
- "Get me out of here! It's not safe!"
- "That guy's after me!" (and sometimes they really were, especially when I lived in dangerous environments and adopted risky lifestyles. Old instincts from cave dwellers over millions of years ago die hard).
- "All women think I am dumb, ugly, boring, and useless."
- "I feel like these fears and feelings are going to kill me, literally."
- "This has got to be hell!"
- "What did I ever do to deserve this?"
- "I'm forever stuck in this mental and emotional hell!"
- "How can I still be breathing and feel this much pain?"
- "I must be making this up! It's all in my mind! No harm is coming to me!"
- "How much of what I'm feeling and believing is real?"
- "How much of it is in my imagination?"
- "Am I really that crazy?"

- "I don't even recognize myself. Why would I do something like that?"
- "I must be stupid."
- "I am damaged goods."
- "People can't be trusted."
- "I can't be trusted."
- "My needs will never be met."
- "I take what I need when I want and enjoy what I can no matter who it hurts."
- "That's not my problem. They're not my problem."
- "I'm going to hell anyway."
- "I have nothing to lose. So why not do it despite the consequences?"

The BIG LIES I Habitually Tell Myself

What did all those thoughts and feelings equate to when I added them all up?

LIES!

These thoughts were and are false beliefs. I eventually realized that these thoughts, and the feelings resulting from them, were actually trying to help me stay safe emotionally and mentally by getting me to "escape" uncomfortable situations. However, the actual result of believing the lies was an unconscious erosion of my sense of security, validation, self-esteem, and love for myself and others.

In the process of uncovering these hidden culprits, I was surprised to find that my false beliefs, assumptions, and interpretations about myself, the world, and the universe, caused almost all of my mental distress. The biggest challenge and solution for me was to face my false beliefs head-on.

Believing Internal Lies Affected My Ability to Survive Physically

Believing these subconscious lies in my twenties and thirties did affect my food, jobs, and housing. Because I didn't believe I was worth anything, I ate less than others until I verged on anorexia. In my case, the lack of food contributed to another extreme addiction: addiction to adrenaline. I found doing and being in extreme situations with other people and acting in extreme ways gave me a feeling of aliveness, and I mistook this feeling for validation.

Mental/Emotional Challenges Take Time to Process

I know now that my obsession with managing painful issues like anxiety took immeasurable time and resources during the deepest part of my mental and emotional health challenges. According to Healthline.com, the average panic attack takes about ten minutes (Elmer, CRNP 2019). I'm here to tell you that, although the attack itself may have taken ten to thirty minutes, the total time involved in anticipating the attack, self-talking to try to ignore a live attack, and shaming myself after the attack, was closer to one hour per incident. And I had several panic attacks a day. Often, I had three hours a day dedicated to handling panic attacks, and that's not even including all the subconscious negative talk that gnawed away at my self-esteem like Chinese water torture.

Realistically, I spent most of my waking hours from age sixteen to thirty-two "ordealing" human interaction. These fears came in the form of agoraphobia (self-diagnosed), paranoia, and post-traumatic stress from childhood traumatic events and other unknown and perhaps inherited causes. I spent the other part of the day escaping from the mental, emotional hell in any way possible.

So, did I try to escape? Absolutely!

Until I found a better solution.

How Do You Tell If Your Thoughts are Influencing Your Survival?

To find an example of how emotional needs influence physical needs, ask yourself these questions:

- What kind of food am I going to eat if I don't think I am worth much?
- What kind of jobs or careers will I pursue if I'm invalidated by my own mind or by people close to me?
- What type of relationship will I enter into if I think I am worthless?
- What kind of people will I connect with if I place my dependence on them for self-esteem, validation, or security?
- What if I lean on external escape hatches like addictions to fill my needs for peace, validation, and love? And will they ever really work? Truly?

Note: Some of our false beliefs (a.k.a. the lies we tell ourselves), while personal to us, are often beliefs that others can relate to. These beliefs are typically negative. True beliefs are outlined later in the "Validation" chapter. If you are ready to jump into the "truth" with both feet, go to chapter 25 on validation now. In this chapter, we have been exercising the habit of hunting down our false beliefs, things that are not true. We will get into that more in the next chapter as well. If you're feeling frustrated, hang in there! Solutions are on the way!

An Example Of How Unconscious Thought Leads to Radical Decisions

Let's look at an example of unconscious thoughts in Jill's life and how she responds to them.

A single woman named Jill is walking down the street when, she sees a man she finds attractive walking her way on the same sidewalk.

As they walk slowly towards each other, she starts thinking of how great it would be to date him. She imagines the type of job he has and the kind way he will treat her. She visualizes the wedding and them living in a big house together with a cute dog.

Next thing you know, Jill spots another woman in real life walking across the street in his general direction, and she panics! Oh no, he's going to get distracted by her! Then, the man looks towards the other woman, and Jill decides he is the cheating type. Jill decides to divorce him in her imaginary marriage and asks for her imaginary dog back. She then crosses the street by the time he reaches where she would have been.

This whole scenario with Jill may have taken a few split seconds, and she will likely forget she even thought about this man a few minutes later. Even later, she'll obsess about the election instead. A constant stream of unconscious thoughts has now determined her options and choices in her real life.

Who knows, maybe this man was available as a potential mate. We'll never know since Jill's thoughts are mainly filled with fears and fantasies about how things could be or how people may treat her.

Today I take time to observe my thoughts as often as possible. I have learned to notice all the thoughts I can catch and **only follow the thoughts and emotions that support and serve my life instead of letting runaway thoughts dictate my life.**

Escape hatches

For me, escape hatches were my number one ally until I realized that they didn't lead to where I wanted to go. So, before I could even begin to examine what was going on inside my head, I had to take a look at how I avoided my problems. I know that I can do one of two things when feeling pain, anger, or overwhelmed:

1. **Escape** – I can try to escape the scary, uncomfortable thoughts and feelings. But escaping gives me temporary

relief only and doesn't make my feelings go away permanently.

2. **Face the fears head-on** – I stop running from my feelings, turn around, face whatever they turn out to be, and find out why I have them. This option leads me to freedom!

So, let's talk about the escape strategies I used to avoid uncomfortable feelings. For me, many of these strategies were in the form of avoidance or an obsession designed to distract me. Examples are romantic relationships or money. Many of these distractions were healthy in moderation and even good for my soul. I needed to eat, sleep, shop, and have intimacy with others on different levels. However, I took some of these healthy visible activities and tried to use them for distraction, emotional security, validation, and a sense of being loved. I took many of my escape behaviors to the extreme, where they triggered emotional and/or mental harm in myself and others.

What about you? Have you ever chosen to escape by using the following methods?

- Drugs
- Alcohol
- Overeating
- Sex or porn
- Gambling
- Shopping
- Video Gaming
- Social Media
- Obsessing over the news or relationships
- Caretaking others too much
- Worrying
- Reading excessively
- Staying in bed most of the day
- Raging
- Cowering or hiding

- Hating yourself or others
- Harming yourself or others
- Lying
- Anything else you can think of? ______________________
  ____

The reality is that many of these behaviors may be helpful and pleasurable, but what happens when you take these behaviors too far? Do extreme escape behaviors resolve your feelings? Let's look at one example of taking pleasurable activities to the extreme to escape feelings.

Example of Watching Videos for Escape

According to Marketing Charts (Marketing Charts 2019), the average person will spend 84 minutes a day watching videos. This doesn't even include half of all the other escapes available to us. 84 minutes equals about 511 hours per year. When you add it all up, the average person will spend over 16 work years (40 hours/week) watching videos over 65 years. I'm sure some of the videos I watch are useful or entertaining. However, 16 work years of my life make me think about the opportunity costs for that time. Heck, I could earn a Ph.D. with that amount of time. Or I could become a master artist or a craftsman. I could also learn several foreign languages. The list goes on.

Why Do We Do It?

The question of the day is, why do we find the need to check out or run to the safety of these escape behaviors automatically when we are experiencing mental or emotional pain? Who knows, underneath it all, what causes escape or all of our mental and emotional challenges. The concept of escape is an intricate and personal experience for each of us.

This question also reminds me of some of the research we discussed earlier from my friend Jodi in chapter 7. She shares about the brain amygdala's natural response to fight-flight-freeze and *why* we do it. She further shares how our adult cognitive brain (prefrontal cortex) can relearn to override that primal response. Somehow this biological explanation helps validate my own PTSD responses, while inspiring me to continue learning ways to rework the pathways in my brain for a more peaceful existence. You can find out more about how stress can result in long term changes in brain "circuits" from J. Douglas Bremner in his journal article *Traumatic stress: effects on the brain* (Bremner 2006, 445-461).

All I know is that many of my emotional, mental symptoms were inherited as well as learned. When I started researching my emotional issues, I discovered other relatives who had struggled with anxiety, phobias, anger, and depression. Many of them used escapes like alcohol, relationships, and work to cope with those emotional or mental challenges. As soon as I realized it wasn't "just me," I was able to start facing these fears one at a time.

Facing Fears (a.k.a. The "Monsters") Head On

Escape? You Bet!

The activities I engaged in to escape, which were numerous and fed on each other, seemed like a vacation from my daily, almost constant, apocalyptic-like everyday reality. So, unlike any movie I have ever seen, my mind and emotions felt utterly out of control. I've never in my life experienced so much drama from any experience in the physical world as I have from the **Drama That Was Generated from My Own Mind and Emotions**.

Back then, I lived in an inner world of hell, fear, overwhelming pain, and hopelessness that didn't seem to match the external world I observed, where people were simply going to school or going to work. Honestly, most of the day, I felt like a subhuman freak, more like an alien who didn't belong in the world and especially in "good" society. I falsely believed I was an imposter and lived every day believing my employer or boyfriend would find out how screwed up I was and fire me.

Why Did I Keep Living?

I may have kept living because of my suicide attempt while drunk at sixteen didn't end in death. My ears were ringing for days from an overdose of pain meds. I somehow got it that taking my own life was not an option anymore. It was out of my hands. Maybe some kind of universal spirit kept me going one more day with a speck of hope that there would be freedom from the mental, emotional hell? Who knows?

Hope Returned!

Hope did return as my mindset changed. Layer by layer, I dug deeper inside to see what was really going on. Ever since I became open to new belief systems, I have grown steadily stronger, healthier, and more peaceful. Now, looking back, all the pain, particularly the emotional and mental pain I was experiencing, has been one of the most outstanding teachers in my life. In fact, these false beliefs ended up being "gold mines" in my path to growth.

Goldmine! You've Hit the Mother Lode!

A mentor shared her belief with me that, our deepest "problems" or unresolved baggage from the past, can be our most important keys to freedom, if we can honestly face them. That is why I have gotten into the habit of welcoming these false beliefs, understanding them, and following them to the freedom they alone hold.

An example of finding gold in an unlikely place is when I

would call my friend and mentor and tell her something terrible was happening. Once I told her I had been laid off from my job unexpectedly and was terrified that I would go broke and have to live on the streets. Her response: "What a gold mine you found! You've hit the mother lode!"

She would help me find my false beliefs, such as "I'm no good. No one wants me. I'm an imposter. Who do I think I am to believe I can earn an abundant living in a job I love? Then, she would say, these are veins of gold. Let's keep following where they lead. As we kept following the veins of gold, they led to the reality that these beliefs were lies, projected in my own head by an internal judge or saboteur or tantrum-throwing child. So, I personalized the false beliefs (a.k.a. lies) as characters like Gremlins from the movie.

I was able to thank each "gremlin," or false idea, for trying to keep me safe, but firmly told them I didn't need their help anymore and I lovingly let each one pass on. Finally, I validated the "Truth" of the situation, which was "I am priceless. I am equally valuable to every other human being on the planet, and I am capable of offering work and services to people and organizations that value what I have to offer."

Coming to this understanding of truth, that I was okay and valuable and could interact as a regulated adult with others, was the priceless gold I had been looking for. This process of mining the gold in my life has led me to quickly face any uncomfortable feeling or hopeless situation with clarity and trust that, if I can be present through this incident or situation, I will be richly rewarded on the other side.

Once I process emotions in one area of my life, I usually never experience the level of feelings in that area of my life again. The issues that come up subsequently seem minor.

> **"The emotional work pays off beyond my wildest expectations!"**
> - Myself

I have seen hope like this return to countless others as well, those who were brave gold miners like you and took a look into their own false beliefs. Such hope leads away from survival thinking towards abundant thinking.

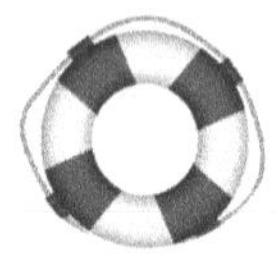

Chapter 17: Survival Mindset

"You simply can't shrink your way to wealth."
- Keith Weinhold, Creator of podcast *Get Rich Education*

My "survival mindset" began with my first real experience as a general maid in the Victorian hotel I mentioned earlier in chapter 10. The first paycheck I earned was impactful. I took myself out to lunch for a grilled cheese sandwich and a Dr. Pepper at a local dime store diner. I felt such a rush at being able to take care of myself in an adult way. That summer, I bought myself some clothes and continued to go out to a diner every workday. I learned right there the awesome power of being able to survive on my own.

This first work experience taught me a few key concepts that contributed to my ideal survival mindset:

- Work can be fun
- Work can be freeing and liberating
- All jobs are worthy no matter what you do
- Be present and shoot for excellence in any job you have
- Work is only hard if you see it that way

- It is empowering to know you can take care of your own basic needs for food, clothing, and more

Frankly, I felt truly alive when I worked at this job. I loved everything from the smell of the pine cleaners to the feel of the clean sheets. I loved to explore all the defunct ballrooms, the old guest registries, and the dusty gambling equipment in the secret basement rooms. I felt responsible and trusted as I cleaned the few remaining crystal chandeliers in the hallways and executive suites. This job laid the foundation for me: I learned to value work as it enabled me to survive by taking care of myself.

However, all this was before I HAD to take care of myself fully. When I actually had to start working to take care of myself and fund my college education, I learned the art of "scrambling."

Scrambling

Scrambling is a strategy or tactic with a hunter-like view of what needs to be done next. I first experienced the art of scrambling when my parents weren't able to pay for my first semester of college. When I realized I didn't have any money to attend college, my internal dialog went something like this:

Freaked-out Self: "WTF! The money is all out! What can I do?"

Advisor Self: "Snap out of it! Get your bearings. Where are you? Where do you want to be? Who might be able to help you? Form a plan."

Freaked-out Self: "I'm all alone. There is no one to help me. I want to stay in college because I don't know what else to do with my life. But... I can't do this!"

Advisor Self: "Get a grip, soldier. March into the office of your dorm and ask for help. Then, go to financial aid and beg for help."

FAST FORWARD 2 WEEKS...

Bingo! After following my internal general, I signed up for emergency financial aid within a couple of weeks. I received enough funds to pay for college tuition and worked in the dorm cafeteria washing dishes to pay for room and board with a bit of extra spending money left over. Problem solved! — until the summer at least, then I had to scramble to find a place to live at the local youth hostel.

Life proceeded along these lines for many years. For a time, I would experience relative stability living paycheck-to-paycheck. Then a change would happen, such as losing a job, and would lead to another round of dust-kicking scrambling, followed by another period of peace. This went on for at least six to seven years until I "stumbled" onto a new way of thinking called the "abundance and prosperity mindset." But first, let's talk about the opposite mindset: the "scarcity" mindset.

What is a "Scarcity" Mindset?

Upon closer examination of my finances, I found that I had been confusing the "survival" mindset, which is genuinely instinctive, with the "scarcity" mindset. When I immersed myself in the scarcity mindset, I always had this feeling that the other shoe was about to drop. This world of scarcity had limited resources and was basically a shrinking pie. I had to continue to fight and scramble for more and more of the shrinking pie's crumbs. If I had a job, I felt like I was always on the edge of being fired.

This scarcity mindset expanded into all other areas of my life as well. If I had a man interested in me and he was available, my scarcity mindset would say something is wrong because genuine relationships are scarce, not available. Then I would conclude that the man was only available because he was boring and unattractive. But if the man fit my scarcity mindset and had to scramble to keep a relationship alive, it felt right. In my mind, the other person was never enough. I was never enough. The clothes I wore, the car I drove was never "it." Maybe another college degree would help. It never did.

Overall, this belief that I would have to "scramble" to stay alive for the rest of my life became the primary mindset under which I operated in all areas of my life; **until I learned, it was possible to develop an abundance and prosperity mindset where there is enough of everything for everyone, no matter what.**

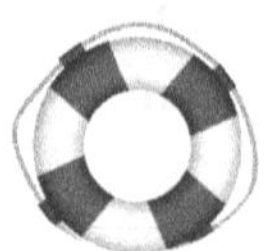

Chapter 18: Abundance Mindset

Abundance and prosperity are available *to me* no matter my income or status.

I found out in my mid-twenties that a true "abundance mindset" involves earning more than I spend and taking personal responsibility for providing for all of my needs. Guess what? Those needs include my emotional needs, no matter my income.

As I mentioned earlier, I joined a friend's financial support group and learned about the abundance mindset by observing my own and other peoples' financial and personal lives. In this group, I saw people who earned three times as much income as I did run into the same problems. All of us had both visible and invisible "needs" that we didn't fully understand. Many of us tried to escape however we could, for example, by spending excess money or engaging in addictive relationships that were not nourishing.

The funny thing was we all seemed to be spending at least 10 percent more than we earned no matter what our income was. Many of us also felt like we were imposters and not "making it." We felt somehow deficient no matter what our income or lifestyle. It all boiled down to our invisible needs for security, validation, and love not being fulfilled. So, our first step in filling these invisible needs was to adopt an abundance mindset, and to do this, we had to learn the principles of abundance.

Abundance Principles

I learned and still believe that true abundance and prosperity thinking is not only possible but fascinating and life-changing! Here are a few of the characteristics of abundance that I now know:

- **Personal abundance and opportunity are here now, always present at this moment** – I can take whatever circumstance I find myself in right now and look for the abundance in it. This awareness of my current level of abundance and prosperity motivates me to form a vision to bring me even more peace, security, validation, and happiness. (FYI, writing this book is completing one of those visions for me!)
- **The answers come in the form of problems** – A solution showing up as a form of a challenge or an issue seems like a paradox but is true for me. If I want to experience more abundance, I need to focus first on the areas in which I feel deprived or pressured. When I get clarity with problems, I gain clarity with the answers. This is particularly true when I share the "problems" or my feelings of fear and deprivation with others.
- **I am not alone . . . ever** – I have learned I can ask **trusted friends or professionals,** who are available and have the knowledge and resources I need, to help me:
    - **Understand where I am at today**
    - **Process my thoughts and feelings** surrounding my situation

- **Establish the facts**
- **Form action steps** I can follow to change my situation
- **Celebrate the milestones** that I reach along the journey to an abundant and prosperous life
- **Figure out what abundance really means to me** by inviting a friend, counselor, or a dream team member to ask me questions to help me find what a happy, joyous, free, and abundant life means to me personally versus what society thinks is right
- **Notice if the results of my actions have brought me true abundance or not and pivot to new actions when needed**

Switching from the Survival to the Abundance Mindset

"I'm afraid to quit my job because I'll barely scratch by on only a million and a half dollars of net worth."

-Friend

It's real! It's possible! I have experienced the transformation of my mindset from survival (or scarcity) to abundance. It feels like the pathways or grooves in my mind have physically and mentally changed. New beliefs, like abundance, displace old beliefs, like scarcity.

One of the reasons I was able to experience this transformation is that, in my heart something kept telling me there must be another way; there must be another reality. I couldn't believe that life, in almost every area, my life was supposed to be that difficult. I was sure I was missing something.

And I was! I'm so grateful that I kept searching until I tripped over the principle of abundance that others had found before me. Thanks to learning about the possibility of abundant living, I have painted a whole new picture of what reality can look like for me. Today, I make every effort to make this new fertile environment available to those around me who show an interest. I don't have all the answers to life's mysteries. But I am willing to become a detective of life and sniff out different mindsets, like abundance, that mainly come in the form of new beliefs.

Note: The primary reason I am writing this book is that today I experience true happiness and prosperity 95 percent of the time, mainly due to this transformation from scarcity to abundance thinking.

Abundance Thinking Starts Here

To begin this process, I first had to **understand all my underlying needs, both physical and mental/emotional.** Learning to uncover my underlying needs and desires was essentially a fact-finding mission. Before I could truly meet each one of my needs, I had to know they existed. I needed a target that I could aim at. For each visible or invisible need that I identified, I wrote down how I met each specific need at the time. After I had a complete sense of my needs and how they were being met, I focused my attention on brainstorming healthier, more abundant ways to fill them.

Using Abundant Options to Fill Invisible Needs Helps Serve Visible Needs as Well

Taking time to review my invisible needs and looking for healthy, abundant strategies to meet those invisible needs, supported meeting my visible needs in more fruitful ways. Again, these invisible needs include mental and emotional needs, such as my need for a sense of security, validation, and giving and receiving love.

Through experience, I have determined that knowing what my invisible needs are and finding healthy ways to satisfy those needs establishes a firm foundation for abundant living. But this is hard to do when I'm hungry or cold. So, although deciding whether to focus on invisible or visible needs first is a chicken or an egg situation, I find if I quiet and calm my mind, clear my head, and focus on the present moment, the answers are right in front of me.

Let's take time now to review some guideposts on transitioning from scarcity to abundance.

Guideposts for Transforming Survival Thinking to Abundant Thinking

As I learned about abundance principles from people, books, and experience, certain guideposts emerged. These "guideposts" or "best practices" made my transition from a scarcity lifestyle to an abundant lifestyle possible. In what follows, I illustrate how I transformed my thinking using my relationship to money as an example.

1. **Clarity is the key to paradise** – I first experienced this concept by tracking my income and expenses for 30 days. Then I categorized each item and was surprised by what I found.
2. **Abundant money exists in all situations** – I discovered that I nearly always have plenty of money to cover my direct expenses with a little extra remaining at all times. I did have to switch to taking the bus to work instead of paying for parking downtown. Thinking of the glass half-full, I saw riding the bus as an opportunity to read. I also had to be willing to take whatever work I could find. This included mowing lawns, dishwashing, cleaning hotel rooms, answering phones for hotels and businesses, working in retail, and eventually finding and following my passion through countless dream jobs with differing incomes.
3. **Redirect my effort, time, and money** – What I found when looking at my survival lifestyle was how I had misdirected my money and efforts. I was robbing Peter to pay Paul. I

acted like the big shot, when giving gifts, instead of paying my monthly bills on time. Along the way, I discovered tools to develop spending plans, pursue career goals and organize my time—tools such as Jerrold Mundis' book, *How to Get Out of Debt, Stay Out of Debt and Live Prosperously* (Mundis 2012), or the Franklin Covey calendar system. These tools rocketed my effectiveness and accomplishments forward, which helped me exceed any goals I set myself.

4. **Focus my attention in smaller time units... a day, an hour, this moment** – Most of my mental and emotional anxiety was centered on fear of the future and shame about the past. Probably the most lasting strategy I have used has been living in "day-tight" compartments: I can plan and have goals, but I only live 24 hours at a time. Lately, through extreme self-honesty, I have reduced this into living in the moment. The present moment is, after all, the only reality that exists. If I can accept and live with this truth, abundance takes care of itself, so long as I am present for it.
5. **Rely on my own internal gauge to find my level of joy and peace in each moment and situation** – I like to observe what I am doing and thinking when I find myself worrying about a painful or confusing situation. I used to panic and freeze up. I had to rely on others' actions, beliefs, attitudes, and emotions to judge and reflect on whether I was ok. I subconsciously thought "they" were right and had power over whether I could be happy and feel fulfilled. I know now that I can use challenging emotions, like fear or worry, to clarify what is actually happening in the moment myself and dig deeper inside to find abundant solutions to fill that invisible or visible need. I can be as joyous and peaceful as I make up my mind to be, regardless of the people or circumstances around me.

6. **Accept things, circumstances, and people as they are, not as I want them to be** – For the longest time, I thought that some person or some condition like my employment was unfair and "should" be the way I saw fit. But ideas like, "If I just work hard, I'll be recognized and become wildly successful in the eyes of the world" didn't pan out most of the time. Hard work could pay off if I had my ladder against the right wall but depending on others to "recognize" and reward my hard work was a dead end. Not having a particular person's or employer's approval, either emotionally or financially, really used to bring me down.

   Today I know it pays to sit still, suspend judgment, and observe my thoughts and the people and circumstances around me, so I can detect my underlying needs and the needs of others. If someone uses a critical or mean tone of voice, I can accept that without reacting unconsciously. Once, to the best of my ability, I determine what is actually happening, I can consciously decide not to take anything personally.

   I can then choose how I want to respond and interact with people instead of engaging in a panicked state of mind or feeling I am a victim to others' actions. Again, I do not have to accept behavior that does not match my values, but I can always accept a person as a valuable human being, even though I may have to do so from a safe distance.

   By accepting others fully for who they present themselves to be, I am free to respond effectively to any situation without compromising my "truths" about my own worth, security, and sense of being lovable. For instance, I can determine if the other person appears to be cooperative and looking for win-win solutions or if they appear to be lying and trying to take credit for work they are not contributing.

Either way, I can intuitively respond if I am willing to see what is happening as clearly as possible, instead of acting out of fear or believing the other person's reality.

7. **Commit to personal growth** – I used to be obsessed with what other people were doing or not doing. I would ask myself questions like, "Why was this person born into this wealthy family?" Or "Why does that person get promoted, and I don't when they stole my ideas and took the credit?" I learned along the way that if, for a moment, I take the focus off of other people or circumstances (including dropping comparison with others), then **I can focus on the one person I can change, *myself*.** Focusing almost exclusively on changing my own beliefs, attitudes, actions, and emotions throws the door wide open to a lot of emotional freedom.

In any situation, the opportunity exists to rise above without feeling superior or inferior. I have learned to look at how I can accept the current reality around me. My experience has shown me how to switch to more abundant visible or invisible tools, like thoughts or relationships, AFTER learning the personal growth lesson from that person or situation. Trust me! You will end up thanking that annoying person or situation for their role in your life if you can learn and grow. And, hopefully, later, you can share what you have learned with others.

So, without any further delay, let's dive into the three invisible needs, **security**, **validation**, and **love**, which can form the foundation for a life of abundance when properly met. We'll cover security first.

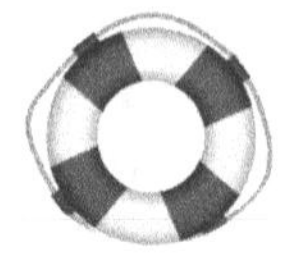

Chapter 19: Security

What does the word "security" mean to you? What crosses your mind when you find yourself in a mental, emotional, financial, physical, or relationship crisis? Do you feel hopeless and grab for a quick fix by buying something? Or do you stop to compose yourself and regain emotional or mental peace? And what about the needs you are addressing? Are they genuinely physical needs, or are you trying to get your internal, invisible needs met for security by getting angry with others or overeating to push back uncomfortable, insecure feelings?

Perhaps a definition of security will help.

What is "True" Security?

True security is a basic emotional, mental, physical, financial, or relationship need. My security needs started in childhood. When I was born, I instinctively expected all my basic physiological, safety, and emotional needs to be met; things such as food, a safe/warm home, clothing, safe hugs, and a few toys, even if only pots and pans. I also believe I instinctively needed a parent or guardian who was happy to see me and lovingly watched over me. I needed a parent to pick me up when I fell and to teach me how to pick myself up as soon as I was able to.

But not all my needs were met as a child, so I had to heal as an adult. In this process of healing, I learned how to parent myself into a regulated adult. As a regulated adult I can engage parenting skills for myself such as paying attention, identifying my unmet childhood needs, and taking action to fill those needs. My regulated adult self is never far away, is reliable and shows up when needed. Today, I can provide safety for myself in the face of physical and mental threats, which satisfies my unmet childhood need for security.

As a regulated adult, I am now equipped to focus on specific values and identify trusted, outside help when I need to. I can now leave behind insecure childhood fears and **trust that all my basic needs are met. I can choose to believe that the world is an overall safe place that I can navigate successfully.** I know this to be true today for me. I believe it can be true for you too.

The way I discovered what security meant to me was first to identify what security is not. For instance, I believed that **real life was "insecure," I had to be on my toes, and "security" and peace were a fantasy**. I know now that is what security is NOT.

Building Insecurity into My Belief Systems

I landed somewhere in between security and insecurity growing up. I always had a place to live, though I moved to different schools on average every 18 months. I also had food, clothing, and some consistent periods of adult care. I know my parents did the best they could with the information and resources they had available at the time. Providing for my physical needs, including food, housing, and clothing, came easily, but providing for my emotional, relational, and financial security needs came much later.

How One of My Insecurity Belief Systems Started

Once, when my cousin and I were both fifteen and my sister nine, we all went hiking by ourselves one sunny summer day on a big mountain in Colorado. At the time, my cousin was pressuring me to climb this mountain and I had too much pride and arrogance to say no, even though I felt the hike was beyond my experience. At first, we had a wonderful, fun, adventurous day, but soon we found ourselves surrounded by ominous grey clouds. I literally could feel the calm before the storm as the air began to get warmer. Then it started raining as we were almost to the top of the mountain. After the first few sprinkles, lightning started, and it was striking too close. We were scared.

We went to a low spot to avoid getting struck by lightning, but then trickles of water started streaming between our feet. My cousin freaked out at that moment, saying, "We're all going to die!" I told her that was crazy and that we would be back in our sleeping bags at home in a couple of hours. All we needed to do was to ride out the storm. I started us on a round of singing "My Favorite Things" from the *Sound of Music*, thinking that would be it.

We were hunkered in our low spot, noticing the water beginning to flow around our feet, when my cousin screamed again about all of us dying. I didn't know what to do, so we ran to the top of a nearby hill to get away from the trickle of water. I thought her fears of us dying were all in her head.

We started to get wet and cold; really, really cold. I had some training in hypothermia and realized that I might be moving into that state. I told my cousin and sister I had to keep moving to stay warm. They fought over the only coat we had, and my sister ended up with it. They opted to follow me.

We started walking and ran into a small stream that was about five inches deep. I told my sister and cousin I thought we should go across it because we needed to be on the other side. My cousin was scared and was chewing on a piece of long grass. To reassure her, I took out a rope we were carrying and told everyone we could hold on to it and help each other if we slipped or had difficulty crossing.

We started to cross, holding onto the rope, my sister going first, followed by me and then my cousin. All of a sudden, a massive wall of rushing water came down on us, engulfing and picking us up like rag dolls. We tumbled head over heels.

But as I floated in the water, I felt calm. It seemed like I wasn't struggling, just rolling over and over and breathing naturally. Then, I remembered hearing about the Big Thompson flood. In that flood, 144 people died because they thought they could outrun what turned out to be a 50-foot wall of water. They were running on foot or driving their cars to escape. I had forgotten that flash floods in the mountains come in waves with vast amounts of water rushing down narrow canyons. These "waves" crash down on anything in their path, twisting cars into unrecognizable hunks of metal.

I broke out of my trance when I grasped we were in a flash flood. I clawed my way out and threw myself against a bank. Once clear, I yelled for my sister and cousin. My sister yelled back, but my cousin didn't. I kept walking beside the river and yelling for my cousin until I couldn't hear my sister's voice from the other side anymore. At that moment, I started running blindly—kind of like a Carlos Castaneda novel in the desert.

I did not know much about God, but I prayed all the way down the mountain and negotiated with God that if we all made it out alive, I would go to church and be a true believer. When I finally reached the street we lived on, the realization set in that we never had to cross that creek in the first place. The beginnings of a survivor's guilt started to creep in.

We didn't all make it out. My cousin hit her head on a rock and drowned. My dad and brother later found her, and all my dad's efforts to revive her failed.

I gave up on God the next day and placed myself lower than everyone, especially women. I decided to live my life for my cousin. I was in shock for a long, long time. The world now seemed insecure. Young people died for no reason, there wasn't a thing I could do about it, and there was no God.

How Lack of Security Affected Me

Six months after my cousin died, I was drinking alcohol heavily and I began the risky behavior of getting involved with and placing my dependence on men, who were a danger to me, for their attention and protection. One day, when sixteen and drunk, I attempted suicide by chewing handfuls of aspirin. I had to rid myself of the unbearable feelings of pain, self-blame, and shame. But my dad and his girlfriend intervened and saved me. My ears rang for days. I decided not to try that again.

I didn't go to counseling, and at the time, there was no internet to learn more about my thoughts and feelings. I continued into my early twenties to lean on alcohol and men for my security. These were my first escape hatches from unbearable pain, shame, and survivor's guilt.

Another escape was to spontaneously sign up to be an exchange student traveling to Germany in my senior year in high school. But the same pattern of dependency on alcohol and men followed me overseas. And another incident in Germany caused my insecurity to mushroom. I was at an American Army base taking an ACT exam for college, and I passed gas (a.k.a. farted) that smelled like the worst sulfur you can imagine. I had been up drinking Ouzo (a Greek alcoholic drink) the night before, and my body was starting to break down.

After I passed gas, all the other students shunned me. I went back to the German high school the next day and embarked on an unintentional habit of experiencing daily panic attacks, becoming paranoid that I would pass gas again.

I'm guessing that all of the events leading up to this first panic attack, including my behavior and survivor's guilt over my cousin's death, contributed to the fact that my body was breaking down from neglect and abuse. I was losing my sense of smell, which led instantly to a vicious cycle of five or six panic attacks a day. This is the core of the insecurity and insanity that I felt for years and years.

Yes, I felt insane at seventeen and tried my hardest to cover my imperfections in order to survive. **I'm here to tell you now, though, that these incidents and how I interpreted them, along with the feelings my interpretations generated in me, turned out to be the best things that ever happened in my entire life.** Why? Because I suffered deep physical insecurity and mental and emotional instability, **I was driven to find a way up and out. And I have.** I feel my life was just like a piece of coal that undergoes extreme pressure and turns into a diamond. I am still here and thankful to tell you I didn't give up the search for true security even in my darkest hours.

Tracing the Root Cause of Insecurity

Have you ever or are you right now struggling for food, shelter, or safety? Did you have your basic needs provided by your parent(s) as a child? In my life and personal research, I've found that if children have one or more unmet basic need, they will instinctively develop coping methods and solutions to meet those physical or emotional security needs.

As children, many of us experienced fear when our basic needs were not satisfied. In addition to not getting some core security needs met in childhood, one or more of our parents may have been absent at times or been in a rage when communicating with us. A child may fear a parent and at the same time have to rely on that same largely unavailable parent for security. This makes things confusing for the child since, from a child's perspective, they may be thinking, "I'm supposed to go to my parents for security, yet my parents might be raging at me, and I feel scared of them."

Faced with confusion, I believe the child misses a critical developmental stage: feeling a sense of security. They do not have an example of security to model, and so they do not learn how to provide for their own security in a healthy and direct manner. As a child, I came up with my own interpretations of what was going on around me, and I found ways to cope. I used to pretend to be magic and built an imaginary nest of security around myself. However, as I mentioned earlier, all of these escape hatches and false sources of security eventually broke down, and I felt despondent.

I have learned that when a child takes "security" into their own hands, they may feel responsible for taking care of their own basic needs and providing for their sibling's needs. As a result, they may start stealing food and other items to provide for themselves and their younger siblings. Sometimes, a child who is taking action to provide for their own physical and emotional needs early in life may also feel responsible for taking care of their parents' emotional needs. Thus, the child may fall into handling adult issues way too early in life, without any true understanding of how to meet their own needs first.

Note: Values that may be reasonable in one circumstance may not be reasonable in another. For example, it may be reasonable for a seven-year old child raised on a farm to collect eggs at six in the morning but it may not be reasonable for the same child in a city to the grocery store by themselves.

I believe my parents had some of their needs unfulfilled as well. In my mind, this compounds the difficulty in stopping the generational cycle since unhealthy ways of getting needs met are passed from one generation to the next.

What changed?

When I reached my lowest point, I finally stopped and took a breath; I jumped off the merry-go-round of habitual thinking and actions. I then got outside help from Connie Klein, who offers psychotherapy in Colorado and is the true "guru" of the upward path for me. With outside help from Connie and others, I learned the concept of **"committing to the upward path in life."**

When I went to counseling with Connie, on a whiteboard she drew a dot on the lower left and another dot on the upper right and drew a straight line to connect the two. She then turned to me and asked: "Are you committed to the upward path in your life?" meaning that I just keep learning and improving in good times and bad.

Do You Want to Commit to the Upward Path in Your Life?

If so, commit to yourself, with someone else as a witness, that you will find and follow your upward path no matter what. Even if you "feel" like you are sliding backward, you are going to treat your survival and quest for peace, love, and abundance in your life like a mission. I know once I made that commitment, the world of abundance, peace, and sanity began to take hold in my life. After committing to the upward path, I found the first step in my journey was to face the demons in my mind, heart, and life that had created my insecurities.

Fear is the "Ringleader!"

My biggest challenges boiled down to fear. I kept feeding that dog of fear for years and didn't know how to stop. In my life, **fear had countless shapes, forms, and creative outlets.** So, if I wanted to make progress on my upward path, I would have to unlearn many old beliefs and learn new ways of thinking and acting in the world.

I Started My Path in The College Library

The simple answer to moving into surviving and even thriving with absolute security was to **start somewhere, anywhere!** For me, it started with a magazine article in our college library, then a book, then a counselor, and then biofeedback and meditation, followed by countless other steps.

I eventually changed my diet and let go of alcohol, caffeine, nicotine and processed foods. I suddenly realized I would have to work hard, as if my life depended on it (which it did!), to find out how to get to peace and abundance in my life. Somehow while mired in the mud of my misinterpretations and circumstances, I peeked out into the fresh blue sky and reached my hand out for help. And help was there! Gradually, I began feeling myself being pulled from the mud, which I later found out was more like quicksand, by all the people and resources reaching their hands out to pull me into their life raft.

Note: To be honest, it has been hard for me to write down some of this experience because I'm so deeply grateful to be sane and happy today that I do not want to risk being pulled back into the quicksand again. But I know now my chances of staying in the sunshine will be greater if I share these experiences with you. We are not alone, even when we are physically by ourselves. This is hard for me to see sometimes when crises arise.

What to Do When Overwhelm Strikes Me on My Path

I have experienced this feeling of being overwhelmed many times over the years. When I felt a surge of fear, I would panic and freeze until I learned how to face fear.

One day, I was sitting in a support group, slowly getting unstuck from the sludge of hopelessness, when I witnessed a woman walk in clutching a doll. She periodically broke down crying and talking in little girl voices when sharing her struggles with the group. I thought she was going completely off the deep end at the time, and I wanted to avoid her at all costs.

But not long after I saw her in the group, I was home alone after a boyfriend had left me. I was terrified to live alone. It was 2 a.m., and I was melting down into an overwhelming panic attack. Well, guess who I was inspired to call that night? I called the woman I had seen hugging the doll and crying in that support group.

Not only did she answer the phone at 2 a.m., but she calmly talked me through the overwhelming panic attack. She told me to pick something up and move it from one room to another. She was teaching me how to ground myself. Through her generous support, I made it through that night by writing on sheets of computer paper nonstop for hours.

I learned a lot about who to trust that night. If I wanted to feel mentally and physically secure, I no longer had to go to people who were acting dangerously. I could adjust my radar on who was safe and helpful for me. Some part of me knew that a woman had to be somewhat secure in herself to show up in a public support group in such a vulnerable state. Today, I can honestly say I would trust my life with this woman. She is a best friend, even today.

Switching to Trust-Based Coping Tools for Security

Over the years, I have learned if I want to experience true security, surrounded by that feeling of safety, peace, and appreciation for everything and everyone around me, I need to commit to lifelong learning and growing. I need to learn to trust who people really are and not fantasize about who I want them to be. I am now skeptical about the assumptions I've had about people and life! I feel like I've earned the highest degree available in life and happiness. Today, the interactions I have with most of the people out there are safe and secure. I have learned how to tell when someone is really in my corner and can help or partner with me versus someone who is unavailable and judgmental.

Trust-Based Tools that Have Aided My Journey From "Insecurity" to "Security"

Although recognizing who may be mutually supportive has been a hallmark of my change from insecurity to security, there are many more strategies that supported this transformation. Here are a few of these strategies:

- **Going for help** – counseling (mental health and career), support groups, countless books, the internet, friends, relatives, and more.
- **Food** – Researching and building a relationship with food and nourishing drinks that work for me has been vital. In this chapter, unlike the purely physical need for food discussed earlier, I am referring to the ability to be present with food by involving all the senses. I can smell a strawberry, taste it and savor its flavor. I can feel nutrients being absorbed into my body as I chew the strawberry slowly and swallow it. I can breathe deeply as I digest the strawberry and become grateful for all the people that made it available to me. For more details on building a true reality, relationship, and experience around eating and food check out The Slow Down Diet by Marc David (David 2015). I love it!
- **Biofeedback** – And other types of physical therapy.
- **Meditation** – One of the single best sources of grounding and sanity for me. Meditation eventually overtook medication as a solution for my panic, anxiety, and paranoia. I am currently practicing Centering Prayer and Tonglen. Thank you, Father Keating and Pema Chodron!
- **Prayer** – Take or leave this suggestion! I find I am happier when I reach out to a bigger force than myself for any

challenging issue or circumstance I am facing. This force is personal and removes the burden of feeling responsible for all the circumstances in my life and others' actions.

Yes, I'm responsible for showing up. One of my favorite sayings attributed to Mohammed by the scholar Al-Tirmidhi (Wright 2016) talks about maintaining spiritual versus earthly minded balance.

Trust God but tie your camel to the tree.

My belief that there is more spiritually going on around me than I am aware of and that I can touch and access this universal power directly, has given me the ability to survive, thrive, and contribute to the world. One well-known prayer that I like is the Serenity Prayer. Here are two versions:

More Common Version of the "Serenity Prayer"
God grant me the *serenity* to accept the things I cannot change,
the *courage* to change the things I can,
and the *wisdom* to know the difference.

The Codependent (Healing) Version of the "Serenity Prayer"
God grant me the *serenity* to accept the people, places, and things I cannot change, the *courage* to change the one person I can,
and the *wisdom* to know that one person is *me*!

Are you wondering how this faith came about given my traumatic experience during and after the flood? Around nine years after the flood, the shock and the cobwebs started to clear in my mind. After trying and failing to reach sanity or peace using other means like school, alcohol, work, men, and adrenaline rushes, I finally decided that some things in my life could not be explained logically and were out of my hands.

With the help of self-help books, such as The Seven Habits of Highly Effective People by Stephen Covey (Covey 1989), I realized that there are things that are bigger than I am, that I may be able to influence but which I cannot control. A nine-foot wall of water coming down on us in the middle of a mountain desert was one of those things that I had no way ever to control. We all did the best we could with the resources we had at the time. So, I concluded that there must be a bigger plan than I could comprehend, and for some reason, that plan involved a young person losing their life before their prime. As writer Richard Bach says:

> "Here is the test to find whether your mission on earth is over. If you're alive, it isn't."
>
> -Richard Bach, Illusions

Like all my other research, I have consumed countless hours studying and following spiritual principles from multiple faiths, including nature, to arrive at something that works for me. Hopefully, you can find your source of strength, clarity, and inspiration to fuel your deepest underlying needs and desires.

- **Medication** – I have taken medication for anxiety here and there for periods of time throughout my adult life. I was totally against taking the medication until a friend said that if my experience was like hers, the medication was NOT going to make me feel high. It was going to widen my experience. I could finally stop going into fight or flight mode over a twig breaking and instead, react only to a more extreme incident such as a car getting too close to me while I'm walking. In other words, she shared that taking medication for depression and anxiety gave her more appropriate responses. So, in patches over the years, I have taken medication for anxiety.

Currently, I'm not taking medication. Instead, meditation has taken over much of the treatment for my anxiety. If I need to take the medication in the future, I will. Again, taking medication is a personal decision. I'm grateful to be medication-free today. It helped me when I needed it. Now, grounding exercises help me!

- **Grounding exercises** – I remember one time when I tried medication for my anxiety, and I actually felt way worse than I had without it. I was laid out depressed on the couch, and I panicked. I felt out of control. I picked up the phone and called the women who had been bringing her doll to the support group again. She taught me this grounding exercise:
    - Rub your hands together, then touch your face.
    - Rub your hands together, then touch your thighs with feet flat on the ground.

I did these things, and they worked!

These grounding exercises exemplify the kinds of ego-bashing actions I had to take to get the seeds of sanity and peace planted in my mind. These seeds eventually grew into a true sense of consistent emotional, mental and physical security.

Again, I love and trust this woman who was hugging her doll and crying that day. I am forever thankful for her help when I needed it the most. My friendship with her is a perfect example of gifts arriving in unexpected packages. She was a sheep in wolf's clothing, turning out to be good for me even though initially, I thought she would be bad for me.

In fact, many of the issues in my life have stemmed from not realizing that bad things for me were *bad* for me: someone I thought was good for me turned out to be bad for me, especially when I didn't think I was worth much. Now I can identify things and people who are "good" for me, or a healthier match as I think of it today, and steer clear of things and people who are bad for me, or as I think of it today—not supportive of a healthy, thriving life. Looking for what is healthy for me in any situation helps me stay grounded, sane, and peaceful.

I look for what seems to work for myself and others instead of what my old beliefs tell me will work.

When in doubt, I ask myself what the next right thing to do is. Then I do whatever comes to mind with the best information I have at the time. Best information includes any ideas others have shared with me when needed.

- **Physical security** – I've tried all types of things to provide myself with a sense of physical safety. I've tried self-defense, concealed gun carrying classes, mediation, and more. The lessons have been long and sometimes surprising.

  For example, I used to be afraid of living alone, even as recently as ten years ago. Then, I lucked out, as I mentioned earlier, by working with therapists and guided imagery which helped me resolve some old fears. At the same time, I went through cataract surgery on both eyes. I had been almost legally blind and needed corrective lenses to drive a car very early in my life. I'm not sure which helped me feel more physically secure, the cataract surgery or the guided imagery therapy. I know that I no longer have fears of being alone during the night.
- **Mental, emotional, and spiritual tools** – What helped me feel more physically safe in the end was the mental, emotional, and spiritual tools I picked up along the way. These were tools I've already mentioned, like meditation, programs,

books, counseling, building a dream team of friends, and consulting with professionals. CHOOSING to live in safer physical homes with lockable doors, no drugs or alcohol, and plenty of insulation for warmth helps as well. For one of my friends, her helper is a kitty named Stuart.

- **Relationship/Sexual security** – My experience again is that abundance, including intimate relationships, came about by being fully open to seeing what was really happening in each area of my life. Like how a shopkeeper takes inventory, I answer the question, "What is working and what isn't working?" regularly.

  I was fortunate to learn how to identify what was working and what wasn't working for me in each area of my life. Through careful experimentation and with support from programs, friends, and counselors, I found relationship values that work for me. I am now enjoying the fruits of a highly abundant marriage with my soulmate and have unbelievable relationships with most family members and many female friends.

  How has my experience around sexual security changed? I used to believe that sex was dirty and painful, and people couldn't be trusted. I know now that sex is clean and feels good in the right environment. I, myself, and other people can now be trusted.

  Overall, I can trust people to be themselves. Through much emotional pain, I've learned that I cannot use or change people to support my need for security. It was my *unwillingness* to accept other people for exactly who they are or what they were doing at the moment that caused most of my emotional pain and insecurity around sex and relationships.

  As a friend once told me, "I can love anyone as deeply as I want to. I may not be able to live with them, however."

This was echoed by a psychiatrist, Dr. Janet Settle, telling me one time that "love is not enough." Frankly, we need to agree on values, have chemistry, and a similar emotional quality to how we communicate, according to Gary van Warmerdam of Pathwaytohappiness.com (van Warmerdam), to experience healthy relationships that work. I believe it. I live it and love it today!

- **Financial security** – I love talking about financial security. It is such a personal topic. I've gone over most of the tools to achieve financial survival and a prosperous and thriving life in the physical needs section. The bottom line for me is that switching my mindset from a survival mindset to an abundance mindset has been the key to unlocking my feelings of financial abundance, no matter what my income or material resources are at the moment.

  I have reached this new life of financial abundance by using the tool of clarity instead of settling for vagueness. To repeat some of the basics from Jerrold Mundis (Mundis 2012), I strive to do the following actions regularly:

  - Keep track of my income and expenses
  - Create an ideal spending plan through vision work
  - Create an actual monthly spending plan that supports my overall vision no matter how much money I have
  - Adjust this plan based on my actual expenses. Again, I had to see at one time in my life, by looking at the facts, that I was not spending enough money on food and realize that I needed to increase my grocery spending.
  - Commit to paying back everything I owe (a.k.a. making things right with creditors)
  - Refuse to take on unsecured debt that is not backed up with collateral
  - Practice being grateful for where I am

- Make sure my expenses are lower than my income
- Be willing to sell anything but my body or family members to make ends meet if I have to. Every person counts. Every material belonging may need to be up for grabs. Material objects are all assets, in the end, and can be sold if need be.
- Understand that my value as a human being is not related to my income or my material wealth. I am a priceless human being, no matter what I own.
- Know that there will always be people with more or less wealth than I have, even if it looks like I'm wealthier on paper. Some people may just be happier than I am.
- Share my finances with trusted friends or professionals for more objectivity and brainstorming
- Believe in myself. I found I was the main person holding myself back because of false beliefs about money, my inner value as a human being, and pressure from others to stay small.
- Know that I am already perfectly okay wherever I am financially today. When I accept that I am perfectly okay no matter my financial state and live within my means, I set the ball rolling towards my vision. I have found the journey to be abundant. Happiness and abundance know no bounds where money is concerned for me today.
- Make sure I meet my basic physical needs, even if I am couch surfing. This practice helps me build a firm foundation to actualize my bigger goals. It's hard to think of vision work when I'm worried about where I will sleep.

Practicing First Principles to Promote Security in My Life

My understanding of practicing first principles is to first stay calm in a bad situation. Next, I break down whatever the problem is in front of me into its most basic elements. What am I trying to achieve? What do I need to accomplish as a bottom line? What are all the possible solutions for fixing the situation in front of me? What parts and resources do I need to make this solution possible? Who can help make these changes happen?

Envy is Absent from True Happiness

I can be happy rather than envious when others experience success. Being happy for other peoples' abundance brings me joy, while fearing there is only so much to go around and I'm missing out brings me pain and insecurity. I know now I've always had abundance and prosperity. I just didn't know it before. The foundation of abundance for me grew from being grateful for what I have. The key is a willingness to learn and grow.

This concept of first principles shows me that any "problem" or "fear," real or imagined, can be overcome by pausing to get clarity on what is actually going on, identifying the gaps that need to be filled, evaluating solutions for those gaps, and then leveraging the experience into an opportunity to forward my own and other's "success" and "growth."

There are countless tools, also known as "strategies," I can use to change my mindset from one of scarcity to one of abundance and security. Of all my options, however, the top strategy I have employed has been to find ways to validate myself. The same concept of clarity that I apply to evaluate and fill my needs for mental, physical, emotional, and financial security I can also use to fill my need for validation: I know I am okay no matter what.

Let's now take a closer look at the vital role validation plays in our lives.

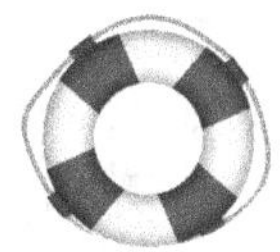

Chapter 20: Validation

"What do we want? The common denominator that I found in every single interview is we want to be validated. We want to be understood."

- Oprah Winfrey

Self-Worth: The Core of My Validation Needs

On June 28th, 2019, Oprah said she had conducted over 35,000 interviews in her career thus far. She shared that after each interview, when the camera went off, each person would ask her, "Was that okay? Did you hear me? Did you see me? Did what I say mean anything to you?" (Winfrey 2013)

I spent a lot of my life asking other people, either with my actions or words, not only "Was that okay, what I just did?" but the more basic question was, **"Am I okay?"** For most of my life, I was dependent on other people validating my self-esteem and self-worth.

It all started somewhere in my childhood. Growing up, I learned that if someone important to me thought what I was doing was "good," then it would mean "I was good," and I felt worthy. I learned to "people please" to get by and to stay safe. I also found myself accepting peoples' criticism and blame and thus took responsibility for things I hadn't done, again to get their approval. I was addicted to their approval for my very self-esteem and would agree to almost anything they said to get that external validation.

No matter what I use
to prop up my self-esteem or fill my true need for validation,
if I base my source for self-esteem on the visible external world,
it will not truly fill my need for internal validation:
to know I am basically okay.

In fact, when I place dependency for my self-esteem in the hands of any other person or thing, I set myself and the other person up for a no-win deal. When that person (or thing, such as how I look or where I work) fails to live up to my expectations and falls through—and it always does—then my self-esteem tanks. When I lose that external validation source I am left feeling scared and hollow inside.

I used to think there was something wrong with me. I tried to keep my head down and not let my light shine out of fear of reprisal, often by people close to me. At the time, I thought, "It must be my fault if they say so. Why would they lie?" Maybe it was our Midwest roots or childhood environment that led me to build this habit of automatically looking to other people to validate my worth as a human being.

At other times, I blamed others for issues that were really mine. It felt like I was on a never-ending merry-go-round. I know now, looking to others for validation only feeds into the lie that I am not worthy. But this is something I had yet to discover.

Eventually, the internal parent and judge in my own mind

took over where others had left off, and I ended up melding my self-esteem and my need for validation to false identities. The validation was conditional on how well I performed specific roles; I refer to these roles as "identities."

Identity

> "There is a deep tendency in human nature for us to become precisely what we habitually imagine ourselves as being."
>
> - Dr. Norman Vincent Peale,
> *The Tough-Minded Optimist*

For most of my life, I struggled with my identity. I thought I was shy, then cute, then a student, then an imposter, a worker, a sub-human freak, separated from my body, my heritage, relationships and more. In the end, these "identities" left me flat. Belief in these identities limited my choices and quality of life. I used to spend a good portion of my time consciously and unconsciously searching for my identities. I just knew if I found out who I really was, the empty feelings in my gut would disappear. Well, they didn't. After many years, I finally made progress when I reversed the question. Instead of asking myself who I was, I started asking myself who I was not.

Who I Am NOT

Figure 13: Who I Am NOT

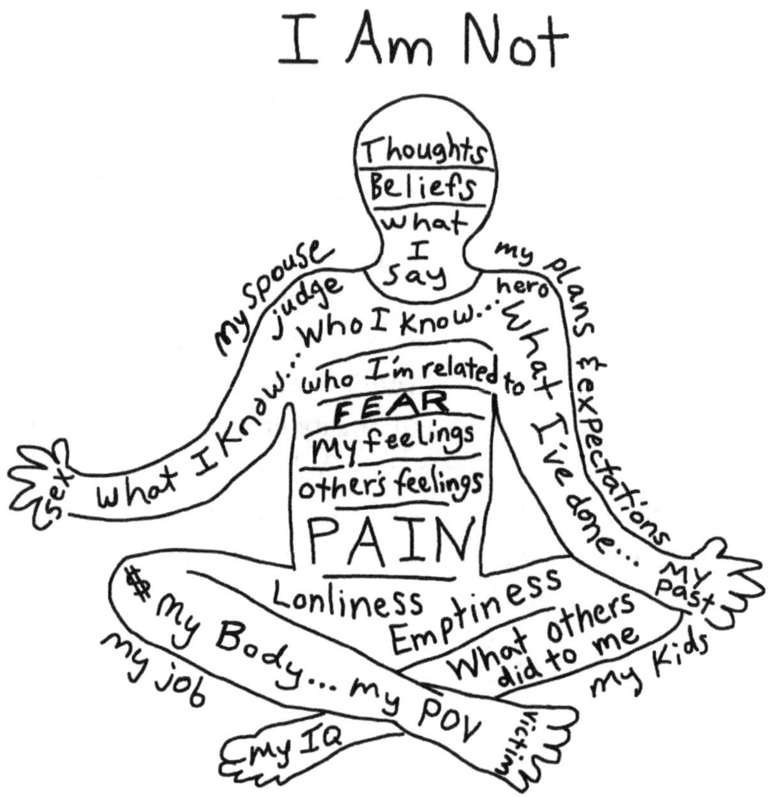

People often self-identify with their job title. "I am an accountant." "I am a race car driver." "I am a nurse." They identify with their roles as mother, father, step-parent, son, or daughter. Many people carry shame from childhood, consciously or unconsciously, believing they are what others have done to them, and adopt a victim identity—e.g. I am a bullying victim. Many of us feel our identity includes our kids' accomplishments. If they do well, that shows what a great mother or father we are and how valuable we are as a person. Right? Not in my parenting book today.

Have you committed or been convicted of crimes and identified as a felon? Have people called you a drunk or a loser or a bully? What about emotions? If you feel sad or angry, does that make you a sad person or an angry person? Do you think your identity is wrapped up in your income? Possessions? Who you're married to? Who you're related to? Are you a Barcelona soccer or a Dallas Cowboys football fan? Where do you live? Who do you work for? What do you eat? After all, you are what you eat.

How much do your thoughts and beliefs play into your identity? If you believe in fortune cookies, does that make you a superstitious person? If you tend to judge people or get angry often, does the archetype of villain or judge identify who you are? Is your identity based on your behavior?

The best way I have found to see who I really am, my true identity, is to start by listing out who I am not.

Who We Are NOT

First and foremost, I don't believe my identity is any of the things listed in the last section. I am not my job or my marital status. You and I are not our IQs or the levels of education we have received. We are not our actions or past experiences. I am not a sum total of all my past mistakes.

You are not a mistake. You are not anything you have done or are doing. Similarly, you are not what anyone else has ever done to you, such as being an abused person because someone abused you.

You are not your circumstances or traumatic events that have happened to you. You are not your thoughts. You are not what anyone else says you are, whether they say you are worthless or priceless. You are not your feelings, whether they be sad, mad, hurt, angry, happy, joyful, confident, or peaceful. You are not your fears. You are not your beliefs. You are not your points of view, such as a victim or a hero or saboteur. Most of all, you are not alone.

Your true essence, self-worth, and who you are, have no bearing on what you or others have ever or will ever say about you.

Here is an additional list of who I believe we are NOT:

- Past or current crimes
- Roles – mom, dad, teacher, lawyer
- Affiliations – gangs, politics, skinheads, etc.
- Educational level – third-grader, college student, etc.
- Race
- Religion
- Money, net worth, material possessions
- Body
- What was done to you or what you did to others

You are NOT your material possessions as they are clearly outside of who you are and have no bearing on your identity. Are you your gender or sexual orientation? I don't think so. Instead, I think my hair color and job title are more like attributes of who I am, not my identity. I do **not** believe these attributes tie to my value as a human being, one way or another.

We often relate to our attributes like gender, roles, and material belongings. Some of these attributes we can change; others are impossible to change, such as age. You and I need to gauge this for ourselves. No one but me can be the final judge of my attributes, especially whether they are valuable or healthy. I color my hair, for instance. Who knows what color it actually is? LOL! Maybe gray would look great on me. Will we ever know?

All of these attributes simply reflect my beliefs or expression about myself and the world. Placing these assignments on our own or another's "identity" can lead to a practice called "othering."

How "Othering" Arises from Placing Labels on Identities

Othering is the practice of aligning with some people who share specific characteristics or beliefs against "others" who share different characteristics or beliefs. Some examples of othering are white vs. black, belonging to a gang, being a fan of a team, and Muslim vs. Christian vs. Jewish vs. Atheist.

When I used to place labels on myself, such as low-income or worthless, I mentally limited my choices in life and created separation from others with my belief system. The labels were driven by internal judgements of myself and other people. It made it hard to survive as I attached my identity to "scraping by" since I was a low-income person instead of "thriving" in life. I felt excluded, judged and worth less than others due to the differences I believed were between us. Bottom line, I didn't feel like I fit into many social and business groups. This is one example of where I was "othering" myself and those outside myself, whether the other people were doing this or not.

Another example of othering can be seen in race relations. In their book, *Racial Formation in the United States*, Michael Omi and Howard Winant "see race as a way of 'making up people' and also as a process of 'othering.' Classifying people as others also classifies the classifier" (Omi and Winant 2014, 80).

Although "othering" may have its quick or convenient uses,

more times than not, it can lead to a sense of tribalism, exclusion, "them vs. us," and war. When I have felt excluded or "othered" by people or even my own internal judge, my mind has often believed the lie that I am inferior and a failure. When this happens, I have felt stuck in a box with a label that I don't identify with. I do not like feeling stuck in a labeled box, so I strive to avoid labeling others.

I have found that aligning myself with external identities or labels that are more "visible," such as gender, hair color, or skin color, is rooted in the fear that I am not feeling worthy enough just for being born. As a child and through much of my adult life, I developed coping mechanisms based on these external identities and used "othering" to cope with the fear of not being okay or worthy enough as a human being.

In my mind, everyone does count, and there is nothing "bad" about anyone, including myself. There is behavior that may need to change or be controlled from time to time. But at base, I believe there are only two real issues either I or anyone else really ever struggles with.

Ignorance or illness. That's it!

So, when I am ignorant of something, I may later realize I didn't know what I didn't know and change my behavior or way of thinking to match my new knowledge. That is why I strive to keep an open mind, remain skeptical, and challenge my own beliefs regularly when presented with further information.

As I shared earlier, I have experienced many illnesses that have come to me in the form of mental or emotional challenges, such as anxieties and paranoias that made it hard for me to function. Other illnesses may include addictions of multiple flavors, including money, that have led many of my friends and me to explore healing options. I'm sure, over the years, my behaviors arising from ignorance and illnesses have impacted other people's lives in ways I wish I could have avoided. I know what I know now. It can only get better from where I am right now. This statement by 'Abdu'l-Bahá sums up a lot of my thoughts as to whether people can be labeled or classified as bad or evil:

> The only difference between members of the human family is that of degree. Some are like children who are ignorant, and must be educated until they arrive at maturity. Some are like the sick and must be treated with tenderness and care. None are bad or evil!
>
> -Abdu'l-Bahá, 1911

Honestly, avoiding "othering," with labels and judgments about who is good and who is bad, is probably the single most challenging job I still face in life. I believe my source of "othering" and "labeling" is my fears.

Fear-Based Coping Mechanisms

Here are some typical coping mechanisms I used before learning to validate myself with more appropriate, invisible resources:

- Going to the hardware store to look for milk – looking for needs to be met in all the wrong places
- Depending on external material sources to prove my worth
- Blaming others for my feelings and circumstances
- Making false interpretations and assumptions

Exercise 1: Exploring Where You Get Your Validation

Answer the following questions, aloud or in writing, to peek into where you may get your validation:

1. Observe where you are currently getting validation
2. Are you seeking approval from another person?
3. If it's a person, are you putting this person up on a pedestal or catering to their ego to build them up?
4. Are you offering all your love and physical or personal treasures to someone in the hopes they will like you?
5. Are the people in your life cherishing you and treating you like you and your gifts are priceless? Or are they treating the gifts you have to offer as trash?
6. If you are getting your validation elsewhere, where do you think it is coming from? Money? Status? Accomplishments? Body? Children? Popularity? Car? Write down the first thought that comes to mind.

The Freak-out

I like disengaging my self-esteem and validation needs from all external sources.

Exercise 2: Ponder This Question…

How do you feel about this idea of not
using external people or things
to support your need for internal validation?

Can you imagine releasing all the connections to your identity and self-esteem: your race, education level, emotions, group affiliation, your body, and more? Do you feel freaked-out? Scared? Terrified? Like being stranded without a boat in the swift currents of the River of Transformation? When you look behind you, are you truly ready to face who you really are today? Have you dreaded truly asking yourself this question on the very deepest level? Are you afraid the answer will be that you are a "loser" or "bad"? Let's see the answer now!

Who Am I Really?

My Answer is:

Figure 14: Who I AM!

You have always been, are now, and will always be a basic core of goodness. No matter what! No matter what! No matter what! That is the great reality I have discovered for myself, and I choose to believe this is true for you as well. Understanding this truth, that I am a basic core of goodness, completely fills my need for internal validation.

I believe each of us discovers that we are basically okay in a unique and personal way.

In other words, no one else can tell me how to find this truth. They can influence me, but, ultimately, I am the one that has to make this inner journey to find this truth for myself.

I Know the Answer, Now What?

Once I discovered and felt my basic core of goodness inside, my #1 job changed to accepting and encountering my basic core of goodness daily so I could move into a truly thriving life. The term "Basic Core of Goodness" was coined by Trappist monk, Thomas Keating (Keating 1994).

Additionally, Heather Forbes, a leading trauma therapist and author, reinforces this concept by offering countless affirmations in her *Dare to Love Yourself* CD series (Heather 2016). Here is an example:

> "I know now, I'm perfectly alright. I've always been alright. I accept that now."
>
> -Heather Forbes

To put things in perspective, the basic core of goodness is how you might see yourself as a newborn baby—perfect in every way, regardless of any health defects, job or no job, body image, etc.

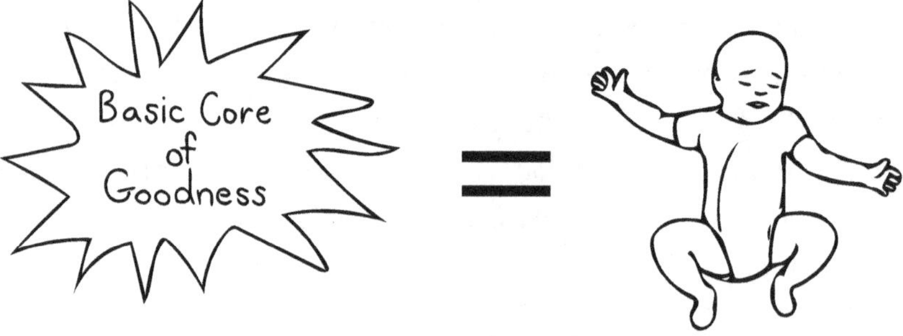

It all boils down to knowing:

You are already okay,
you were always okay,
and you will always be okay.
Okay?

My basic core of goodness interconnects with my feelings, beliefs, and relationships with family and friends. My core of goodness also interacts with my external environment. This dynamic includes what has been done to me in the past and what I have done to others. My work, accomplishments, and education are also greatly impacted by acknowledging and accepting my basic core of goodness.

Here is the main point: You can interact with beliefs and thoughts and jobs and people and even choose to spend time with people with similar views. However, **the state or condition of any of these external factors never changes the principal fact that YOU ARE A BASIC CORE OF GOODNESS, and so is everyone else.** Nothing you say or do, or anyone else says or does, can ever change that.

Believing I Am a "Basic Core of Goodness" is Practical

Practically speaking, basing my foundation in life on this principle, "I am a Basic Core of Goodness," has helped me establish a firm bedrock for my upward path. When I accept and validate my priceless value inside, I attract and choose healthier and more abundant jobs and relationships to myself.

Accepting my basic core of goodness is fueled by an absolute power of love instead of the illusionary power of fear.

Exercise 3: How Do Your Beliefs Influence the Job/Career You Pursue?

1. Sit quietly, away from all distractions
2. Ask yourself:
   "If I think I am worthless, what kind of a job or career would I expect to get?"
3. Next, ask yourself:
   "If I believe in myself and know, in my heart, I am a basic core of goodness, who cannot fail and is equal in value to all other human beings, now what kind of a job or career would I pursue?"
4. Did you feel an internal shift during this exercise? Did you think of different jobs or careers for question 2 than you did for question 3?

Forming our identities from external sources, as well as from our own negative feelings, thoughts, and beliefs is normalized in our society. What is the benefit of detaching from this norm and dropping the judgment against myself and others? Everyone involved benefits when I stop and clearly see what is happening in any given situation and assess what needs to happen next to achieve a thriving, winning outcome for all.

Exercise 4: Experience Your Basic Core of Goodness by Seeing and Feeling the Beauty Inside and Around You

1. **Be present in this moment** (smell the air, touch the blanket, see the sunlight)
2. **Appreciate everything immediately around yourself** (smile, tell the flowers and leaves how beautiful they are, acknowledge your body, birds, trees, roof, clothing, sanity, a friend, etc.). An example of appreciation is an affirmation by Heather Forbes about the body:

"I love and care for my body as it is my oldest friend"
-Heather Forbes

3. **Realize the great reality that all is well and always has been well and always will be well.**

The Takeaway Is a Paradox

Appreciating people and things in the physical world supports my feeling and belief in my own basic goodness inside.

Even though our value and true being may not be tied to our physical bodies, jobs, relationships, or net worth, we must remain present with our bodies, jobs, relationships, and financial well-being. This concept may be difficult to accept, since society has conditioned us to believe that our value lies in material things such as our bodies.

It is by caring for and being present with my body, for instance, that I recognize dangers when they come up and put down boundaries for protection when I need to. Wouldn't you rather listen to your body than just fall into being mentally or physically abused or drinking too much alcohol that cuts you off from feeling your aliveness and basic core of goodness inside? Eckhart Tolle refers to this as focusing on our inner body, where that feeling of life and being alive can be felt (Tolle 2004, 112).

Connecting to the Aliveness Within

Stop right now and notice what you are feeling inside. Can you feel your own aliveness and goodness? Can you feel where it sits? Do you see the aliveness in a plant or a person nearby? Can you now feel the powerful, beautiful aliveness inside yourself? If not, don't worry. It has taken me a long time to know I am alive and okay no matter what. I have patience with my learning process today. I hope you do not give up on finding and feeling the aliveness and beauty inside yourself until you get there!

Once you can feel the basic core of goodness inside yourself and bask in your own glow, you will start spotting signs of life everywhere around you, including the opportunity to see the aliveness and goodness in all other people as well. Don't forget to enjoy the journey to your goal of self-validation. The trip will happen either way. You might as well enjoy the ride.

Oh No! Chasing Self-Validation is Too Stressful for Me!

If I can practice being present with my body, it will warn me when I am under too much stress from old beliefs and worries or a real danger in front of me. So, the adage stands that you can keep your head in the clouds (pursuing your basic core of goodness) as long as you keep your feet on the ground. That is to stay grounded in your body and aware of the people and world around you.

Trust-Based Life Coping Strategies

- **Going to the grocery store for milk** – I mentioned going to the hardware store for milk earlier. Going to the grocery store for milk instead, means shopping for and placing my dependence on the correct resource for the correct need. I have learned over many years that to fill my need for validation, I need to go to invisible sources such as:
    - **Being in the present moment**
    - **Accepting my basic core of goodness internally** just for being alive
    - **Observing the life force** exploding from nature and the people around me. For example, I have a daily practice of

seeing and thanking the trees and flowers for their beauty and oxygen so I can live.

- **Don't take anything personally** – If someone says something I feel triggered by, I follow the 5th agreement suggested by Don Miguel Ruiz, which is to "become skeptical, but learn to listen" (Ruiz and Mills 2010). Then I can decide whether I share their belief on a subject or not and know how to use that information.
- **Thankfulness** – I list what I am grateful for first thing in the morning, the last thing at night, and as many times as I think of it during the day.

Exercise 5: Create an A-Z Gratitude List

If things get tough, try writing an A-Z Gratitude list. For example, A for apple crisp, B for breathing… Z for Zen Buddhism.

- **Identify, observe, accept and fully embrace the fact that "You are a basic core of goodness no matter what"** – As you may have guessed, accepting this truth almost single-handedly converted my thinking from scarcity to abundance. The more I thought about it, the more I saw the truth in this statement. I'm reminded of this simple truth whenever I see a baby, with all its beauty and basic core of goodness just for being alive. I have always felt honored to be in the presence of a baby, including my own children.
- **Dis-identify from external validators and invalidators** – This process took me a lot of time and countless hours of therapy, mental and emotional, and spiritual program work, as well as deep meditation. It all boiled down to not looking for one speck of my self-worth from my relationships, job, income level, body image, and my own or my kids' accomplishments. It simply meant to accept my basic goodness and pricelessness as a core fact. I have and do practice

unconditional validation of myself daily, especially in the face of people invalidating me from the outside or my own invalidating thoughts from the inside.

- **Taking regular inventory of my actions and needs** – I take responsibility for carrying out the actions necessary to validate myself and get all my needs met in healthy ways. Again, I felt like a victim of life and circumstances most of the time. When I narrowed down all the reasons things did end up working in my life, it was the concept of "being at source," as one of my best friends put it.
- **Being at source** – Being at source to me means that if I want to overcome my self-esteem issues or anything like panic attacks or PTSD, I need to take personal responsibility for all my feelings, reactions, beliefs, attitudes, actions, needs, and circumstances (see more detail on the "being at source" concept in chapter 1, section *Acceptance of Gaps without Blame*).

  I've found being at source also means if I want to feel or experience some aspect of life, like love or abundant work, that is new to me, then I need to do the things others before me have done to reach the inner and outer state of life that I admire. When I've done my research, I can experiment with getting a specific desired outcome met in my life and thus get through any issue in front of me.

Example: Being at Source with an Anxiety Disorder

When I struggled with anxiety attacks, I made a complete list of my anxiety symptoms and how I felt while experiencing those symptoms. I wrote down where they were occurring and how often I panicked. Next, I sought out resources I thought could help me answer my questions on anxiety. I found people like Mary Lou Stevenson, a mental health counselor, The Anxiety and Phobia Workbook (Bourne 2020), and the book Complex PTSD (Walker 2013).

Next, I experimented with the solutions I found. I participated in a biofeedback program and took anti-anxiety medication for a while. Then, to eliminate the panic attacks, I transitioned from medicine to deep meditation, such as Tonglen with Pema Chodron and Centering Prayer through the Contemplative Outreach network.

Looking back, I'm not sure which of the fifty things I tried to eliminate my anxiety actually worked, but eventually, they did; and I am 99 percent anxiety-free today.

- **Learn from my "failures"** – Learning from my own problems or "failures" has been my most outstanding teacher, bar none. In fact, it has been as an adult that I have experienced many of the worst events of my life—such as witnessing our dot-com business tank in the early 2000s.

  Whenever the dust settled and I got some emotional distance from those experiences, I noticed that they taught me the most valuable lessons about what to do, what not to do, what I wanted, and what I didn't want in my life. Lost relationships or jobs that I may have thought were indispensable later turned out to be blessings for everyone involved.

  I trust the crooked path. It has straightened out for me and led to a world of abundance in all areas of my life. My life gets better and better every day.

  Don't forget the earlier principle, **"You cannot do it wrong."** As my friend Laura reminds me, "Even paths that we thought were mistakes, are not mistakes. They are all opportunities for learning lessons."

- **Try affirmations** – Here's another excellent affirmation for validation by Heather Forbes:

"I recognize now it is my responsibility to love and validate myself, knowing I am alright. I know now that I've always been alright. It's just that no one ever told me. But that doesn't mean I didn't have it already."

-Heather Forbes

There's Peace, But Wait! There's More!

If all I ever achieved in my life were to fill my instinctive, internal needs for security and validation in healthy ways, I would likely have a wonderful, peaceful life. I learned to thrive **because I stretched myself even further and dove into learning, understanding, and practicing unconditional love from healthy internal sources. I've broken through the ceiling into a more expansive and deeper peace and happiness than I never knew existed.**

I believe and I admit I'm still a novice and am learning more every day. In the next chapter, I share the meager information I have gained so far about unconditional love. Please join me in exploring this last invisible need called "love."

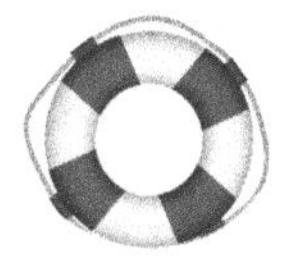

Chapter 21: Love

What is love? We all know we need it. I have confused love with a lot of other things over the years. Currently, I define "true love" as the deepest act of accepting and appreciating ourselves and one another, no matter what.

True love is a feeling I get when I think of myself or others as tiny newborn babies. We are all born perfect. We are all cute, no matter what anyone says. Now, as a regulated adult, I can serve as my own internal parent. I can and have learned to provide this unending sense of love for myself by tapping into my own and all other universal life forces.

Love Starts with Me

My crooked but perfect path has led me to open up to the experience of deeply loving and cherishing myself. I have learned to love myself primarily by applying healthier, more direct ways of filling my internal, invisible needs for unconditional love. My deepened capacity for self-love has enabled me to love everyone else on the planet, without conditions, 95 percent of the time! Not bad!

This ability to love myself unconditionally, no matter what, builds on the awareness that "I am a basic core of goodness," as discussed in the previous chapter on validation. I have found that by truly learning to love and cherish my very essence, I can express love and validate others in a safe, abundant way.

If I can feel true love for myself,
I can feel true love for you!

This statement is true for me because I know now how to give and receive love. I can observe the feelings that flow through me when I am giving and receiving love.

So how can I get some of this self-love? I create this inner feeling of love by focusing my awareness on the present moment. With each breath in and out, I feel the love for myself taking hold. For me, self-love is an ever-deepening emotional and even physical "feeling" of warmth and light that spreads slowly and peacefully through my whole body, mind, and soul.

Exercise 1: Practice Creating the Feeling of Self-Love

One way I can create a sense of self-love is to lie down in my bed and feel the mattress's firm support. I have also practiced this by lying on the ground if I am camping. I feel warm blankets or earth embrace me. I imagine a wide beam of light entering the top of my head and gradually, but steadily, washing down through my body to my toes. As the light passes through me, each muscle becomes warmer, loosens, and relaxes into the full support of peace, life, and the universal power of love.

The power of love is greater than a tsunami and hotter than an erupting volcano, yet it is gentle and unending. Love feels like I am being held in the soft, warm, strong, supportive embrace of a protective sage. I am being nourished and cared for. Overall, I have a deep feeling that I am safe, okay, and loved in every sense of the word, no matter what! And so is everyone else at all times.

When I am ready to return to the physical, visible world, I begin wiggling my fingers and toes. I gently stretch all my muscles like I'm a cat just waking up, and I open my eyes to the beauty surrounding me.

I feel peaceful, hopeful, happy, and refreshed after creating the feeling of love inside.

The Feeling of "Love" Is Available 24/7

Amazing news! I can generate this feeling of love whenever I want to create it, just by sitting or lying down with my eyes closed any time of day or night. Therefore, the deepest form of true love is available to me 24 hours a day, seven days a week, 365 days a year. Just like biofeedback training, when I learned what tension felt like by flexing my muscles tightly and then releasing them, the feeling of love is always available now that I have trained myself to know how it feels and how to access the feeling when I need it.

Today, I do not have to "wait" for someone else to tell me they love me to get this feeling. True love does not require me to earn it from them either. Instead, I access this feeling of love with each breath I inhale and exhale. It's kind of like a soft hug on the inside, gently flowing in and out of my entire body.

The more I practice actively giving and receiving love with myself and others and setting aside time to practice creating love internally, the easier it becomes for me to call up this feeling when I need and want to. I am extremely thankful for this most vital life lesson.

Practicing Gratitude Creates the Feeling of Love and Peace Within - I Am Here

I have also learned to generate this feeling of love through a gratitude meditation you can find in Gary van Warmerdam's "Lesson 1: Gratitude" podcast found on Pathwaytohappiness.com. In his gratitude lesson, Gary provides a deep, guided meditation, teaching how to feel and experience deep gratitude both inside and outside yourself.

By practicing the level of gratitude presented in the podcast, I have trained myself to create my own love-based emotions rather than automatically accepting the emotions my habitual mind comes up with. As I mentioned earlier, the unconscious, habitual thoughts I often have are generally based on old fears and beliefs. Since I have learned to generate a feeling of gratitude, I've noticed I can also generate the feeling of love when I want or need to. This ability to practice creating the feeling of love anytime allows me to have greater control over my emotional state of mind.

Because of general practices like this for self-love and gratitude, I feel I'm filled with light and love most of the time. It doesn't matter what my job accomplishments or family connections are. I may get rattled emotionally here and there, but overall, I feel a sense of openness and spaciousness both inside and outside myself. I feel like I am part of a rich inner and outer world. I feel connected to flowers, leaves, and even the strong concrete supporting my full weight as I walk on the sidewalk. I also feel the human connection to every person, both alive and dead. I feel loved, lovable, and cherished, no matter what! I call this feeling unconditional love, and I can generate this love myself 24 hours a day, seven days a week, 365 days per year.

Unconditional Love

Technically, I see unconditional love as loving or being loved without conditions. A friend once told me, "I can love anyone, anywhere, and in any circumstance from any distance. I may not be able to live with them or physically interact with them, however." I do believe in the concept that love is to be given and received unconditionally. Love is meant to flow, not to be hoarded or left stagnant, but also not to be treated lightly and abused by ourselves or others.

I can love everyone on the deepest levels, no matter what they've said or done or what I've said or done. If I stop and take the time, I can see each person's bright source and core of goodness.

How Does Unconditional Love Work with "Bad" People

My definition of "bad" has changed over time. I used to believe people who harmed me in some way, whether real or imagined, were "bad," and they didn't deserve love, at least not from me. I no longer believe people are "bad" or "scary." I believe we are all lovable and have an inner essence connected to the source of all life and each other. Instead of "bad" people, I believe people suffer from various physical and mental illnesses as they struggle with real unmet needs, just as I struggle with my own illnesses and unmet needs.

Just like money and physical health, some of us have more or less mental and emotional health than others at any given moment. Some of us are still acting out of "instinct" and unconscious habits that continue to lead us to look in all the "wrong" places for our self-esteem, validation, security, and love.

Many of us are also learning how to rise above our habitual ways of buying into and acting out of fear every day. I see a great mass of people around me, on social media and in the news, who are shifting to more loving, kind, and accepting ways of relating to people or difficult circumstances in their lives. Everywhere, people are converting adversity into a gold mine of learning and abundance.

The change in belief from conditional to unconditional love is likely the cornerstone of my sanity, peace, happiness, abundance, and security.

How Did I Shift from Fear to Love-Based Reality?

I work daily on shifting my beliefs to truly loving myself and everyone on the planet, no matter what they have said or done. This shift has taken years. The tools I used to make this change appeared in deep daily research and experimentation focused on learning and applying principles of unconditional love to my own and others' lives. I used to be afraid that if I gradually let go of fear, defensiveness, and judgment of myself and others, it would literally kill me. Before beginning the practice of unconditional love, I sat up most nights in fear that I would be cut down either physically or emotionally by a "bad" person.

What I've found to be true, however, is that through diligent practice of unconditional love, I can recognize real dangers more reliably than constantly pre-judging others and using defensiveness and anger to keep myself safe.

Unconditional love has made it easier for me to say "no" when I need to. Sometimes I need to disagree with another person's criticism and not take their anger towards me personally. Today I can recognize and say "yes" when the situation is win-win for everyone involved. Since I do not believe I have any control over other peoples' emotions, I can love everyone, even if I disagree with their angry tone of voice towards me. I probably won't go to lunch with them though. Some people I love unconditionally but from a distance.

Advanced Unconditional Love with People Showing Anger

Practicing unconditional love with someone who is acting angry or trying to convince me my reality is completely off, is like a martial art. I used to get so defensive and full of pride in these "hostile" situations. Today, I am not actually trying to defeat anyone anymore. I am merely practicing being extremely present and expressing love where I can. If and when I see a verbal or physical kick heading my way, I can lean to the side, and the person's foot goes right on by when I am not there, presenting a hard surface. It's their own energy, momentum, gravity, and anger that brings them down in the end. Allowing another person to fall due to their own momentum, can also give that person a priceless opportunity to grow. I've grown myself through these gold mine opportunities.

I do not have to participate in another person's reality of blame and conditional love directed towards me. Instead, I can follow the international singer, Selena Gomez (Gomez 2007).

> "Kill Them with Kindness."
>
> -Selena Gomez

Unconditional Love For My Enemies Does Not Include "Taking Abuse"

Let's take a moment to clarify this point. When necessary, I believe in taking any action available to stop someone I think is harming me or others and not just "take the abuse." In fact, if I find myself staying in a relationship with someone who threatens or blames me for their unhappiness, I can accept that the emotional quality they express towards me does not match my values. I can then choose to communicate my needs or choose not to be around them. Again, loving people from a distance is easier for me under such circumstances.

Even when I maintain distance from a person who sees me

as the source of all their problems, it's still possible for me to see their core of goodness and express love the best way I can. I have learned to see the best sides of people, but without risking my safety or adding fuel to their rage.

Don't Take Things Personally Ever

Today, I know I have a choice with all of my reactions. I do not have to get defensive or angry with anyone, anytime, anywhere. I can protect myself by staying unhooked from what they are doing and saying as little as possible. I do this with the total commitment to Don Miguel Ruiz's 4th Agreement (Ruiz and Mills 2010):

> "Don't take things personally."
>
> -Don Miguel Ruiz

I've actually taken a class on how "not to take things personally" on pathwaytohappiness.com. By not ever taking anything personally, I find I am happier and more peaceful than I have ever been before. I am further mindful that others may be in so much pain that their only coping mechanism is to lash out at myself and others. This practice of not taking things personally includes accepting the reality of that person's behavior and circumstance just as it is and not how I fantasize it to be.

Also, by not taking anything personally, I am more present mentally and emotionally. I am calmer and, therefore, more able to really see what is happening. By seeing what is really happening, I can better detach my self-esteem from the other person's opinion of me. I can listen and accept what they are really saying and determine if I want to change my part in the story, or I can, just as quickly, decide I disagree with their assertions about me and get on with my life without lingering self-doubt or hatred for myself or the other person.

It took me years to sort out if I was worthy or not, as I struggled with unconscious beliefs that others' opinions about me were more accurate than my own. Fortunately, today I have found clarity and guidance on how to proceed in any situation I normally would have taken personally in the past. And yes, I am way, way happier by not taking things personally.

Trying to Change Someone's Opinion of Me is a Losing Battle

I have not been successful in getting people, who get angry and blame me for their problems, to show love towards me when they are unavailable.

Why is this so? I always thought I could work misunderstandings out with anyone, anywhere, any time. Wrong! Like myself, when I am panicked and overwhelmed, there are times when my ability to treat myself or others with respect, admiration, and kindness may not even be on my radar.

When I'm calm, though, I can understand that someone who is criticizing me may not even be directly mad at me. They just may not possess the love-based tools that I have chosen to develop. What has shocked me in the past is that the person invalidating me may even view my kindness as a weakness, while I see kindness, vulnerability, and respect as a strength.

Don't Waste Each Other's Time if There is a Mismatch

Here is a principle that helps me keep perspective when attempting to give or receive love with someone who seems unavailable:

> "Never waste your time trying to explain who you are to people who are committed to misunderstanding you."
>
> -Dream Hampton

Remember, the Hardware Store Does Not Carry Milk

In addition to unavailable people, visible things I list below may seem to offer feelings of love, rest, or occasional nourishment, BUT you will not find the real milk—i.e., true love—in them for long. Instead, you will find the bait but not the nourishment if you depend on these "visible" sources for your deepest, eternal, personal, and perfect feeling of love.

Things That are NOT the Source of Self-Love

- Romantic relationship – It can be a sacred space where love is expressed but is not a direct source of unconditional love in itself
- Marriage or marriage partners
- Friendships
- More and more and more money
- Possessions (aka stuff and more stuff)
- Prestige
- Accomplishments
- Co-dependence (a.k.a. getting others to be dependent on you, so you feel important)
- Being right
- Being smart
- Alcohol and drugs
- Food
- Living on the edge (adrenaline rush)
- Violence
- Gambling

- Sex
- Porn/romance novels
- Gaming
- Binging on TV or the Internet
- Work and your job
- Manipulating, lying, stealing, and overall "tricking" others
- Criminal acts

I have mistaken many people, things, and circumstances as providing me with a feeling of love in the past, but, in the end, none of these external sources has been a source capable of filling my actual need for unconditional love.

But these "Things" Cover My Basic Needs, and They're Fun!

You know, I can't argue with that. Instead of these things being the sources of unconditional love, I believe they are actually the fruits of love. In fact, most of the false sources of love listed above, like food, not only cover vital needs in the material world but bring pleasure and enjoyment to each of our lives. **The main issue is if my motive for going to these sources is to find love.**

And it's not just my motives but **the extremes I was willing to go to when "trying" to get my invisible, internal love needs met.** Looking back, these extremes seem staggering. The truth is, I can enjoy external things in moderation, but if I try to rely on them to provide for my self-love needs, they will ultimately fail me.

In the past, when I found that my self-love needs were not met, I would find myself trying even harder to get more from these external things. If that didn't work, I tried to control my partner or switch relationships. The harder I tried to force a person or another external thing to satisfy my natural need to give and receive unconditional love, the harder I would fall emotionally when, inevitably, the external source failed.

Starting a romantic relationship is one of the most common strategies I used in the past to try to fill the empty, lonely, hollow place inside myself that blocks my **"real need to give and receive unconditional love."** The reason I am highlighting the false use of romantic relationships to fill our internal needs to feel loved, is that, for me, **participating in relationships that are NOT win-win has the power to send me back down the rabbit hole of struggling to survive again.**

Romantic Love is great, but Cannot Fill my Need for Self-Love

"Love is not enough."
- Dr. Janet Settle, Specialist MD
in Integrative Psychiatry

When Dr. Settle told me that "love is not enough," I interpreted it to mean that while I can experience rich, real, and deep love for another person, I can still decide not to marry that person. In other words, just because I felt love didn't mean that this person was the "right" person for me.

Before learning this principle, I thought "love," and especially "my love," were big enough forces to fix the other person or the relationship. I now have accepted that my "love" is not big enough to fix another person's issues or serious relationship incompatibilities. In truth, our values may not be the same, which can occur, for example, in the way we communicate with each other. One person might want to share everything about their day, while the other person may want to be more private. One partner may use patient, kind, and welcoming tones while the other person may communicate in a more abrupt, blaming, or even angry tones.

When people bring vastly different values and communication styles to a romantic relationship, the partnership may or may not last long-term. Each person in the relationship may complement the other when things are going "well." On the other hand, if the underlying difference in values and communication styles is too large, a sense of confusion, hurt pride, and disappointment may arise, leading to separation.

Take the Pressure of Filling Self-Love Needs Off of Romantic Relationships

It's taken me decades to realize that **it is vital to take personal responsibility for providing my own self-love, validation, and security, instead of expecting another person to fill these basic internal self-love needs.**

Expecting a Romantic Partner or Any Other Person to Fill Self-Love Needs Doesn't Work

What happens when I try to get these needs for self-love, validation, and security from my spouse or partner? When I **expect** a romantic spouse or partner to provide my underlying love-based needs, I'm expecting them to give me something only I can give myself.

In the past, when my needs for self-love didn't get met this way, I tried even harder to convince the other person they were not doing enough or offering the right kind of love for me. They could try 24 hours a day, seven days a week, 365 days a year to fill these needs for me, and it still wouldn't be enough because internal self-love can only come from my own internal sources. For years, I tried to convince various partners to provide me with approval or attention to fill my need for self-love. It never worked, and I felt empty and let down. In return, I believe they felt pressured, maybe judged, and only loved conditionally. I have since found this type of relationship is not a mutual partnership based on love, admiration, and respect; it is based on false dependencies instead.

The pressure I may put on my romantic relationship, stemming from dependency on another, can take a toll on everyone involved, including children and adults.

Unconsciously, underneath it all, I used to believe I was unlovable.

Looking back, my partner could have told me every day I was priceless, and his affirmations still wouldn't have been enough to fill my needs for self-love. In fact, in some twisted way, I used to think a man was weak for loving me unconditionally. I'm convinced now that no amount of external attention would ever have been enough to fill my needs for self-love.

When I place dependency on a romantic partner to fill my internal needs for self-love, I just end up feeling emptier inside. Feeling empty, I would unconsciously seek out romantic partners who were unavailable: they couldn't express love and would be angry at times. I've tried to get these people (like my parents when they were unavailable) to display affection or say and do things I believed showed they loved me. The false logic was, if someone who does not know how to express love can change and prove they love me, then that proves I am lovable. When I failed to get love from unavailable partners and people, I would see it as evidence I was unlovable. This false evidence was a lie I told myself unconsciously for years.

The truth I know now is that I am lovable simply because I exist, whether anyone else chooses to be close to me or not.

So, where did this dependence on another person for self-love start?

The Missing Love Links in Childhood

As a child, I had a real need for unconditional love from my parents. I needed attention and approval. I needed to be loved just for being alive. My parents could still teach me how to behave when a change was needed, but if my parents neglected me, then I would feel I was a burden; if they only showed me love when I won a race or got an A, then **I learned that love is conditional and needs to be earned. I know now that THIS IS A LIE!**

As a child, I really did need someone to hug and love me just for being alive. I needed my parents and older adults to look happy and not irritated to see me when I walked into a room. I needed to be shown I was lovable, at least until I could learn to love myself.

But people are only human, and **as all of us parents know, we can just do our best. And our best is enough**. As an adult, I can acknowledge gaps in love from my parents or caretakers and grieve the fact that I grew up thinking I wasn't lovable. I'm sure I've neglected some of my kids' needs for unconditional, consistent, present love as well. (Sorry, kids!)

On many occasions, while growing up, I felt I was a burden and not cherished, valued, or protected. I know now that **no matter how loving, validating, and safe my parents were or weren't, I need to take personal responsibility NOW as an adult to provide for these internal, emotional, invisible needs.** Taking personal responsibility for filling my own inner needs for self-love is part of the maturing process. I believe it is natural for a child to start with dependence on a parent to reflect love. The child eventually needs to develop independence for providing self-love. The regulated adult can be interdependent and give and receive love to and from others provided each person has an independent foundation of self-love already developed. According to Stephen Covey's *The 7 Habits of Highly Effective People* (Covey 1989, 68), taking responsibility to love myself first and then others is the basis of true love for myself and everyone I interact with.

True Love Begins Through Loving Myself

> "We can see that we can love ourselves with no conditions. When we love ourselves, now we can give. We can love. It isn't important if they receive or do not receive our love. What is important is love coming out of us. Because the body is feeling that love. And that is what the body loves the most, the feeling of love coming out." (Ruis and Tha God 2020)
>
> - Don Miguel Ruiz, A Conversation With Don Miguel Ruiz and Charlamagne Tha God

True love starts by exercising my love muscles daily, which to me, it is like meeting myself in silence and nature and feeling the force of life move through me. In silence, I know, accept, and follow these truths:

- **I am priceless and lovable and always have been just for being alive**
- **I can cherish myself, my being, and my life**

By learning to "rise in love" instead of "falling in love," as Don Miguel Ruiz puts it, the force of love in me can see the force of love in you. We can both receive and express love and validation in safe ways and acknowledge that we are all, in essence… made with love.

Is God Love?

> "God is always coming. He's never too late. I saw no way I could get there, but God made the phone ring. I almost got $1000 out of nowhere. That's what happened to me. That was my moment of never giving up. That's when I learned that faith is everything. That you have to remain faithful."
>
> -Steve Harvey, "The Apollo Story"

Like Steve Harvey, some people believe God is love and that there is more going on in life than meets the eye (Harvey 2019). There is purpose and direction underneath it all. I've seen it most clearly as the "life force," especially in my darkest hours in a rock bottom space where no one else was available to support me.

I can see this life force in all humans, creatures, and organisms most of the time. I can see it in the leaves falling on the ground in the autumn and appreciate the gift of life we all originate from and flow into. I don't understand this life force but understanding it doesn't seem to be required. I just remain open to having faith in life, God, myself, and others. This basic view works for me. My path is to believe in something bigger than my job, relationship, or finances, which I can tap into for wisdom, clarity, and direction. It may not be for everyone, but it works for me today.

Another way of looking at this concept of God, or the life force, can be found in studying consciousness. I practice being conscious and present in the moment as much as possible. As Eckhart Tolle shares in his book, *The Power of Now*, everything can be dealt with and moved through if I am willing to stop and be present (Tolle 2004). The answers seem to be available when I am calm. In a quiet state of mind, I can face rather than buy into fears. I do this by being present and listening to the still voice deep within myself. The answers ultimately lie there for me.

Inside myself, I feel a sense of peace and security, knowing I am well and loved no matter what happens to my mind or body. This feeling is priceless to me and is reflected in this statement from A Course in Miracles (Schucman 1975, 24).

> "Nothing real can be threatened. Nothing unreal exists.
> Herein lies the presence of God."
> -A Course in Miracles

During the times in my life when I thought there was no creative force available to tap into, I leaned on material things like jobs, relationships, alcohol, and money. One by one, each of these external things I thought were supporting my self-esteem, security, and validation, failed me. Only this connection to the life force, which seems to underlie all inner and outer beauty, provides for my food, clothing, and shelter, connects me to everyone and everything on the planet and beyond! This love-based, life force energy has come through for me in every challenge I have ever faced. I see this life force as the deepest light and love I feel within myself,

This life force shows up in the form of principles such as kindness, patience, personal growth, teamwork, generosity, clarity, wisdom, mindfulness, trust, peace, forgiveness, acceptance, and unconditional love of one another.

Now that's being rich!

Chapter 22: Hopefulness

"And will you succeed? 100% guaranteed! Kid, you'll move mountains."
- Dr. Suess, *Oh, the Places You'll Go!*

Hopefully, having read this far, you are experiencing more clarity and hopefulness in your own life. Perhaps you have begun making a list and started taking steps to resolve some of the most significant pressures in your life. Maybe you have a real sense now about what is working or not working.

Are you hopeful, energized, and ready to draft your Personal Plan?

If you do have a pretty clear idea of how to proceed, you may want to skip now to Part IV of the book which outlines how to develop a personal plan. When forming your personal plan, try reviewing the plan elements before starting the exercise steps.

In Part IV, you can either work the action plan steps from the beginning to the end, or pick only the exercise steps that work for you and leave the rest behind. You can always come back later to the parts of the plan you did not complete if you feel you are not achieving the goals and results you wanted. The point is, you know better what your needs are than I do.

In my case, my main life goal has been to fill my own visible (physical) AND invisible (mental and emotional) needs to the point of abundance. I myself have completed all the steps I suggest in the next chapter. All of the work I have completed has led me directly to a happy, abundant, hopeful, and prosperous life.

Are you still feeling hopeless, skeptical, or just plain stressed out?

Take a moment to assess how you feel by asking yourself:

QUESTION:

On a scale of 0 to 10—0 being stress-free, serene, secure, and clear-minded and 10 being completely out of control, hopeless, and insane—where are you at right this moment?

ANSWER:

If you are at a 0-6, low to moderate anxiety level on this stability scale and not experiencing a lot of stress, go to the Quick grounding exercise for moderate anxiety at the end of this chapter.

If you feel you are at a 7-10, high to extreme anxiety level right now, go to the Deep grounding exercise at the end of this chapter.

If you are still feeling down, depressed and skeptical about your personal ability to build an abundant life, keep reading. I will briefly share my transformation experience with you in the hopes that you may find inspiration for your own life. You may want to search for other inspiration and opinions as well.

I Used to Feel Hopeless Most of the Time Too!

Yes, that's right. It took me quite a few years to start seeing the light at the end of my tunnel and *even trust that there would be an end to the tunnel.* I felt like I was either trying to solve the day's crisis in my life or waiting in fear for the next crisis to show up (and they always did!).

If I wasn't dealing with an immediate crisis, I felt sorry for myself for one reason or another. I then justified finding creative, unconscious, habitual ways of escaping instead of facing my fears. For example, instead of drafting a resume, I would hang out with my friends and complain about my lack of money. True story!

Or even better, I would be broke and take someone else to lunch to act like a bigshot and build up my ego, which I confused for self-esteem. Later that month, I would be begging my student loan company for a forbearance (a.k.a. delay in my payments).

(SIDE NOTE: My personal opinion is that "the powers that be" make it way too easy to get too much unsecured student debt. Funding higher education is an area we could all work on.)

Underneath it all, I really didn't think I had the power to change my life. I thought I just had to accept the way things were.

But somewhere along the way, I decided to admit I didn't know all the answers and started looking for the answers anywhere I could. I started with articles and self-help books. Then, I added a counselor and support groups. That was the beginning, and this is where I landed: in abundance in all areas of my life!

The Abundant Life I Enjoy Today

I am happy today. I am delighted. I feel peaceful, calm, clear-minded, secure, and hopeful over 90 percent of the time. My life feels abundant and prosperous to me. My every-day contentment and happiness has been available to me even though my income has dramatically swung up and down during my life. So, the income level has not been the biggest component that determines the peace I feel today. Instead, I believe the two most significant factors that started me on my path to feeling abundant are:

1. Taking personal responsibility for my happiness through the exploration of my life challenges and causes of pain and,
2. Realizing I wasn't going to fix challenging issues solely through my own efforts.

How Did I Reach This Abundant Life and How Do I Maintain It Today?

In the beginning, when things were at their lowest point, all I could do was take one action towards improving my life and circumstances on any given day. If I could go to bed that night, reviewing the one thing I did for myself that day, it was a successful day.

Later, I added more tools in my day to further my upward path and self-exploration. I ended up with simple routines for about ten things a day to build more happiness and abundance and maintain peace and sanity. I openly admit to being a self-help addict, so bear that in mind when I tell you that I easily spend around two hours a day maintaining my happiness. Some decisions are easier for me now because I have changed my beliefs to be more abundant. Here is a sample list of some of the beliefs and actions I include in my day to fill my visible and invisible needs. I generally pick a few a day to focus on as they come up.

Daily Action Items

- **Loving myself completely and unconditionally**
- **Partnering with friends, family, and other dream team members** for mutual support, including voluntary accountability to bookend tough decisions and mark milestones.
- **Providing for my family's visible physical needs** (e.g., food, shelter, clothing, safety, warmth, sanitation, and more)
- **Providing for my own and children's invisible needs** (e.g., mental, emotional, security, validation, and love)
- **Clarifying my finances to empower me to make choices**
    - Be mindful of my short and long-term goals
    - Ensure my income exceeds my expenses
    - Make "win-win" agreements or choose "no-deal" (Covey 1989)
    - Record all my income and expenses (Mundis 2012)
    - Create and use a spending plan (Mundis 2012)
    - Avoid unsecured debt (debt not backed up with collateral) (Mundis 2012)
    - Provide value for what I receive if not a gift (e.g., if couch surfing, offer to do dishes, clean home, etc.)
    - When financial pressures arise—DO THE MATH—two ways to solve it:
        - Increase income
        - Decrease expenses
- **Be the solution, not the problem**
- **Think and act to produce win-win solutions for everything I do or choose "no deal" (Covey 1989)**
- **Assume everyone is doing their best**
- **Fix the "process," not the "people" (Deming 1982, 23-24)**
- **Accept people and circumstances as they are, not how I fantasize them to be (Mellody, Miller, and Miller 2003)**
- **Give up on life being "fair"**

- **Guard and focus your attention**
- **Take full responsibility for my beliefs, emotions, abundance, and circumstances within my control**
- **Be accountable to myself and others** (e.g., partner with others to support doing scary or tough projects within a deadline for both of us, a.k.a. "bookending")
- **Give up the illusion of "Free" and join the "Tipping" economy**
- **Become a sponge** – Learn from everyone and everything that presents itself as a learning opportunity on what to do, not do, and what to be and not be
- **Rebalance and reset daily** – e.g., double-check priorities, what needs to be done when.
- **Organize, clean, and maintain myself and what is in my control around me**
- **Drop the Judge** – including the internal judge towards myself and others, and the judge of the judge
- **Facing, accepting, and healing any pain or fears within**
- **Healing the past to free up the future**
- **Let go of the internal victim, judge, villain, hero, princess, prostitute (people-pleasing), and any other internal characters sabotaging myself and others** (Gary van Warmerdam, podcast Self Mastery Class I, Archetypes www.pathway to happiness.com).
- **My "enemy" and I are on the same side of the ring against both of our character limitations, a.k.a "egos"**
- **Love is peaceful and not violent**
- **Do not judge my progress by my feelings; I'm always doing better than I feel**
- **Create my own feelings through practice** – e.g., gratitude
- **Do service work regularly** – includes the idea of giving away to keep it

- **Pray**
- **Meditate**
- **Exercise**
- **Connect with family and friends**

The chapters in the next part of the book are all about forming your own plan for your Upward Path. You can work on these exercises on your own or find a friend or professional willing to be there as a cheerleader and accountability partner. Meanwhile, use the following grounding exercises if panic comes up at any time in your Upward Path.

Resources: Grounding Exercises

Before beginning your plan, consider trying one of these grounding exercises depending on your current emotional/mental stress level.

Exercise 1: Quick Grounding for Moderate Anxiety

1. Stop and sit down if you can
2. Pause and think about where you are right at this moment
3. What are your mental and emotional thoughts and feelings? Observe
4. What are your external physical circumstances and conditions? Observe
5. Are your current thoughts or circumstances affecting your mental and emotional well-being?
6. Or are you feeling peaceful?
7. Breathe and reflect on what you are facing right now, not what you fantasize your reality to be physically, mentally, and emotionally.
8. Are you afraid or confident?

9. Breathe in again and as you inhale, ask yourself where your pressure is
10. As you exhale, ask yourself what you can do about it right now
11. Write down what your pressures are and the action items you can follow to relieve them

Note: Sometimes, the best I can do is breathe in and out for a few minutes and observe my feelings as they come up. Then when I feel more grounded, I can work on my action plan.

Exercise 2: Deep Emotional Grounding When Feeling High Anxiety or Overwhelmed

1. Sit right now and put your feet flat on the ground
2. Rub your hands together, touch your face
3. Rub your hands together, touch your thighs with your feet flat on the ground
4. Start breathing in for four counts, hold for four counts, then breathe out for four counts
5. Breathe into your abdomen like you are breathing into a flexible bottle in your stomach/midsection
6. With the in-breath, breath in all the grey smoke and fire and claustrophobic yuckiness that seems to be engulfing you; then, with the out-breath, breathe out cool, refreshing, peace, and light. (This is a piece of the Tonglen practice from Pema Chodron). Do not get lost in the in-breath.
7. Repeat these steps until you feel a sense of calmness begin to set in. (**Note:** If you are high or drunk, this may not completely work. Try walking around the block. Go to detox. Get somewhere safe where you can detox). **Note:** There is always time available to get clear-headed. Stop and take that time now.

8. After you feel adrenaline subsiding and your breathing becoming more even, open your eyes and look around at all the objects and people around you. What do you see? What can you be grateful for?
9. Write down any of this experience or concerns and fears that come to mind. By writing them down, you get them out of your mind and prepare for some type of action just by acknowledging them.
10. Share your experience and concerns with a trusted friend or professional.
11. Take a break (your choice on the length of time).
12. Do the immediate next "right" thing you can think of to do. Stop if you need to and repeat this grounding exercise.

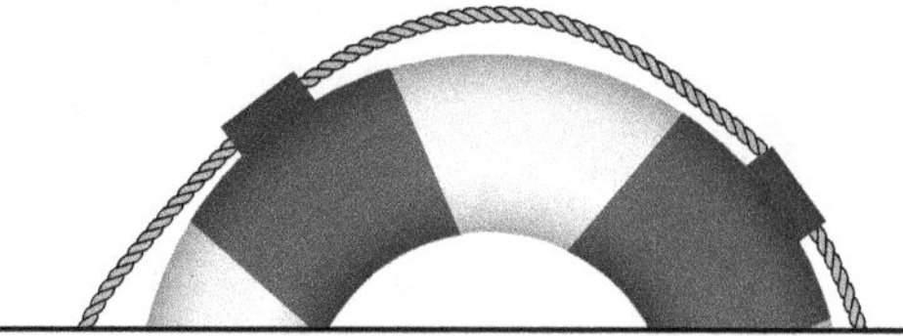

Part IV: Your Personal Plan

Here we are! Your turn!

In Part IV, we walk through exercises to offer you clarity, abundance, and overall happiness. I can tell you right now that knowing you are open to investigating your life and applying principles that will transform your life, is the primary reason I wrote this book.

I have worked with many people over the years in many different fields spanning business to education to career navigation and web development. Far and away, the most excited I get is when I witness the spark lighting up in someone's eyes and their excitement when they tap into the possibility of a purpose and direction for themselves.

It happened just last weekend. I saw the son of a friend while volunteering at a food bank. He had just graduated from college. When I asked how he was doing, he seemed down and discouraged. It has only been a few months, but I could tell he hadn't landed a job yet in this fragile economy. I told him something I learned in a small business class over 30 years ago from my professor at CU Boulder:

"Opportunities are like streetcars.
They just keep going by."

The young man commented that I had a positive outlook on things, and I said, "Yes, I do." As he left the volunteer job, he smiled and threw me the peace sign. I could see him shift to hopelessness and possibility within a matter of minutes. It's not what I said; it's that he found hope inside himself. I was just the messenger.

Okay, onto your story! Here are some principles to consider that will support your planning process.

Chapter 23: Principles for Your Personal Plan

- **Start somewhere! Anywhere!**
- **Accept, validate, and be thankful for where you are right now.**
- **Form a plan.**
- **Get help.**
- **Continue to assess and improve your situation.**

All Needs Are Woven Together

As you start on your plan, it may seem overwhelming. It may seem pointless to start in one small invisible area of need when there are many looming "real crises" in your life. But, in my experience, both the physical, visible needs and the emotional, invisible needs are tied together. If one of these needs gets satisfied to any extent, it can help your other needs.

Satisfying One Need Helps Feed the Other Needs in Nourishing Ways

Most of us do not "fix" or "heal" all our needs 100 percent all at once. Sometimes, we focus on our food and eating patterns and then find our emotional moods balancing out more. Other times, we focus on getting our emotional validation, or "feeling we are okay," in abundant healthy ways and, as a result, find our finances improve. Balance helps survival overall but finding new fruitful ways to satisfy even one need, like finding a stable, safe home, can automatically help all other needs.

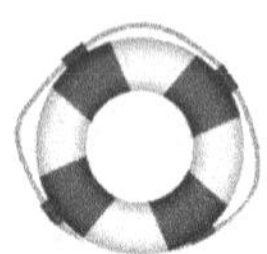

Chapter 24: Drafting Your Personal Plan

"Our actions in the present build the staircase to the future. The question is whether that staircase is going up or down."
- Craig D. Lounsbrough

Your personal path is a plan customized especially for you. You create your customized path in response to your own circumstances, present and past, those which may affect your well-being. Your path also includes your own deepest underlying desires in life.

No one else can create this personal path for you, but there are armies of support people standing by, both inside and outside your current family and friendship circles. You also have resources such as books, movies, schools, and the vast internet universe. These resources and guides are navigators to help you plan and bridge the waters and obstacles that come up in your personal River of Transformation.

However, you are the only human being alive who can determine what your "thriving life" looks like and decide the steps and lengths you are willing to go to reach the happy, joyous, free, abundant, and prosperous thriving shores.

The primary reason I wrote this book was to support YOU,

specifically to help you draft the blueprint you will carry out, leading you from a life of scarcity to a life of abundance. Remember, your path includes identifying and creating a plan, following the plan, and pivoting or correcting the plan when necessary.

We will start by committing to a path that can lead you to an Upward Path for your personal life. Making a conscious decision for change, dramatically improves the possibility of change in your life. Trust me in the process!

So, let's get started with Step 1, Committing to Your Personal Upward Path.

☐ Step 1: Decide to Commit to Your Own Upward Path

Your first action item is to commit to your own upward path. Don't think about this too much. Just ask yourself this question:

"Am I willing to commit to the upward path?"

☐ Yes ☐ No

If Yes, Commit to the Upward Path

1. Check the "Yes" box above.
2. Go to the diagram below and draw a line from the lower-left dot to the upward right dot. (**Note:** The line can be straight, in recycling spirals rising up over time, or however you visualize your path to be.)
3. While you are drawing the line, say out loud:

"I fully commit to the Upward Path in my life, at all times, with all people, and under all circumstances."

4. Take a deep breath and sign Your Personal Upward Path commitment form.
5. Now, every time you come to a crossroads, a decision, a fear, or a strange conversation, ask yourself if the thoughts and actions you are about to take are leading you towards a thriving life or back to the scarcity life. Are you on the upward or the downward path?
6. Remember, you don't know what you don't know. If you find yourself on the downward path, pivot, correct, and get back on the upward path.
7. Carry on! Persist! "Never, never, never give up," as Churchill said.

Form 1: Commitment to Your Persoanl Upward Path

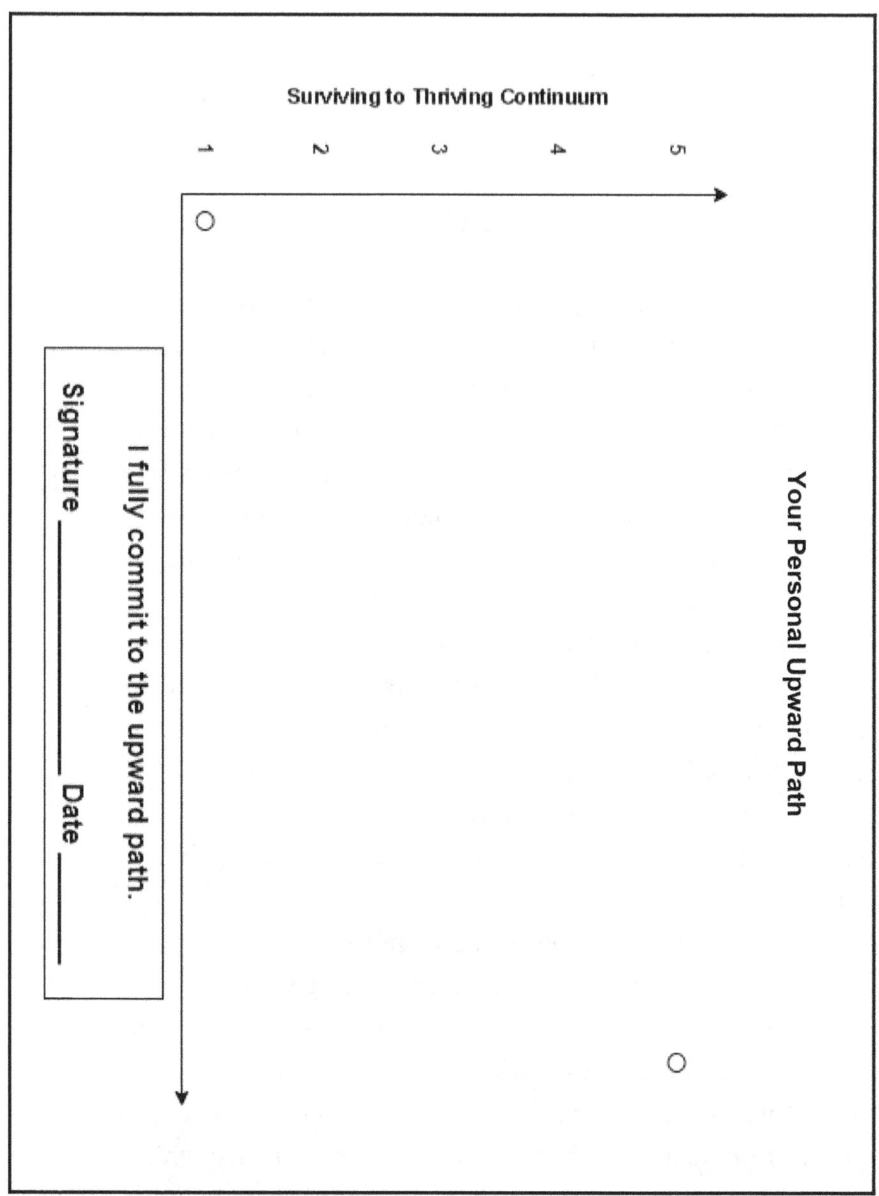

Congratulations if you committed to your own upward path!

Note: If you selected "No" and do not want to commit to your Upward Path right now, keep going with the exercises that do speak to you or jump to Chapter 31 "In Conclusion… The Beginning."

Your next big commitment relates to how you see yourself deep down.

☐ Step 2: Accepting You Are a Basic Core of Goodness

This step encourages you to make a conscious choice to build a positive foundation for your life. Are you going to unconsciously base your life on fear and the false belief that you are a mistake, worthless or damaged goods? Or are you going to base your life path on a foundation of love, that you and everyone else out there is a basic core of goodness to be unconditionally loved, appreciated, and valued no matter what? (If you need to change the words to match what works for you - no problem!)

It's worth noting that accepting you are a basic core of goodness doesn't mean you won't make mistakes and need to change direction from time to time. It means you consciously choose to focus on the best in yourself and others. Then you work to change the processes or circumstances you can control or influence if they need to be changed. Ideally, I suggest making these changes together with the support of others.

If you desire to make some changes but the people around you are not supportive or are even sabotaging your efforts, you can choose to accept others for what they do or say, even if you disagree. You may not be able to work or live with everyone, but you can still appreciate their essential goodness and not stay angry towards yourself or them. Accepting people I cannot change while taking care of my boundaries is much less stressful than trying to force changes where I have little or no influence.

So, are you ready to commit to a love-based foundation in your life? If **YES**, sign your name on the *Commitment to a Love-Based Life* form below.

Commitment to a Love-based Life Foundation

I fully accept that my basic core of goodness

is my true self,

at all times, with all people, and under all circumstances.

Name: ______________________ Date: ____________________

Form 2: Commitment to a Love-Based Life

☐ Step3: Where are You on Your Upward Path at This Moment?

Before you develop your Personal Upward Path, we need to know where you are in various areas of your life. Pay special attention to the areas of your life you would like to change. I recommend using a separate journal or notebook to allow plenty of room to explore these questions. Start by answering these to determine where you are.

Form 3: Where Am I Now?

- Where am I now?
  - Financially ______________________________
  - Physical Security (e.g. home) ________________
  - Physically/Healthwise______________________
  - Socially ________________________________
  - Family_________________________________
  - Partner ________________________________
  - Mentally _______________________________
  - Emotionally _____________________________
  - Spiritually ______________________________
  - What feelings and thoughts come up when I reflect on my current life and choices? ____________________

    ____
- How did I get to this place in my life?
- Do my insides (self-esteem, values, beliefs, deepest desires, etc.) match my outsides (physical, social, financial, and security health)?
- What is the image I believe I am showing the world? How do I think the world sees me?
- What lengths am I willing to go? What effort am I ready to make to match my outside life with my inside values and underlying desires?

Taking Inventory

When you are ready, refer to the form below and rank how well you feel your needs are being met (a.k.a. "status") in each of these four areas on the Basic Life Inventory form below.

I like to use a 10-point scale to help identify how I'm doing in each area of my life. For instance, on a scale of 0-10, 0 being a hopeless or crisis state and 10 being an abundant state, where do I feel I am in this area? You can also use percentages. For example, I feel like my finances and relationships are 60 percent of where I would like them to be; however, I feel like my physical health is only at 20 percent, while my mental, emotional state has tanked to 5 percent. Also, list the top "pressures" you are facing in each area.

The form divides into Visible and Invisible needs. You can estimate in general how you feel your life is going in each area. Below I've listed examples of what you could consider in each category.

Examples for Visible Needs:

- **Business/Financial** – Jobs, income, expenses, net worth. You may include travel here, or it could go into mental/emotional or social.
- **Social/Family** – Spouse, partner, child, extended family, community involvement, neighbors, and church group.
- **Physical Health** – Physical condition, illness, food availability, clothing for warmth, exercise, and possibly housing and safety tools like security cameras. (Note: housing could also be in business, financial or social, wherever it makes the most sense to you.)

Examples Invisible (Emotional/Mental/Spiritual) Needs:

I am combining all the invisible needs into one column for this exercise. Feel free to separate them if it works better for you.

- **Self-esteem, validation** – How valuable do I feel I am daily: priceless or worthless?
- **Security** – Do I feel like all is well mentally and emotionally, or do I fear the other shoe is going to drop when I wake up each morning? Am I in constant anxiety and panic or depression, or am I feeling calm, and all is well in my life and the world?
- **Love** – Do I give and receive love daily with myself and others? Or do I fear love and believe it only leads to pain? Am I connected to at least one other person or a pet, or do I feel alone most of the time?
- **Spirituality, Meaning, and Purpose** – Where do I get my vitality and sense of peace? Do I go to internal and "bigger" sources for my deepest strength in life, purpose, and meaning, or do I look to external people and circumstances or addictive options to escape and feel some momentary peace? Often my inner strength stems from nature, art, religion, meditation, prayer, vision work, and more.

Note: Remember to "Drop the Internal Judge" when you fill out this form. You are simply on a fact-finding mission to see where you are starting from today. What is your stock in trade? For instance, if the four areas above were about fruit production, you would figure out what is working, and what would you have to send to the compost pile to change or improve your fruit production, a.k.a. life. The more clear-headed and honest you are with yourself in this phase WITHOUT JUDGEMENT, the more likely you are to set a firm foundation for your survival plan.

Form 4: Basic Life Inventory

Visible Needs			**Invisible Needs**
Business/Financial	**Social/Family**	**Physical/Health**	**Mental/Emotional/ Spiritual**
Status: (0-10 scale or %)	Status: (0-10 scale or %)	Status: (0-10 scale or %)	Status: (0-10 scale or %)
Pressures: 1. 2. 3.	Pressures: 1. 2. 3.	Pressures: 1. 2. 3.	Pressures: 1. 2. 3.

EXAMPLE Basic Life Inventory Form

Visible Needs			Invisible Needs
Business/Financial	**Social/Family**	**Physical/Health**	**Mental/Emotional/ Spiritual**
Status: I feel stressed out and hopeless with my finances and income. It feels like I never have enough money. I barely get by and don't get to do fun things without sacrificing something important. It would help to have a car. Rating: 3 out of 10	Status: I feel happy about my family and friend circle. My kids seem happy and are doing well in school. My partner and I are emotionally connected. I'm part of several groups in my career field and volunteer at the soup kitchen. Rating: 8 out of 10	Status: I'm doing poorly on Physical health and could really improve my nutrition and exercise routine. I could get more energy during the day if I could improve this. Rating: 5 out of 10	Status: I suffer from anxiety and panic attacks. It affects my ability to sleep and sit still in classes and conference rooms. Rating: 2 out of 10
Pressures: 1. Don't know how much I spend 2. Barely make ends meet 3. Have too much debt	Pressures 1. I do not have enough time 2. 3.	Pressures 1. I have no time to cook or exercise 2. I feel tired all the time 3. I can't go to sleep	Pressures 1. Feel trapped by anxiety 2. Experiencing low self-esteem 3. Limit my prospects due to anxiety

☐ **Step3: Where Do You Want to Be?**

Drafting a "mission" may seem like a waste of time. But, if you try to kick a ball into the goal, how likely is it for you to succeed if you:

A. Line up the goal first and then kick the ball,

OR

B. Just kick the ball anywhere and hope it makes it in?

Forming a mission or, as I like to say, "recording what I know my main purpose is in life," creates a "target" towards which I can aim.

So, if you are ready to draft your mission, fill out the form that follows.

Form 5: Life Mission

My Life Mission/Vision Statement

____

____

____

____

____

____

____

Name: ____________________ Date: ____________________

What Are Your Goals/Underlying Desires to Support Your Mission

Once you know what your mission is, forming goals may help you get closer to your target. I start creating goals by considering my mission for each visible and invisible area of my life, as shown in the inventory form of step 3. Then, for each area, I ask what goals I can set to improve that area. For example, if in my inventory form on step 3, I wrote that my current emotional, mental status is sitting at a two, I ask what goals I can create to help me get to a four or a six?

Take time now to create at least one goal in each of the visible and invisible areas of your life in the *Deepest Underlying Desires* form below. This form helps determine how you will achieve your mission in life in concrete, practical steps. The super fun part of this exercise for me, is to visualize and write down the rewards I can see myself enjoying when I achieve my goals. These rewards reflect what my deepest underlying desires are.

For example, I might have an underlying desire for financial security. So, I aim to find a career that will support my family and myself without going into massive debt. I also have a goal of learning basic investing so my money can work for me. I might decide to start my own business. The rewards I look forward to might be a home that is paid off or mortgage-free. I might enjoy more free time for artwork or volunteering. What rewards would you like to see in each area of your life?

Form 6: Deepest Underlying Desires Form

Visible Needs			Invisible Needs
Business/Financial	**Social/Family**	**Physical/Health**	**Mental/Emotional/ Spiritual**
Goals: 1. 2. 3.	Goals: 1. 2. 3.	Goals: 1. 2. 3.	Goals: 1. 2. 3.
Rewards 1. 2. 3.	Rewards: 1. 2. 3.	Rewards: 1. 2. 3.	Rewards: 1. 2. 3.

Note: Simple goals are just fine. Realize there are times when you may only have a single "primary goal," like achieving sobriety or finishing a college degree. If that's it, then that's OK!

Also, the actual rewards may not be exactly what you expect. A specific man may not want to marry you, or you may find you cannot have children biologically. However, I have found that where one door closes, another opens—for example, maybe you adopt or become a fantastic coach. In the end, all my deepest desires have come true, but none of the rewards look like I imagined them to be. I know now I've always had abundance available to me. Dreaming big, usually with a greater purpose beyond just fulfilling my own needs, helped make my desires a reality.

☐ Step 5: What Will It Take to Make the Change?

Transforming from the scarcity/surviving life to the abundant/thriving life in one or more areas of your life (e.g., finance, mental/emotional health, or marital happiness) will require you to assess your current knowledge level, skills, beliefs, and motivations. One of the most effective resources I have run across for sizing up my skills and knowledge is the book What Color is Your Parachute by Richard Nelson Bolles. Government career sites can also be helpful for this. At a minimum, I suggest you create a list of the skills you have and skills you think you need to gain to reach your goals. You can make "gaining a new skill" a goal in itself.

Below is a worksheet to help you assess where you are with your knowledge, skills, beliefs, and motivations and what you want to gain to reach your goals.

Form 7: Filling the Gaps

Gaps to fill to reach mission and goals	
What do I already have?	**What do I want to add in order to change?**
Knowledge today: __________ __________ __________	**Knowledge I want to gain:** __________ __________ __________
Skills today: __________ __________ __________	**Skills I want to gain:** __________ __________ __________
Old beliefs: __________ __________ __________	**New beliefs I want to adopt:** __________ __________ __________
Motivations today: __________ __________ __________	**Motivations I want to change:** __________ __________ __________

Once you determine the level of your knowledge, skills, beliefs, and motivations in each of your visible and invisible areas of need, you can log and estimate what additional knowledge, skills, beliefs, and motivations you will want to acquire to convert that area (e.g., mental/emotional health) from surviving to thriving.

This practice will help you track the personal assets you have now and what new assets you want to add to each area of your life as you grow towards your goals, mission, and vision.

Fake It Till You Make It

There are times when you know that you want to or need to do something different in an area of life, but you're having a tough time making the shift to the new way of thinking. When all else fails, you can "fake it till you make it."

Often faking it for a short while and acting as if you are committed to your Personal Upward Path, can get you through a discouraging block. Try to remember: **you can do something you resist or even hate for a short while that would kill you if you had to do it forever.** I find this principle true as long as I remember action is the healthiest way to progress towards my thriving life.

Make Hay While the Sun Shines (Work on Things When Times Are Good)

When you feel clear-headed and have energy, time, and money do what you can to plan and execute your Personal Upward Path. There will come a day when you feel bad and want to give up. It takes all the self-parenting and trust in your sources of strength during the good days, to help you weather the challenging days and to refrain from temptations of crossing your bottom lines "when to yield would mean heartache." -Alcoholics Anonymous

Assembling Your Dream Team!

One of the most powerful tools you can have is to assemble your Dream Team. Your Dream Team will be comprised of a group of individuals and organizations that can help you find and reach your goals.

Here are some of the traits and descriptions of people I have added to my dream team, mentioned previously in the Build a Dream Team section of chapter 3:

- **Win-Win Thinker** – People who thrive by seeing me thrive as well as themselves. We admire and celebrate both of our successes.
- **Gently honest** – They do not "people-please" to boost my ego but share their perspective on my strengths and weaknesses with me, especially as related to my goals. They ask before sharing to see if I am interested in feedback.
- **Reliable** – They show up when they say they will, as best they can.
- **Knowledgeable** – They have expertise in an area that I do not. (e.g., professor, accountant, counselor, job coach, athletic coach, etc.)
- **Accomplished** – They can mentor as they have already achieved the goal(s) I have or know how to help me achieve my goals.
- **Practicing and Supporting Accountability** – I tell them what I will do and then check back with them to let them know if I completed my task. I refer to this as bookending or sandwiching a task.
- **Welcoming** – They are excited to see me.
- **Accessible** – They are people I spend time with regularly and/or who I have access to.

Once I pick the people I would like on my dream team, I confirm that each person wants to support my success and gather their contact information. (See Dream Team Form that follows).

Form 8: Dream Team

Name	Company or Organization	Relationship	Address	Phone	Email	Website	How can they help?

☐ Step 6: Into Action – Launching Your Personal Path

You are now ready to put your plans into action. Here is a basic launchpad for your Path:

- **Pick one area of your life** to work on (e.g., Business/Finance).
- **List the goals and the deadlines** on your **Starting Point Form** for the selected area.
- **Identify the top decisions with deadlines on the Starting Point Form** to reach each goal—e.g., If I have a goal of moving to another geographic area that fits my lifestyle and values better, such as fishing, then one of my top decisions is which state, city, or neighborhood to move to with easy access to water.
- **List the Starting Point Form's top actions** to follow up on the decisions to reach your goals. Consider including personal boundaries you will need to set or adhere to for success. Action items for the above example might be asking others for ideas on where to live or searching the web for areas boasting great fishing.
- **Consult with your Dream Team.**
- **Invite a Dream Team member to be your accountability partner for weekly check-ins.**
- **Execute your tasks,** scheduling your tasks on a calendar to meet the deadlines.
- **Track your results** from your actions/completed tasks on your Starting Point Form.
- **Evaluate results** against goals/mission/vision.
- **Pivot and change** tasks/goals/mission/vision when needed.
- **Complete cycle** above again.
- **Teach others** how to reach missions and goals like yours.
- **Celebrate** (See **Personal Award Certificate** you can fill out for accomplished goals).
- **Start new goals in a new life area** (e.g., Social, Physical, Mental, etc.)

Form 9: Starting Point Form (Goals/Decisions/Actions)

Starting Point in Area ___________

Goals	Deadline
☐ ______________________________	__________
☐ ______________________________	__________
☐ ______________________________	__________

Decisions	Deadline
☐ ______________________________	__________
☐ ______________________________	__________
☐ ______________________________	__________

Actions	Deadline
☐ ______________________________	__________
☐ ______________________________	__________
☐ ______________________________	__________

☐ Complete! Date Completed________

☐ Celebrate! Celebrate Date!________

Name: ____________________ Date: ____________________

Form 10: EXTRA: Quick Decision

Quick Decision

Surviving to Thriving Continuum

Dependence

Independence

Interdependence

Time

Your Thriving Life Mission:
(Win-Win)

The Thriving Line

Your Surviving/Unconscious Life Outcomes:
(Win-Lose, Lose-Win, Lose-Lose)

Is your choice
Above
or
Below
The Thriving Line

One way to celebrate completed goals is to present yourself with a **Self-Acknowledgement Certificate.** Don't forget to invite your **Dream Team** members to your celebration!

Note: This certificate is blank and allows you to fill in your name or someone else's name. You can also fill in the date and the signature of the person offering the certificate. I've also added another certificate (from EveryoneCounts.World), right after step 12 in the chapter, that I invite you to use if you are working through this process on your own.

Form 11: Completion Certificate - Blank

☐ Step 7: Challenges You May Face on Your Journey

Fears

We could almost just leave this section at that—fears. Everyone understands fear on some level! Fear is the most common obstacle most of us face on our Upward Path journey. It may be the only real obstacle at the end of the day.

Fear appears in countless situations and with people and things in your life. Some of us live in constant fear - anxiety, panic attacks, phobias, paranoia, fear of failure, fear of success, fear of people, economic insecurity, not being liked by our loved ones or peers, and on and on. No matter what the apparent cause of anxiety may be, it often feels like it is real and never-ending. We're mainly referring to imagined or inflated fears. Some fears are needed, such as fear that helps us jump out of the way of a moving vehicle.

Fear and pain are often old coping mechanisms. When old fears band together in the form of characters like the internal bully, judge, or victim, an immense amount of fear and worry about the future can be unleashed inside us. Worst-case, the fear can paralyze you. During these times, you may not feel you can function. You may withhold your best efforts, through procrastination and self-sabotage, to stay in a comfortable and safe place and "avoid" disappointment. As you can see, fear is probably the biggest obstacle you can face on the Upward Path. So, take a page from Mark Twain and act regardless of fear when fear is not needed.

"Do the thing you fear most, and the death of fear is certain."

- Mark Twain

Feeling Stuck

Somewhere along your Personal Path, you are going to feel stuck. You won't know whether to turn left or right when you hit a crossroads on your next decision or next step. This is the time to pause and get a new point of view from a higher vantage point. You can remind yourself again of what your true underlying desire is on the current path. Ask yourself what the next right thing to do could be. Ask someone else, who has already been where you are trying to go, what they would do in a similar situation.

Trick: If you want an opportunity to grow and strengthen your decision-making skills, think of your dilemma from your best friend's perspective. Imagine your best friend (or someone close to you) is going through the same journey and runs into the same decision or issue you are facing right now. **Here's the catch: instead of asking your friend what you should do, tell them what you would do if you were in their place**. And watch what happens. Often, doing this exercise yields a very different result from what you might have expected. Be ready to be surprised; it's truly amazing. The expectations we often hold ourselves to are so much stricter and more perfectionistic than the possibilities we can see for our best friend. So, try it; you might like it!

Don't Want What Is

We all may want things to be different in our lives (e.g., better-paying jobs or a happy marriage). In fact, that is the primary purpose of this book: to help change the way things are and improve our lives mentally, physically, socially, and financially. Again, we see a paradox. By accepting things exactly as they are in this moment, you will stand on a firm bedrock of reality which can be a springboard to the changes you want to make in your life.

For instance, you may want to eat like you are at a banquet

overflowing with food but only have a can of beans and some rice at home. It's ok to visualize the perfect banquet. At the end of the visualization, just say to yourself and the universe the following affirmation inspired by Shakti Gawain in her book, Creative Visualization:

"This or something better is manifesting itself for the best of everyone involved."

Then treat your beans and rice as though they are the banquet. I assure you, someone somewhere in the world is feeling that way about your beans and rice right now.

Need Something or Someone to Be Happy?

This idea of needing something, someone else, or your circumstances to be different before you can be happy misses the central point. Outside of natural grief, trauma, and recovery, I believe it is totally possible to be happy, joyous, and free at this moment, no matter the circumstances around you.

Much of the grief, anger, and fear around us is based on disappointments we experienced in the past. I believe this is primarily due to having expectations about how things should have been and not accepting how they really are.

Another issue comes in when constantly thinking of the future. Do you spend time, like a director in a movie, running worst-case scenarios through your mind? Remember what John Candy's character shares in the film *Cool Runnings*:

"If you're not enough without it, you'll never be enough with it."
- John Candy, Cool Runnings

Therefore, if you want to be happy, joyous, and free most of the time, start the "**being present in the moment**" habit.

"Cold Pricklies" Versus "Warm Fuzzies"

Have you ever tried to get someone who doesn't seem to like you or is critical and invalidating (a.k.a. "cold prickly" attitude), to like you? Have you ever felt like no matter what you do, the person with the cold pricklies is never satisfied with you or what you offer? Do you feel like you are always trying to provide them with warm fuzzy attitudes?

This is an excellent opportunity to accept someone as they are vs. taking someone else's attitudes, actions, feelings, or beliefs as a personal affront to you. Suppose you choose to be kind and tolerant, no matter what other people act like most of the time. In that case, you'll likely attract others who have similar values, such as believing in Win-Win outcomes or at least respectful communication.

Note: There is a beautiful children's book from the 1970's called The Original Warm Fuzzy Tale by Claude M. Steiner.

Personal Invalidation Based on Perfection

You may ask yourself why you should take a risk and put yourself and your work or heart out there. Maybe you used to think that what you have to offer society isn't enough, and therefore, you're not enough. You may be thinking, "Who do I think I am putting something out there?" Or, "Who am I to let my light shine? I don't have anything to offer that anyone will want!"

The reality is, **if you do not share what you alone uniquely have to offer in this world, you run a bigger risk of withholding your spark from people who really need you and what you have to offer.**

So, my question to you is **"What do you have to lose anyway?"** Put something out there in the world and let the world decide how it will fit in, how it will help, and what they will do with the talents you share. (That's what I'm doing right now writing this book!)

Comparing Yourself to Others

Again, people are different. Really different! We each have a unique path. Comparing yourself or your talents and offerings to others is totally an illusion. Comparing yourself to others doesn't work! It will only set you up for resentment towards yourself and others. So, I recommend that you **drop the judge** when it comes to comparing yourself to others. Strike out on your own trail and remember… Everyone Counts, and that includes YOU!

Deep Breathing as a Strategy in a Crisis

When the overwhelm button is pressed down hard in your life and you believe you're a failure and that your life is falling apart, **stop and breathe**. Breathe deeply from the diaphragm, just below your chest, envisioning the air you are breathing in filling an expanding bag or balloon in your lower gut (a.k.a. between your solar plexus and your sacral area chakras). Think of what you are most grateful for and how it makes you feel. The deep breathing and practice of gratitude in the present moment makes it nearly impossible to feel high levels of anxiety. Breathing exercises can usually restore my peace and perspective in a short period of time.

☐ Step 8: Check If You Are Still on Your Path

Measure Your Results

One of the best ways to determine if you are still on your Personal Upward Path is to stop periodically to measure your results during the process. Compare the **metrics** (a.k.a. measurable outcomes) against your goal. Did you desire a 10 percent income increase in three months? Is your income 5 percent or 20 percent higher at two months? Did your income go down by 10 percent instead?

Getting clarity on the measurable results of your goals (such as reviewing your Basic Life Inventory or your Deepest Underlying Desires form) helps with direction. Look for signposts along the way as well. For instance, if you change your tone of voice with your spouse from irritation to kindness and appreciation, notice if you laugh more together.

Schedule "Check-In Moments" on Your Calendar

By scheduling as little as 15 minutes per week or per month to review the progress you are making towards your goals, you get in the habit of clarifying whether your strategies are working or not. It's so easy just to plow ahead once you have momentum. There is comfort in continuing to do automatic tasks. But what if your new strategy is costing you money while your old strategies were earning money? If that happens, you are just losing more money faster. Without regular check-ins, it's like being an ostrich with its head in the sand. Anything could be happening around you, and you wouldn't know.

What do you do if a strategy you are using moves you away from your goal instead of towards it? You pivot!

☐ Step 9: Pivoting from Regression/Recycling

"Make sure you remember the Fun of It!"
- Michele Feigen, Fine Artist and Art Teacher

What if you fail to reach your goals or notice you are getting off track? Does this make you a failure? Should you give up? NOT! Start by remembering that having far-reaching visions, goals, action items, knowledge of where we want to be, and plans to get there are all fantastic. The danger comes when you start taking the process too seriously and buy into the internal Judge or Taskmaster.

The truth is, we may lose the battle by not reaching a specific goal, but we win the war if we stay on our Personal Upward Path and enjoy the journey to a thriving life.

Who can judge if the right thing happened or not? If you think a task will take you two days, and it takes two weeks, maybe that was the perfect amount of time needed. Being overly critical and invalidating your process, especially when you are in the home stretch of a goal (like I am right now writing this book), takes the fun out of the goal. It is important to bask in the joy of what you are doing instead of shaming yourself or others for non-achievement. Be gentle with yourself and take regular breaks. Above all, stop being so hard on yourself when you notice your internal taskmaster is hard at work.

Remember, all is well now, no matter what you get done or don't get done. We cannot push plants to grow faster in a field or a baby to be born in half the time. Creative endeavors like your vision need time to marinate and bake, as well as to plan and implement. So, bring to consciousness the belief that you are a basic core of goodness committed to your Upward Path. Remember the affirmation by Heather Forbes earlier,

"You are perfectly alright. You've always been perfectly alright and you always will be perfectly alright."
- Heather Forbes, Dare to Love Yourself CD

☐ Step 10: Joining the Community Path

Where Our Lives Intersect and Support One Another's Paths

The community path differs from the Dream Team path. On my community path, my main focus is to engage and connect with various groups and communities to be of service, give and receive support, and network. The community path ideally benefits everyone involved. On the other hand, the Dream Team comprises individuals and professionals who are primarily focused on supporting me.

You might ask why you should get connected to community groups, resources, services, or volunteer work? By taking time and attention to connect with others and provide mutual support, you can help stabilize your own and another person's reality as a person who is a foundation of goodness.

When you are connected to others and receive support from one another naturally as needed, you will see that everything is falling into place instead of feeling everything is falling apart. It's all good. It will turn around, especially if we can all accept our circumstances exactly as they are at this moment, knowing they are temporary.

Many people think because they are struggling themselves, they don't have the strength or talents to help others until they get their own act together. This is not true in my experience. In fact, here's a paradox: I find that helping someone else figure out their problem or situation allows me to work through my own issues. Watch how teachers learn their topic on a deeper level by teaching others.

So, take a moment now and note on the "Community and Volunteer Opportunities" form below how you are engaged and can engage in a community.

Form 12: Community/Volunteer Form

Community & Volunteer Connections

Organizations/Group Memberships	Since the year
☐	
☐	
☐	

Volunteer/Service work opportunities	Schedule
☐	
☐	
☐	

Networking activities (WIN-WIN)	Schedule/Deadline
☐	
☐	
☐	

Name: ____________________ Date: ____________________

☐ Step 11: Assemble Your Plan

Print and gather all the forms you have filled out in this chapter (e.g., your Commitment to Your Personal Plan and your Mission/Vision statement). Staple or punch holes in the printouts and assemble the pages in a notebook for reference.

Another great way to view and follow your Personal Path is to post the pages you want to see daily on a wall, mirror, refrigerator, or the back of your bedroom door to serve as reminders of your Upward Path and progress made.

☐ Step 12: Celebrate the Completion of Your First Personal Upward Path

Congratulations! You've reached step 12 of the Personal Upward Path. You've reviewed the principles of this book, assembled and launched your Personal Path, and assessed where you are now with the goals you have set. I want to personally honor you for your hard work, persistence, and willingness to be open to new beliefs and ways of operating in the world. Please fill in your name on the certificate which follows and **accept my deepest heartfelt congratulations for making it this far!**

Have other significant people on your Dream Team sign this award as well, and then find a way to celebrate your achievement of completing the development of the Plan for your Upward Path! You deserve it!

Form 13: Completion Certificate - EveryoneCounts.World

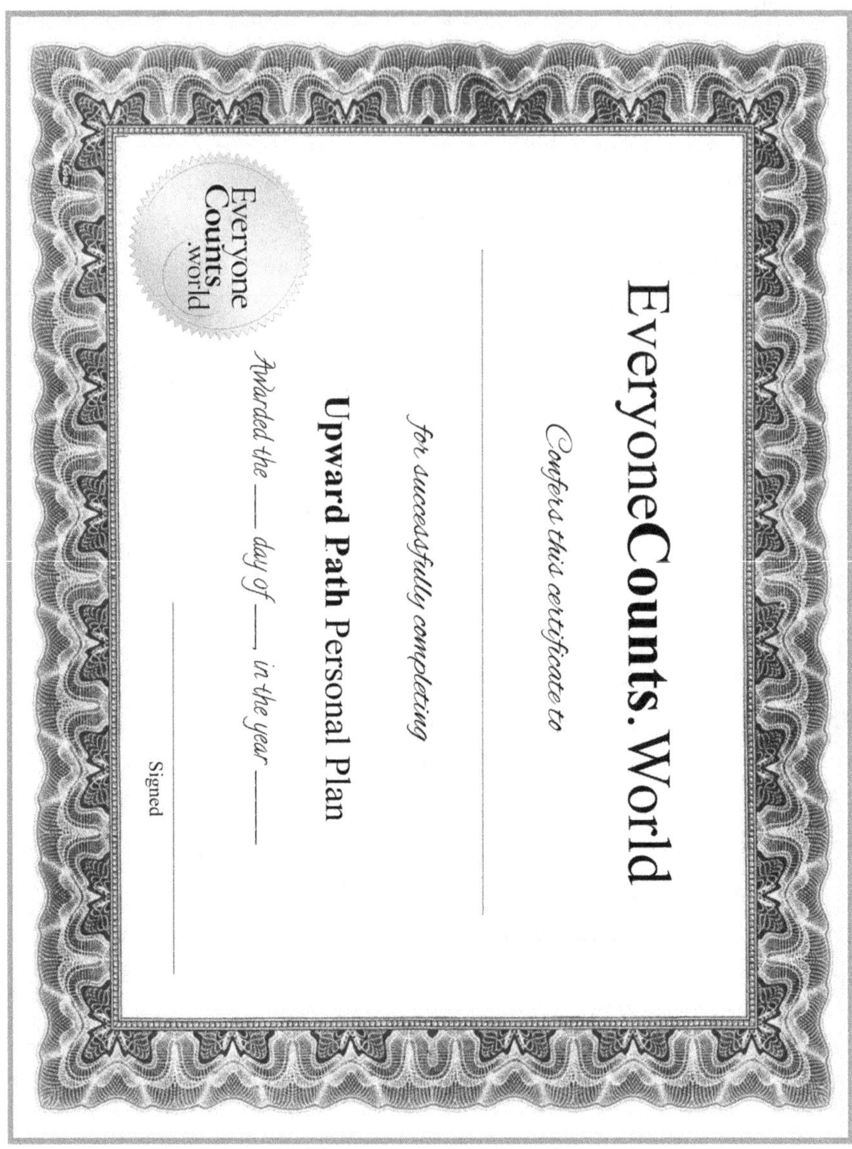

Ongoing Work

Daily Inventory

I find taking a daily inventory of my life a practice that grounds and helps me maintain my balance and fuel my thriving life. I have developed the habit of "seeing where I'm at" using the Basic Life Inventory Form in step 3 above. You can either write your review or go over the form in your mind.

I take the perspective of a fruit stand owner who must take daily stock of my inventory and does so by looking at and touching a small portion of the fruit in my stand to determine if it is fresh and sellable. Is the fruit unripe and needs to be held back a few days? Is it starting to perish and needs to be put on sale to move it more quickly? Or should it be donated to a nearby food bank? When I find a portion of my fruit or life beliefs have already begun to spoil, then I send old beliefs to be composted and look for new ways of thinking. How much fruit do you have? Do you have enough for your customers at this point in your sales cycle? Or do you need to order more from local farmers? The farmers I go to for new ideas on how to see the world are other authors, friends, counselors, and mentors. I also look at movies, online videos, and other sources.

Daily Maintenance

Take time each day for essential personal maintenance in your visible and invisible need areas you have the power to influence. Remember, you can find dream team members in the form of individuals and organizations that can help you navigate ANY choppy waters you encounter along your path. Let's clarify the four daily maintenance areas of life that you may want to track.

Tracking Visible Needs

- **Business/Financial Needs** – Keep tabs on your finances. Get in the habit of tracking all the money you receive and spend, in whatever form it comes (cash, paycheck, debit card, credit card, crypto, etc.). Start a spending plan and use it. Also, take time to work on any projects you have personally (e.g., organizing your home, shopping, planning, finding a new career, joining a club, etc.). Read and journal in these areas regularly.
- **Social/Family** – Take stock of your close business, family, spiritual and educational relationships, and friendships. Notice and record what is working and not working in each of these relationships. Develop plans for changing what needs to change in your life. Schedule time with people. Celebrate and appreciate people. Even a greeting card can brighten someone's day. Change relationships when needed. **Focus on your part of the inventory to ensure you are not just blaming others when you can make changes. Otherwise, you may find yourself in the same movie and drama throughout your life but with different actors.** Journal and review your social interactions and relationship adventures.
- **Physical Health** – Take time to identify the physical health areas that you would like to track and possibly improve or change. Evaluate your eating patterns; plan and remember, "You are what you eat." Where are you with exercise? Do you have a routine, or do you need one? Have you been to the doctor for a check-up in the past year? What about the dentist? Have you looked at your wardrobe lately? Anyone can take time to find clothing that fits and is clean. Splurge and ask a friend to be your personal shopping assistant, even if you shop at the local thrift store. Balance is the key here. Journal and review your physical and medical wellbeing to stay fresh.

- **Mental/Emotional/Spiritual** - This area is primarily for you. Schedule time daily to reflect on your mental, emotional and spiritual health. Read some inspirational or motivational literature at least once a day, maybe first thing in the morning and at the end of the day. Learn and practice mental, emotional, and spiritual routines that can help you keep an even keel in the changing weather of time. Inventory what you respond to better: meditation, prayer, reflection, yoga (crosses over with physical), breathing, tapping, rocking back and forth, religious practices and worship, twelve-step activities, empathy, compassion, acceptance, and love of yourself, the universe and others.

  Being in and enjoying the present moment ROCKS and solves many mental, emotional, and spiritual issues. It's all we have. It eliminates the fear of the future and regrets from the past.

Persist!

Never, never, never give up on your Personal Upward Path. Stay in the present to avoid regrets from the past or worries over the future. Enjoy the journey in your thriving life. **Do not question your value as a human being or your basic core of goodness, even for an instant.** If you do experience self-doubts, simply observe your thoughts and watch them drift away. Fighting them only makes them stronger.

Remember, you may feel crazy at times, but you're not crazy. Trust this.

"You can't judge your progress by how you feel.
You are always doing better than you feel."
- A friend and mentor overflowing with wisdom

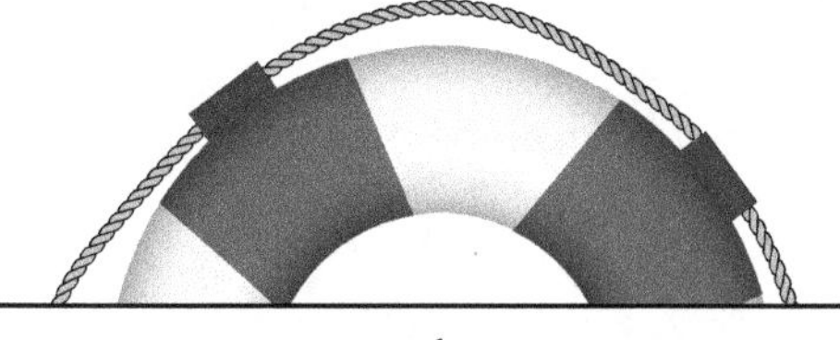

Part V: What's Next?

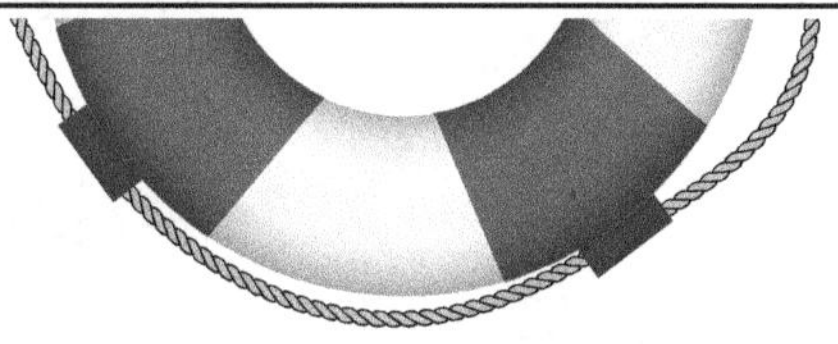

Chapter 25: Community Survival Up-Close

> "I always tell people that you can call me anything that you want. You can call me Arnold. You can call me Schwarzenegger. You can call me the Austrian Oak. You can call me Schwarzie. You can call me Arnie. But don't ever ever call me a self-made man."
>
> -Arnold Schwarzenegger

The experiences I have shared so far have largely been about how I found and followed a personal plan of surviving, which led to thriving. But how does this really work? If I strive and survive myself, is that the whole story?

How many of you reading this book right now are surviving or even thriving? Did you get there by yourself? Who helped you? Who hired you? Who taught you what to do, who to be, what to have in your life to survive and thrive? If you find yourself thriving and yet half your neighbors are standing in a food line, literally trying to physically survive, have you won? Have you really survived? Just because you have a job in a teaching or tech field that seems secure today, do you look down on those who are cycling-out of traditional manufacturing or service jobs that are at risk? Do you consider yourself thriving just because you've got two cars, a three-bedroom two-bath house, and plenty of money to outlast any world pandemic or economic crisis?

This chapter on community survival is perhaps the most important I've written so far. Even though I've personally struggled in the past to survive and fought hard to get to a thriving life, I still don't forget what it's like when it's tough. As I mentioned in the finance section, it seems that often I, and possibly you, have gained material security and wealth and then become obsessed with losing it or thinking it isn't the right kind of material wealth we need. Sure, we might donate now and then to a cause or take groceries to someone in need, but are we really part of the solution?

Transforming Economies

I like to remember that economies change. I have learned to change work to adapt to the times. I myself have lived through at least four significant changes in industries throughout my career. I was selling something called "film" and finishing services for 35mm cameras back in the late 80's. Don't know what those are? That's the point. Later, I worked as an employment recruiter finding jobs for computer programmers and web designers. That seemed like a secure up-and-coming profession. Then, online services like Monster.com came out, and our business dropped by 50 percent almost overnight, and I was let go. I experienced the same in real estate and higher education as well.

Now we're all seeing it in auto manufacturing, finance, telecommuting, and even in service industries, such as fast food, as companies automate as much as they can. Combustion engines are going electric. Cryptocurrency is making a move in finance. Fast food restaurants are becoming self-serve and automated.

As a community, we owe it to one another to start tracking and developing economies that provide the basics for everyone and support people to change careers as and when needed that fit current models. I believe we are all responsible for improving the smooth transition from one economy to the next.

We Are All Part of the Solution

For some reason, it has been my calling to learn to scramble through all these changes and adopt a surfing mentality. The bigger the economic wave, the bigger the possibility becomes, the greater the ride, and the longer the run. But unlike surfing waves, these "economic industry" waves are more like tsunamis. These waves have the force to financially knock out millions of people across the globe in one fell swoop.

I am not a fan of trying to stop waves, but instead accepting and surfing them, whether technological, social, or economic. I have trained myself to choose to see change as a real adventure or a carnival ride. In the end, change is the only true constant.

An example of accepting and going with a wave is letting go of the horse and carriage mode of travel and switching over to automobile manufacturing when the industry naturally took over.

Note: There may be times when old industries will recover, like vinyl records coming back in-fashion, or when it may be useful to retrain ourselves in old methods that bring advantages, such as growing vegetables or canning fruit.

Instead of fighting new waves, I propose we find ways to get together with everyone involved and see how we can make the new industries even stronger, prosperous, equitable, and cleaner by including everyone's participation and benefit in the solution.

At the same time, I think it is important for each of us to observe if the economic wave seems like the right thing to do in the long run for the planet or not. If not, we need to do everything humanly possible to stop those waves from consuming us (e.g., nuclear disaster).

I believe we all need to get involved if we see new economic waves that include large-scale violence or benefit only a handful of people. In such cases, the benefit to the few overwhelms the fundamental human rights of the many. If spotted, this is a wave that our communities may need to find ways to redirect.

I do my best to do this by taking personal action. If it looks like a company is eroding competition, I might boycott that company and look for alternatives. I'm not into protesting publicly, but rather privately and with real money, though I support peaceful protests that help bring real issues that impact many people to the forefront.

I also like to invest in companies and funds that follow my family's dearly held values. We are into the long-term investment, not short-term gains alone.

Now Is the Perfect Time to Retool

In the early part of the twenty-first century, we are experiencing major transitions due to robotization, pandemics, space travel, natural disasters, and more. Around the globe, an unprecedented number of people are out of work.

Why not take this time, both personally and from a business standpoint, to retool for new industries taking over? We could work together to gradually transition out of the older industries, which are shedding workers, into new win-win industries together. Things are slow right now anyway. I have a habit of retooling my skills as the need arises. One thing I can count on is that technology and circumstances will continue to change over time. I want to be prepared to pivot when I need to while trusting that many basic skills will transfer to new industries.

Employers Retooling?

Are you an employer? Where are your products in their life cycle? Are you hiring fewer employees due to automation?

Suppose your family has owned a factory for generations and you see your industry at risk of going down. You may be able to weather the downturn for a generation or two, but what about your employees? Why not talk with the people working with you. Allow them to help you develop innovative solutions from their own day-to-day lives that might help themselves and the company and your customers?

Why not find a way for your employees to experience some of the upsides financially and find other ways to motivate them? I've observed people pull through with incredible ideas and efforts if they feel they are an integral part of the solution and will participate in the upside alongside you, the employer.

You probably have an incredible team. Your company, together with its people, may be a well-oiled machine. Why not turn those efforts into something truly extraordinary? Sure, you help them succeed in the process. Who knows? You will likely gain something, which is better than the nothing that you may be facing right now. You may even be surprised by the creativity and economic possibilities for you, your employees, your family, and your community by working together, synergizing, and giving it a shot.

Employees Retooling

What is your current situation? Have you lost a job? Are you having trouble seeing how you will be able to keep a roof over your head in the coming months with your industry at risk? Are you responsible for others? Children?

These questions have kept me up and scrambling, and so, I have gotten into the habit of strategizing what I can do next to take care of myself and my family. I have earned degrees, but I have also been on the lookout for opportunities to learn new trades. Case in point, this is the first book I've ever written. I've also learned how to code in HTML and CSS, as my husband and I plan to launch an app soon. I NEVER THOUGHT I could learn HTML, and I'm not a spring chicken!

I know that if our income goes south, I have another robust tool now to offer employers. Learning new skills can help my community too. When I become more stable mentally, emotionally, and financially, I can buy other neighbors' products and services and become a contributing member of my community. It can also help employers that really need the help.

Note: Many companies in tech, for example, may offer stock options. Consider this opportunity. Also, consider launching your own new business with products or services that you could offer your community at this time for sale or trade.

Teaching Our "Kids" How to Support Themselves Legally

One of my values as a parent has been to teach my "kids" (now young adults) how to support themselves financially. When I started planning how to teach my kids to become financially self-supporting, I looked back to my own childhood for clues.

I started by babysitting my younger sister and then moved to lawn mowing and minor construction demolition and cleaning somewhere between eleven and thirteen. By fourteen, I started working part-time at hourly jobs in hotels and restaurants and kept going until I was seventeen. By eighteen, I was fully self-supporting and putting myself through college on the 5½ year plan, and that was it. I never moved back to my childhood home again. However, much later in life, my family members offered to help pay for my master's degree—which I completed—and I still thank them for their generous gift.

My work life may sound like child labor to some. Both of my parents, however, grew up on farms. Who knows when they started working, but I imagine it was incredibly early in life and much more intensive than my work history?

So, it worked for me to work from an early age and put myself through college. I decided to change my strategy for teaching my own kids about supporting themselves financially, however. I supported my kids not working a paid job during their school years or their first year in college. Instead, I wanted to encourage them to stay focused on school instead of working a conventional job during their school years. I've told them their grades and extra-curricular activities are their jobs right now. This is the opposite of the way I grew up.

My goal is to ensure that these young people can support themselves and their families with professional or entrepreneurial work down the line and practical jobs like I started with in restaurants and hotels. By observing their accomplishments in high school, I know they do have the full ability to earn income as well. The big thing I impress on my family is we want each person to be fully self-supporting after college. I also want to ensure none of us are forced to work in industries we don't believe in because we are desperate for money.

Industries I Avoid

I have tried to avoid and encouraged my immediate family to avoid careers that specifically focus on alcohol, drugs, gambling, illegal, or sex trades. I have seen many friends and acquaintances "go down" in these trades. Thankfully, I have also seen just as many of my friends bounce back after leaving them. I also know a few individuals who are happy and prosperous in such trades. Of course, alcohol may be served in restaurants, and you or your kids may be fine serving drinks for a living.

One of the biggest reasons I avoid these trades is that I find it very difficult NOT to consume these products if I am working around them all the time. There is a saying— if you go to a barbershop enough times, you're likely to get a haircut.

I have found that if I end up "over participating" in these trades, I end up acting out unconsciously in my thinking and decisions. I lose clarity, and I tend to act more impulsively instead of thoughtfully, resulting in my decisions moving away from my true values. Things can happen that I do not expect. I can also lose my dignity and self-esteem, which are hard to recover once lost. If I check out and then try to check back in, I may start from a lower point than before I checked out. I'm super protective of where I place my attention today. Life is just too short to miss out!

These trades can make a massive impact on a community as well. I've seen small towns vote to legalize gambling, for instance, and over 90 percent of the same people who voted feeling compelled to leave town after the casinos took over. This isn't good or bad. It's just essential for each of our communities to make conscious, explicit, long-term decisions when considering starting any new industry. I like to think at least ten if not a hundred years down the line.

Today, I like being present most of the time. I like to work in industries that advance myself and others and are a win-win for everyone involved. If I had to, I would go back to mowing lawns all day long rather than working in some of these trades. Lawn mowing has dignity and purpose for me.

Finding Your Own Bottom Lines

> "You need to stand for something, or you'll fall for anything."
>
> -Aunt Marie

The trades you choose to avoid may be completely different! Please know I have no judgment about what works for you! My intent is to press on you to know and stick to your values. Find your own bottom lines that you do not want to cross and do whatever you can to stick by those values, even if you only have one can of beans in the cupboard. This principle holds if you are starting your own business, especially during a transition to a new economy, like artificial intelligence or mass robotization.

Diamonds in Our Community Backyards

Just as new products and services are valuable, so are the people and knowledge from more traditional industries. It's so easy to say, "Wow, look at that company or community. They really figured it out, and they are blossoming while we're dying on the vine." NOT TRUE!

The opportunity to ensure your community's survival and guarantee its thriving heartbeat can often be found in your own backyard. If coal mining is no longer a viable business in our community due to the increase in solar energy offerings, we can get together as a community and answer this question, "OK, what else is there? What could we do that would bring all of us up and out of poverty?"

Maybe we have a massive amount of trash and industrial waste. That could be the start. Let's retool and become the biggest waste recycling community in the world. Let's make it cheaper for manufacturers to buy our recycled plastic than producing more from oil. Or let's pick a new industry like computer programming and become the best high school within ten counties for "kids" who can code. Maybe these kids can help community businesses make the leap from in-person to digital while retaining a personal touch. I know one kid and family who are doing this!

One of the most fun examples of finding diamonds in your own backyard is a photographer known as Mary McConnaughey from Boca Chica, Texas, known as Boca Chica Gal. When SpaceX moved operations into her neighborhood, and though she and many of her neighbors were worried and unhappy, she started photographing the developments at the space company. She captures videos of the daily progress on the spaceships, activities of the workers, and exciting launches. She contributes to a larger community of space fans like the Marcus House report on YouTube. Here's what Mary has to say about how she got her start in space journalism:

> "A lot of it is just right place, right time, being observant.
> You have to pay attention to what's going on.
> You just have to be patient and ready and wait."
>
> -Mary McConnaughey, BocaChicaGal

I'm guessing there are dozens of people involved in making these dreams of building a space news agency come to life. We can find meaning in a lot of places by being observant, as Mary says.

How Can I Help My Community Survive and Thrive?

> "What can I do?"
>
> - Song by Laurie Dameron

My friend Laurie Dameron wrote a beautiful song called "What can I do?" to help people start thinking of what they could do to change their habits and care for the environment. Once I heard her song, I just couldn't get those words out of my mind. I experienced posing this question to my community a few years ago.

I lived in a small town and worked as an academic and career navigator for a college and job center called Workforce. One day, the top social agencies in town discussed how we could work together to help our clients succeed and, more importantly, not fall through the cracks. The attendees came from education, corrections, social services, housing, and other life support agencies and businesses.

Two of the questions we posed that day were "What can we do to move the needle in core areas of our community, such as helping more high school students graduate from college?" and "What can we do to support people coming out of correctional institutions to successfully re-enter and help grow our communities?" Then, we had a state agency present a dynamic web app that helped us pull together our efforts and achieve these goals.

The idea was that each client any of us had would have an online digital plan. We would all be on their dream teams, and if a client went to one agency, they would be referred to the other agencies that could help them succeed on their unique, personal path. This was a holistic approach that I'm proud to say our community went for and implemented to a large extent.

Although I believe this idea of collaboration between agencies worked, I also believe that there is always room for continuous quality improvement. You can learn more about putting community plans into action by reading Edward Deming's 14 Points for Management.

Overall, I will say we did seem to work together, the best we could, to be like a relay team helping our local clients move from scarcity and challenging circumstances to abundant lives. There is more work to be done there, I'm sure, and I now live in a large urban area far away. However, I'll never forget how we all worked together in my hometown to make big changes.

I believe if each person, who is surviving and thriving, took as much time as the average unemployed person is spending on the phone right now trying to get jobs and financial benefits we all promised them, we could solve the world's problems... together!

Chapter 26: In Conclusion: The Beginning

Here we are. The end of this journey together for now. This book started simply talking about survival. And I hope we have achieved that together. The type of survival I was sharing involved moving from feelings of being a total victim of circumstances in your life to a place of curiosity, hope, and a sense of prosperity and abundance for you and others.

We have talked about making this journey regardless of the people and circumstances around us. I no longer believe my growth and possibilities are limited by any identities I have adopted based on my past trauma, race, gender, income level, and so on. Instead, I am heading to a place of real action and peace based on total unconditional love for myself and everyone else.

You Are Not Alone

Know this, YOU and your life inspire me daily. Though we've never met, I feel we have now. I agree with my best friend, Dr. Sue Nesbitt:

"If I ever think there is someone I do not like,
I believe it's because I don't know them well enough yet."
-Dr. Sue Nesbitt, Ph.D., Professor Human Services

So, if your mind tries to gather evidence that you are that one person who is unlovable and worthless or believes the LIE that you need to EARN your worth as a human being, then observe and accept that thought. Thank your false thought for the service it has given you over the years. Then visualize letting that thought go and feel the warmth of the truth and reality of your basic core of goodness beginning to glow and grow inside of you.

This is the same core of goodness I feel within myself right now, thinking of you not just surviving but thriving in every way possible.

There Is Always More Abundance Available

On a personal note, throughout this book's writing, it has been challenging to focus on "survival and scarcity" because I have been fortunate enough to have worked through many of the deeper survival issues. I consider my current ability to truly live and grow an abundant life to be like striking gold.

To Find the Gold, You Have to Move a Lot of Dirt

I feel like I have been mining for gold my entire life; the mental and emotional kind of gold. I did this by moving tons of dirt that showed up in the form of visible and invisible "unmet needs" or "issues." This search for peace and happiness in all areas of my life (a.k.a. The Gold) has required countless tools, a massive crew of people, and tons of energy.

At first, I found thin veins of gold that I almost overlooked because they appeared like problems or "red flags" in my life. Those "red flags" at first looked like "crises" or deeply unmet physical and mental/emotional needs. By observing, clarifying, and overcoming the red flags or problems I ran into, I have been rewarded with the golden rewards that come in the form of sanity, peace, connected relationships, and abundance in all areas of my life.

Taking Full Responsibility for My Happy and Abundant Life Turned the Tide for Me

The magic happened when I started turning my attention inward to explore why I was experiencing a problem versus blaming someone else or society for my problem. Transforming to a regulated, adult point of view from a victim's point of view has made all the difference in my thriving life. I found the solutions deep inside myself from my own efforts, along with tons of support from my Dream Team!

Thank You!

One of the most important strategies I have employed in the past thirty-plus years has been the tool of daily gratitude. Today, I say that if I have personally ever met you or read a book or viewed a film you've produced, know this: you've made a difference in my life no matter what the circumstances. I thank you, the reader, right now! I am a better person because all of you have touched my life in some way. **Thank you!**

Hang onto Your Socks! You're in For a Ride!

Your journey from survival to thriving can be just the beginning of an extraordinary life, regardless of how the results measure up to your ego or other people's standards. You can succeed just because you say you are succeeding, no matter what things look like to you right now. However, if you really want to feel that sense of thriving instead of just surviving, DON'T STOP NOW!

As a wise friend once told me: **"You think your life is good now? This is just the tip of the iceberg of what is available if you keep going and growing."** I took that to mean I needed to keep digging, learning, risking, and growing no matter how good or bad life appeared in the moment.

Another man told me in a therapy group: **"How good do you want it? That's your limitation."** And did it matter that I made a lot of so-called "mistakes" in my life? No, it didn't. In fact, the hurdles I've had to climb, jump, and wrestle my way over have all been the most powerful rocket fuel for my growth, whether I liked it or not.

The Crooked Path Works Too!

So, when I look back on my life, the path does look pretty crooked. It hasn't been smooth all the time, physically, financially, emotionally, or mentally. I didn't go from A to B to get to C. I went from A to Z to get to C. Even though I didn't take a straight path to survive and thrive, I can look back now and realize it took every single twist and turn to get me to where I am today. It makes sense now. No regrets. I am forever grateful for the crooked path which has led me to where I am today:

One of the happiest and luckiest people on planet earth, maybe in the universe.

There Is Now!

The ultimate truth I found is that, even in the direst circumstances, I can know and live in happiness, peace, and freedom and grow personally, no matter what others say and do or what my circumstances are.

It may require:

- The deepest level of love and acceptance for myself and others that I cannot even imagine right now
- Acceptance of a current reality that seems totally unacceptable to me
- Willingness to change the things that I can as they come up
- And gaining the wisdom and knowledge to understand what I can and cannot change

As Victor Frankl put it:

"They can hurt my body, but they can't hurt me, who I really am."
-Victor Frankl

I believe this philosophy includes my ability to give and receive love from whomever I want, whenever I want, even though they may refuse to talk to me, or I may not be able to live with them. This change, going from dependence on people or circumstances for my self-esteem and freedom to self-love, is one of many changed beliefs that have led me to my "turn-back moments."

Don't Miss Your "Turn Back Moment"

> "Everybody has a turn-back moment. You have a moment where you can go forward, or you can give up. But the thing you have to keep in mind before you give up is that if you give up, the guarantee is, it will never happen. That's the guarantee of quitting. It will never happen, no way under the sun. The only way the possibility remains that it can happen is if you never give up no matter what."
>
> -Steve Harvey, "The Apollo Story"

There are no words to describe how hard this concept has been for me to learn. For decades, my mind resisted, with everything it had, the possibility of self-love to become real! I believe my mind was trying to help me "stay safe" by not expecting too much of myself and others or my circumstances.

In my case, it took being willing to think completely outside the box and becoming open to any new beliefs or resources that could help. I call my turn-back moment my "transformation."

One day a unique and talented counselor, Connie Klein, asked me, "Are you willing to commit to the upward path in your life?" She actually drew this diagram out on a whiteboard like the one I included in your Personal Plan chapter. "*Yes,*" I said. "*I am willing to do anything to get sanity in my life and stay on the upward path, even if I backslide from time to time.*" **That was my turn-back moment.**

That's how I became open to all possibilities to stay on my upward path, and that's how I was gradually able to tap into the universal love that I believe is the essence of all of us.

This philosophy of changing my beliefs about self-doubt and not giving up, especially not giving up on learning to love myself, is the biggest decision I believe I have ever consciously made.

-My story

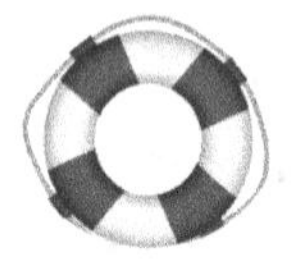

A Final Note

"Hey, I don't have all the answers.
In life, to be honest, I've failed as
much as I've succeeded.
But I love my life. I love my wife.
And I wish you my kind of success."

-Dicky Fox, Business/Life Guru
from the Movie Jerry Maguire

Does this book have all the answers? No, this book doesn't have all the answers. I hope it is helping you raise the right questions, though. These are questions that spark curiosity and hope in your mind and heart, leading you to venture out into the unknown reaches of the universe, also known as:

Your own abundant, prosperous, happy, free, and peaceful life no matter what!

Please, take care on your journey and remember you are not alone. Life is basically good. An abundant life can happen for you today, no matter what. I know it because I agree with Elon Musk when he says:

"I think it's possible for ordinary people to choose
to be extraordinary."

-Elon Musk

How am I, as an ordinary person, choosing to be extraordinary? By aligning my personal mission and actions in the world with the mission Buckminster Fuller embarked on after his transformation:

"an experiment, to find what a single individual could
contribute to changing the world and benefiting all humanity."

- Buckminster Fuller, The New York Times

From one "ordinary" person to another: **thank you from the bottom of my heart** for taking your precious time to read this book. Please pass it on or pay it forward to others if you think reading this book could support their health, happiness, prosperity, abundance, and success. Please consider what you can do or say, large or small, to change the world and benefit yourself, your family, community, and humanity.

Auf Wiedersehen! Until we meet again!

-Toria

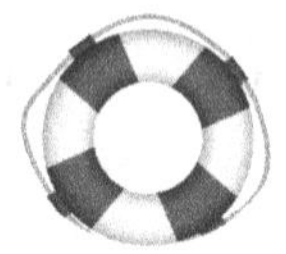

Bibliography

AAA Foundation for Traffic Safety and Brian C. Tefft. 2016. "Acute Sleep Deprivation and Risk of Motor Vehicle Crash Involvement." AAA Foundation for Traffic Safety. http://publicaffairsresources.aaa.biz/wp-content/uploads/2016/11/Acute-Sleep-Deprivation-and-Risk-of-Motor-Vehicle-Crash-Involvement.pdf.

Abdu'lBahá. 1911. "Paris Talks." The Bahá'í Faith. https://www.bahai.org/library/authoritative-texts/abdul-baha/paris-talks/1#733601770.

ACLU. 2017. "Anti-Camping Ordinances - Important Case Law and Frequently Asked Questions." aclu-wa.org. https://www.aclu-wa.org/docs/anti-camping-ordinances-%E2%80%93-important-case-law-and-frequently-asked-questions.

Alai, Safa. 2020. "Full Stack Grow." Udemy. https://www.udemy.com/course/full-stack-grow/?referralCode=7AD13A1EE70C6CFBBEE5.

Alpha Leaders and Elon Musk. 2020. "Elon Musk BEST Motivation 2020! | 10 Rules for Success." YouTube. https://www.youtube.com/watch?v=N0bj4UZ3zWg.

American Red Cross. n.d. "4-Person, 3-Day Emergency Preparedness Kit." American Red Cross. https://www.redcross.org/store/4-person-3-day-emergency-preparedness-kit/91053.html.

Bach, Richard. 2001. *Illusions: The Adventures of a Reluctant Messiah.* Eastbourne, East Sussex: Gardners Books; Reprint edition.

Bolles, Richard N. 2020. *What Color is Your Parachute.* New York City: Ten Speed Press; Revised edition.

Bourne, Edmund J. 2020. *The Anxiety and Phobia Workbook.* Oakland: New Harbinger Publications, 7th Ed.

Bremner, Douglas J. 2006. "Traumatic stress: effects on the brain." *Dialogues in Clinical Neuroscience* 8, no. 4 (Dec): 445-461. 10.31887/DCNS.2006.8.4/jbremner.

Brinlee, Jr, Chris. 2016. "How to Live Out of Your Car." outside-online.com. https://www.outsideonline.com/2138841/how-live-out-your-car.

CALIFORNIA DEPARTMENT OF FORESTRY AND FIRE PROTECTION, CAL FIRE. n.d. "Benefits of fire." fire.ca.gov. Accessed March 5, 2021. https://www.fire.ca.gov/media/5425/benifitsoffire.pdf.

The Center for Nonviolent Communication. n.d. "Center for Nonviolent Communication." Center for Nonviolent Communication: What is N-V-C? Accessed March 5, 2021. https://www.cnvc.org/learn-nvc/what-is-nvc.

Cilley, Marla. 2002. *Sink Reflections.* Bantam trade paperback reissue ed. Vol. 1. 1 vols. New York, NY: Bantam Books.

Conwell, Russell H., and Project Gutenberg. 2008. *Acres of Diamonds.* N.p.: eBook #368 Charles Keller and David Widger.

Covey, Stephen R. 1989. *The seven habits of highly effective people: restoring the character ethic.* Vol. 1. 1 vols. New York, NY: Simon & Schuster.

Cramer, Cramer. n.d. QuoteTab. https://www.quotetab.com/quotes/by-jim-cramer.

"Current World Population." 2021. Worldometers.info. https://www.worldometers.info/world-population/.

David, Marc. 2015. *The Slow Down Diet: Eating for Pleasure, Energy, and Weight Loss*. Rochester, VT: The Healing Arts Press.

David, Marc. 2015. *The Slow Down Diet: Eating for Pleasure, Energy, and Weight Loss*. Rochester: Healing Arts Press; 2nd Edition, 10th Anniversary.

Deming, W. E. 1982. *Out of the Crisis*. Cambridge: Massachusetts Institute of Technology.

Eastwood and James R. 2015. "KEEP YOUR HANDS WARM WITH NITRILE GLOVES- QUICK TIP." Eastwood. https://garage.eastwood.com/eastwood-chatter/nitrile-gloves-in-cold/#:~:-text=Since%20nitrile%20gloves%20are%20non,the%20event%20of%20a%20spill.

Elmer, Jamie. 2019. "How Long Do Panic Attacks Last?" Healthline. https://www.healthline.com/health/mental-health/how-long-do-panic-attacks-last.

Emerson, Clint. 2016. *100 Deadly Skills*. Survival Edition ed. New York, New York: Atria Paperback.

Gerber, Michael E. 2004. *The E-Myth Revisited: Why Most Small Businesses Don't Work and What to Do About It*. New York City: Harper Business: Updated, Subsequent edition.

Gomez, Selena. 2007. *Kill Them with Kindness*. Champaign: Polyvinyl Records.

Harvey, Steve. 2019. "The Apollo Story | Motivated +." YouTube. https://www.youtube.com/watch?v=9igSh9IwMAc.

Heather, Forbes. 2016. *Dare to Love Yourself*. Boulder: Heather T. Forbes.

"The Hobbit 2 The Desolation of Smaug Trailer." 2013. YouTube. https://www.youtube.com/watch?v=9XPqQ09-1Bo.

Hostels Worldwide. n.d. "Hostelling International." hihostels.com. Accessed March 5, 2021. https://www.hihostels.com/pages/global-initiatives.

HuffPost and Leigh Campbell. 2017. "We've Broken Down Your Entire Life Into Years Spent Doing Tasks." HuffPost. https://www.huffingtonpost.com.au/2017/10/18/weve-broken-down-your-entire-life-into-years-spent-doing-tasks_a_23248153/.

Johnson Hess, Abigail. 2017. "10 ultra-successful millionaire and billionaire college dropouts." CNBC Make it. https://www.cnbc.com/2017/05/10/10-ultra-successful-millionaire-and-billionaire-college-dropouts.html.

Keating, Thomas. 1994. *Guidelines for Christian Life*. London, United Kingdom: Bloomsbury Publishing.

Kenny, Rogers, and Genius Lyrics. n.d. "The Gambler Lyrics." Genius Lyrics. https://genius.com/Kenny-rogers-the-gambler-lyrics.

Kris, Deborah F. 2018. "What's mentionable is manageable: Why parents should help children name their fears." The Washington Post. https://www.washingtonpost.com/.

Lauer, Katie. 2020. "Tiny homes community opens in San Jose." sanjosespotlight.com. https://sanjosespotlight.com/tiny-homes-community-opens-in-san-jose/.

Maharishi International University and Jim Carrey. 2014. "Full Speech: Jim Carrey's Commencement Address at the 2014 MUM Graduation." YouTube. https://www.youtube.com/watch?v=V80-gPkpH6M.

Makohen, John. n.d. "What are the best places for homeless people to sleep?" quora.com. https://www.quora.com/What-are-the-best-places-for-homeless-people-to-sleep.

Makohen, John. n.d. "What is the cheapest, safest way to live homeless in New York?" Quora. Accessed 03, 2021. https://www.quora.com/What-is-the-cheapest-safest-way-to-live-homeless-in-New-York.

Marketing Charts. 2019. "Online Video Consumption Continues to Rise Globally." Marketing Charts. https://www.marketingcharts.com/digital/video-110520#:~:text=The%20global%20forecast%20estimates%20that,rate%20of%2032%25%20per%20year.

McLeod, Dr. Saul. 2018. "Erik Erikson's Stages of Psychosocial Development." simplepsychology.org. https://www.simplypsychology.org/Erik-Erikson.html.

McLeod, Dr. Saul. 2020. "Maslow's Hierarchy of Needs." simplypsychology.org. https://www.simplypsychology.org/maslow.html.

Mellody, Pia, Andrea W. Miller, and J. K. Miller. 2003. *Facing Love Addiction: Giving Yourself the Power to Change the Way You Love.* San Francisco: HarperOne.

Movieclips Classic Trailers. 2017. "The Terminal (2004) Trailer #1." YouTube. https://www.aclu-wa.org/docs/anti-camping-ordinances-%E2%80%93-important-case-law-and-frequently-asked-questions.

Movieclips Coming Soon. 2013. "The Hobbit 2 The Desolation of Smaug TRAILER 1 (2013) - Lord of the Rings Movie HD." YouTube. https://www.youtube.com/watch?v=9X-PqQ09-1Bo.

Mundis, Jerrold. 2012. *How to get out of debt, stay out of debt and live prosperously*. 2012 Bantam Books Trade Paperback Edition ed. Vol. 1. 1 vols. New York, NY: Penguin Random House. January 1, 2003.